PER CENT
A History of Interest

PER CENT

A History of Interest

REVISED EDITION

Fernando S. David

To order additional copies of this book, contact:
Xlibris Corporation
1-888-795-4274
www.Xlibris.com
Orders@Xlibris.com
37326

To my parents

"Many writers . . . spoke glibly of wages per hour, rent per acre, and profit per cent as if these were comparable magnitudes."

Joseph A. Schumpeter

CONTENTS

PROLOGUE

The payment of interest goes very far back in the history of mankind. It could date from around 10,000 B.C. when people became farmers. Farmers early were known to have lent seed against a promise to receive at harvest time more than what was lent. Grain often served as primitive money.

Certainly, by about 3500 B.C., the institutional lender had appeared in Mesopotemia. The great temple-bank of Uruk and the temples of Sumeria and Babylon, grown wealthy from tributes, began to lend silver and grain at relatively low rates, while the temple of Samas lent at a fixed average rate. In China, in 400 B.C., the Buddhist monasteries, endowed by rulers and the rich, established the empire's oldest credit establishments, the pawnshops, to help the poor.

With such origins in subsistence, religion, and welfare, it is not surprising that lending and borrowing had strong ethical implications. Since antiquity, the morality of interest-taking drew the attention of men's minds. Attitudes swung from total permissiveness to full prohibition. More commonly, they ranged between these absolutes. The eradication of interest payments proved impossible. Prominent men decried them. At the same time, they themselves lent or borrowed with interest. On the other hand, excessive rates of interest were clearly intolerable. There was always the underlying issue of justice and charity.

As thinkers debated the rightness of interest, they were inevitably led to probe its nature. In seeking answers to whether interest should be paid and, if so, how much, it became necessary to know what interest was in the first place. The horse had to be repositioned before the cart.

But as scholars ascertained the essence of interest, frequently in a negative manner by discovering what interest was not, they found themselves going again into new territory. They began examining what determined the level of interest rates. Metaphysical inquiry, which had been induced by ethical questions, led to economic investigation. Subsequently, economic findings bred political policies. The interest rate became a major monetary tool of governments. Eventually, the fuller understanding of the nature of interest and the forces shaping its rate helped evaluate its morality, thus closing a large and laborious circle of thought.

This intellectual journey from ethics to metaphysics to economics to politics began around 1800 B.C., when Hammurabi, the Babylonian lawgiver-king, simply limited interest rates. It continues to the present day, when economists, armed with empirical research, construct complex mathematical models in an effort to understand (and forecast) the behavior of interest rates and their impact on an economy.

Famous men, such as Aristotle, Thomas Aquinas, Adam Smith, John Stuart Mill, Karl Marx, and John Maynard Keynes, participated in this quest for knowledge. Other seekers were moderately prominent, like John Locke and David Hume. A large number were quite obscure, familiar only to the specialist. But their contributions were of signal, if not watershed, import—names such as Bernardino of Siena, Leonard Lessius, Jacques Turgot, Jean Baptiste Say, Knut Wicksell, Eugen von Bohm-Bawerk, Irving Fisher, and Frank Knight. Many were academicians. But jurists, ecclesiastics, rabbis, civil servants, bankers, and merchants made equally impressive contributions. The divining tools used were as varied as these men, ranging from biblical interpretation to philosophical deduction, from differential calculus to plain business insights.

As it was probed, interest became a bedrock idea in economics, linked to such fundamental notions as value, capital, income, prices, production, profits, rent, and spending and saving. It became part of the theoretical center of capitalism.

With this pervasive importance came extended controversy. Interest was decried by the classical Greeks, regulated by the Romans, condemned by the medieval Church, prohibited by Islam, discarded by pure socialism, and rationalized by modern mainstream economics. In 1939, an Austrian economist wrote that the explanation of the interest rate "gives rise to more disagreement among economists than any other branch of economic theory." Twelve years later, a book on the theory of investment could still begin with the observation that "the theory of interest is . . . in a state of great confusion."

The debates, however, were grounds for constructive advance. The analytical achievements of one age taught the next. As in all scientific study, the generative trend was compelling, and to see the progressive march of ideas through nearly thirty-eight centuries is as inspiring as it is instructive. There were mistakes and repetitions of course, blind alleys, variants, and deviants. A 1981 Nobel Prize winner economist recognized the study of interest as not really a straight arrow, but as having loops around itself. Frequently, for instance, showing how interest rates were determined led close to defining interest itself.

Despite the periodic cycles, logical continuity persisted in the drive toward a full and unified exposition of interest theory. In this forward movement, the realities of the marketplace were both a constant spur and a powerful guide. By the 18th century, the core economics of interest were established. By the next century, they were fleshed out in coherent structures. Disputes would arise periodically, but they were often concerned with empirical details of what determined interest rates and what they in turn affected. Towards the middle of the 20th century, the edifice of interest theory had been built, and there was general agreement among economists. Equally important, the age-old moral issues of interest had been clarified and laid to rest.

PART ONE

HISTORICAL OVERVIEW: PRACTICE AND MORALITY

Chapter 1

THIRTY-FIVE CENTURIES

The principles of interest theory reached over the centuries have gained wide agreement among economists today. Key notions have been shaped definitively from ideas propounded in progressive filiation. Current analysis, using complex mathematics, is largely engaged in the finer points of doctrines related to interest, such as capital stocks and flows, production processes, or time preference indices.

The long intellectual journey occurred against the background of prolonged ethical questioning of interest. From ancient times to the end of the Middle Ages, the taking of interest or the charging of excessive rates were generally considered immoral. Today, prohibition persists, but on a lesser scale. Usury laws have been lifted in most countries, although some remain.

Early records of lending with interest in the cities of Asia Minor date from 1941 to 1902 B.C. Individuals entrusted money (typically two minas or a multiple) to a traveling merchant who promised to return twice the amount upon his return after a specified period of time. Any further profit was shared either equally or on a one-to-two ratio.

Disapproval of interest initially dealt with excessive rates. The world's earliest, systematic legal document, the Code of Hammurabi, written about 1800 B.C. in Babylon, imposed, together with price and wage controls, maximum rates of interest—3.3% for loans of cereals and 20% for loans of silver. If higher rates were charged, debts became cancellable. Around 600 B.C., the two rates were unified at 20%. The Code, besides limiting interest rates, permitted interest-free loans of consumable goods, with or without penalty for nonpayment. It also allowed interest to be paid through labor services in case of default. The Code forbade compound interest.

In general, Babylonian cuneiform told of 10-25% interest for loans of silver and 22-35% for grains. During the ascendancy of the Assyrians in the region around 730-630 B.C., loans without interest became more frequent, but penalties for failure to pay were attached, ranging from 40% to 141% of the borrowed amount. The high rates were self-defeating. Meant to discourage borrowing, they made lending attractive.

In Greece, interest was generally freely determined since the time of Solon (c630-560 B.C.), the greatest statesman of his time. Only two exceptions are known. The Temple of Delphi, which acted like a central bank, once mandated a 6% ceiling. An Athenian law fixed additional interest due on a default at 18%. The rates on normal loans, which usually carried monthly payment dates, ranged from 6% to 18% a year, with lenders asking 36% from risky borrowers. The typical rate was 12% (one drachma per mina). A rate of five obols or 10% was considered a favor among friends. Xenophon wanted Athens to establish a fund that would lend to individuals at 20%. Mortgages earned 12-18%. Other types of credit fetched rates of 10% to 62%, with outlier rates of 200% to 9,000%. A miser was known to collect 25% a day from shopkeepers.

Following the revival of maritime commerce in 370 B.C., bottomry loans, which entailed greater risk for the lender and some of which were really partnerships or insurance coverage, earned from 12.5% to 30%, depending on the length and destinations of the voyages, the character of the borrower, the security, and political conditions. But higher rates of 40% to 100% have been recorded. By 160 B.C., sea loans dominated credit activity. Money changers were transformed into deposit bankers, an evolution that could be traced back in time from Babylon to Phoenicia to Lydia to Ionia and finally to Athens.

The Temple banks, with their treasure amassed from donations, continued as a major alternative source of funds that was relatively cheap, because the people had a say in the determination of interest rates. Athenians paid 6% on sums borrowed from Athena and other gods around 430 B.C. They paid a mere 1.25% a century later. Greek interest rates trended downward between the sixth and first centuries B.C., partially as a result of a sharp increase in the stock of coins during the reign of Alexander the Great. Thus, the Temple of Delos, which usually lent on a long-term basis (five years) and regularly charged 10% just before the Peloponnesian War, saw its rate shift from being below the market average to being above it. At this point, demand for Delian credit shrank.

For another ancient people, the Hebrews, who were active moneylenders during their sojourn in Egypt from 1750 to 1447 B.C., interest became a religious matter. Mosaic law forbade interest, with the prohibition shielding more people over time. The Torah's older books, Exodus and Leviticus, dating around 1250 B.C., appeared to oppose the taking of interest only from the poor and needy. Exodus stated: "If you lend money to My people, to the poor among you, do not act toward them as a creditor: exact no interest from them." But in Leviticus, the admonishment read: "If your kinsman, being in straits, comes under your authority . . . do not exact from him advance or accrued interest . . . . Do not lend him money at advance interest, or give him your food at accrued interest."

The Book of Deuteronomy, written in the seventh century B.C., widened the prohibition to lending of money, food, and other commodities to all Hebrews, poor or not. "Thou shalt not lend with interest to thy brother: interest of money, interest of victuals, interest of anything that is lent upon interest." Deuteronomy also introduced a double standard: "Unto a stranger thou mayest lend with interest; but unto thy brother thou shalt not lend upon interest." The duality would generate arduous interpretation and conflict through the ages.

In India, lending is mentioned in texts from 2000-1400 B.C. Hinduism, which began in the early sixth century B.C., subjected interest to guidelines vaguely based on fairness. Its highest caste, the Brahmans, could not lend with interest "except to exceedingly wicked persons who neglected their sacred duties." If lending to the four highest castes occurred, only 1% to 4% interest could be charged. The interest was lowered as the caste of the borrower rose. For all others, maximum rates for unsecured loans were set at prohibitive levels—100% for gold, 300% for grain, and 800% for goods sold by weight. For secured or "use of pledge" transactions, 15% was the norm.

The total amount of interest payments was also scrutinized. Should interest payments cease after one year or after the principal had been doubled? At any rate, the Brahmans ordered payments stopped during interregnums. Despite permitting interest, Brahmanic law likened the taking of interest to selling with false weights and measures and called it "false money value," much as Jewish Talmudic law would do centuries later. By the second century, however, the unacceptability of interest had devolved to merely rates above legal and social limits.

Ancient Rome's early history probably contained a period when interest was absolutely prohibited. Ancestral tradition indicated a custom, enacted into law, that a thief had to pay twice the value of a stolen article, but a creditor was liable for four times the interest charged. The law apparently failed to curb the payment of interest and did not endure. In 450 B.C., the famous Twelve Tables codified Rome's traditional oral law and prescribed, in the course of laying down rules for the treatment of borrowers unable to meet their obligations, a maximum monthly lending rate of 8.3% (*unciarium fenus* or one-twelfth) and a limit of 100% a year for all Roman citizens. Interest ceilings during the Roman Republic (510-27 B.C.) were altered periodically. They ranged from 4% to 12% and from 4% to 12.5% during the Roman Empire (27 B.C.-476).

Lending, while disreputable ("would you take interest, would you kill a man?"), cut across all segments of society, and infractions of the regulations, including recourse to subterfuges like lending through a non-Roman citizen, were widespread. Checking debtor rolls, which could be bequeathed, was a morning ritual of the rich household. Moneylenders nonchalantly regarded laws limiting interest as "boiling water that soon cools off." Roman theater ridiculed the "silver man" who, once paid, "flees from the forum more quickly than a hare when it is let out at the games."

According to Plutarch, Cato the Elder (254-149 B.C.) staked money on mercantile loans, charging 12-48%. Julius Caesar (100-44 B.C.)

borrowed heavily to advance his political career. All this occurred in an environment where Roman senators were not supposed to lend at more than 6%. Loans were widely made to the rest of the empire, for which payments were often collected by the Roman army. Marcus Brutus (85-42 B.C.), the conspiratorial senator, was made infamous by Cicero for lending to the cities of Cappadocia and Salamis at a 48% rate, the same rate charged by pawnbrokers who were notorious violators of the law. The younger Aggripina (15-59 A.D.), mother of Nero, "had money out to provincials at such high rates that panic and insurrection broke out in Britain when loans of forty million serterces were called in."

Christianity, a religion rooted in Jewish beliefs and decreed by Constantine the Great in 313 to be tolerated throughout the Empire, viewed interest as intrinsically evil. The transaction was a sin. In its patristic period, Jerome (331-420), the translator of the Bible from the Hebrew original, and Ambrose (340-397), bishop of Milan, contended that the tribal Jewish prohibition of interest was universally applicable. The scriptural word for brother, from whom interest could not be exacted, carried the wider meaning of "sharer in nature, co-heir in grace, every people." Jerome decried interest charged in both money and commodities lending, and he urged lending freely, even to enemies in the spirit of the Gospel. Augustine (354-430), the renowned bishop of Hippo in Africa, considered interest no better than legalized theft and "beyond just entitlement."

The Church, influenced by the otherworldly teaching of its early theologians and concerned by the spread, particularly among the poor, of onerous consumption debt, reflected the strict interpretation of the biblical passages on interest in the pronouncements of its popes and Councils. In 305, 314, and 325, Councils prohibited the clergy from lending with interest or else be deposed. In 444, Pope Leo I wrote the first papal ban, which became part of canon law. In 345, 1139, 1179, 1274, and 1311, Councils forbade the practice to the laity.

Local Councils passed similar prohibitions, such as the Council of Reims in 1049 and synods at Gerona, Spain in 1068 and 1078. The Second Lateran Council of 1139 proclaimed this sweeping decision: "We condemn that detestable, shameful, and insatiable rapacity of money lenders, which has been denounced by divine and human laws and throughout the Old and New Testaments, and we deprive them of all ecclesiastical consolation, commanding that no archbishop, no abbot of any order, nor anyone in clerical orders shall, except with the utmost caution, dare to receive usurers; but throughout their life let them be stigmatized with the mark of infamy, and unless they repent let them be deprived of Christian burial."

The Third Lateran Council in 1179 largely repeated the pronouncements of 1139, including the denial of Communion to usurers and the refusal of their offerings. In 1148, Pope Eugene III decreed that mortgages were usurious, if the fruits of their pledge given to the lender did not reduce the principal.

In a decretal in 1187, Pope Urban III quoted a passage in the Gospel of Luke ("but love your enemies, do good, and lend, expecting nothing in return") as the absolute reason against interest. He accordingly decided two cases on the basis of mere intention to profit. This interpretation precipitated a debate. Was the Lucan text not to charge interest a commandment or, given its Sermon on the Mount context, a counsel that urged charity to the extent of not even anticipating the repayment of the principal? Some took the incident of Jesus driving the money changers out of the Temple to support total interest prohibition. But a number of scholars understood Christ's words as a counsel. Others took them as a counsel with regards to the principal and a precept as to the interest. For a few, a Latin textual variant that wrote the last phrase as "despairing [worrying] of nothing" removed any reference to interest altogether.

In 1274, the Council of Lyon noted that laws against usurers were inadequately enforced. It ordered rulers not to let usurers dwell in their territories. Foreigners practicing usury are to be expelled. It also nullified the wills of usurers, which do not contain instructions for restitution. Restitution has to be actually executed before Christian burial is allowed. Violators of this burial rule shall themselves be penalized as usurers. In 1312, the Council of Vienne reiterated that interest contradicted divine and human law. It ordered the rulers of Christendom to repeal secular laws that allowed interest and to desist from passing similar pending ones. This last exercise of conciliar authority marked the high point of the medieval Church's absolute opposition to interest. Clement V, the reigning pope, declared: "If anyone falls into the error of believing and affirming that it is not a sin to practice usury, we decree he be punished as a heretic . . ."

The Penitential of Archbishop Ecgbert (735-766) in England typified the Church's stiff position. "It is forbidden to all believers to lend money or goods for any unjust interest . . . . but anyone who makes a loan . . . must do it for love and out of necessity, just as he would wish that it were done to himself. If anyone do this out of wicked avarice, the sacred books prescribe for him a fast of three years, one year with bread and water and two according as his confessor prescribes for him . . . If a bishop or an abbot or a priest or any minister of God whatsoever makes a loan of money for interest . . . he is not worthy to receive the Eucharist, before he is amended, as it is written above, that is to say through a fast of three years."

English monks ignored the interest prohibition as borrowers. A contemporary account contrasted the behavior of some Cistercians and Cluniacs in Wales. The former were frugal and grew rich, while the latter, whose Order was founded around 1077, lived luxuriously and lost their wealth. The Cluniacs, rather than "recede in the smallest degree from their accustomed good fare [twelve to fourteen dishes] . . . would suffer the richest lands and the best buildings of the monastery to become a prey to usury . . ."

The states in Europe, emerging from the Dark Ages, acknowledged the spiritual leadership of the Church, though increasingly pitted against it politically. Canon law was generally accepted as superior to civil law. Local councils and rulers, starting from the Carolingian kings who ruled France, Italy, and Germany from 613 to 987, banned interest through ordinances (capitularies). Charlemagne forbade usury to clergy and laymen in 789. His successors condemned interest, although largely on paper. In practice, they opposed little more than lending money at high rates in times of food shortages.

The Capitulary of Nijmegen in 806, which defined usury as "where more is asked than is given," associated interest with dishonest profiteering, such as the hoarding of "grain or wine . . . for two denarii and holding it until it can sell again for four denarii, or six or even more . . ." Much of the Carolingian restriction involved small on-the-spot exchanges of a self-subsistent agricultural society. Transactions on a large scale or impersonal trade among distant places were yet to come. The pre-10th-century economy, it has been argued, was not far removed from that of the Hebrews when they received the Mosaic prohibition.

Interest continued to irk the popes, because they worried about the proliferation of Christian moneylenders. Beginning to outstrip their Jewish colleagues by the 12th century, they were likened to Judas Escariot, willing to betray Christians for 30 pieces of silver. Some of them went to the extent of masquerading as Jews in connivance with princely patrons. The ecclesiastic Bernard of Clairvaux (1090-1153) used the expression "to play the Jew" for Christians who asked for interest.

In 1159, Pope Alexander III used the idea of a spiritualized tribute as justification for interest in Christian lending to infidels and heretics. But he was adamantly opposed to lending to Christians. In 1163, he decreed that mortgage loans were usurious and ordered churchmen to withdraw from the practice, presumably as both lenders and borrowers. Innocent III at the Fourth Lateran Council, known as the Great Council of 1215-16, was vexed that some Church and civil authorities, "with no eye for God," invited Jews to their towns and supported their lending. He threatened borrowers with forfeited security and prison.

Among the popes, Gregory IX published probably the most sweeping condemnation of interest. Around 1140, Gratian, a Camaldolese monk in Bologna, assembled and integrated with his expositions a large amount of existing Church legislation. The collection, known as the *Decretum*, contained 29 scriptural and patristic citations against interest. Gratian, invoking Ambrose, had a broad definition of interest. It was any return on a transaction greater than the original investment. The *Decretum* generated copious commentaries, but these lacked sustained arguments that interest was against the natural law. Three popes, Gregory IX, Boniface VIII, and Clement V, codified the *Decretum* in 1234, 1298, and 1317, respectively. It became the basic manual of canon lawyers until superseded by a new code in 1917.

In his five-volume *Decretals* of 1234, Gregory IX labeled both cleric and lay usurers as infamous, ineligible for public office, honors, or to testify in court, whose wills were invalid, and who could not be pardoned unless restitution were made or whose day in court could not be delayed by appealing to other courts. Gregory IX expanded his list of offenders and directives. Clergy who buried usurers in sacred ground were also guilty of usury. Heirs of usurers had to return interest earnings or be penalized as usurers. Judges could try usurers without complaints filed by the borrowers. Landlords were forbidden to rent houses to usurers. Rulers were enjoined to expel them from their lands forever.

Raymond of Penafort, a Dominican canonist, helped write the *Decretals* of Gregory IX. He thought that the leading authorities on interest did not sanction it for anybody—Jew, Christian, or pagan. He understood Ambrose with a telling transposition: "From him demand usury, O you, whoever you may be, whom you rightly desire to harm: but you ought rightly desire to harm no one; therefore, you ought to demand usury from no one." Civil courts occasionally exercised a kindred sentiment, upholding Mosaic law to the extent of prohibiting interest among Jews themselves. In 1272, an English tribunal voided a starr between two Jews on the basis that "Jew ought not to take usury from Jew, in like manner . . . Christian may not take usury from Christian."

A theologian, William of Auxerre (1160-1229), using the absolute ontological phrase *in se et secundum se*, declared that usury was wrong in itself and according to its very nature. He had several reasons. One was that usury was like killing, but worse, since killing under certain conditions was justified. Another was that it violated the precept of doing to others what you want done to yourself. In his *Divine Comedy*, often understood as theology in poetry, Alighieri Dante (1265-1321) repeated the unnaturalness of usury. Asking his guide, Vergil, why usurers were so horribly punished, he was reminded of the usurer's lazy trade: "Having read the beginning of Genesis, that humans were empowered to make their way and earn their bread . . . . By taking another road, the usurer puts his hope elsewhere and in doing so despises nature . . ."

There was no mistaking the intrinsic evil attached to interest in the Middle Ages. Pope Leo I intoned that interest was the death of the soul. It was a continuous sin. An author of dialogues in 1220 had his monk character say: "Every other sin has its periods of intermission; usury never rests from sin. Though its master be asleep, it never sleeps, but always grows and climbs." A contemporary manuscript repeated this observation: "the oxen of usury work unceasingly . . . and since usury is an endless sin, it should in like manner be endlessly punished."

Justice demanded punishment for evildoers. Dante consigned usurers, these "woeful folk," to the seventh circle of hell, relatively far down in the pit, in the company of sodomites, crouched on burning sand, dusting off raining flakes of fire, and moaning endlessly. A fellow poet, Geoffrey Chaucer (1342-1400), subsequently described how these usurers were quickly dispatched to their deaths and hell. In his *Canterbury Tales*, the Friar recounted the tale of "an archdeacon, a man of high degree, that boldly did execute, in punishing of fornication, witchcraft, defamation, adultery . . . of usury, and of simony also . . ." Jacques de Vitry (c1160-1240), true to his fame as an itinerant preacher of the time, was more gruesome in telling the usurer's fate. A usurer, he narrated, had one-third of his moneybags buried with him around his neck. His family, wanting to get at the money, opened the grave. They saw demons filling the dead man's mouth with coins that turned into burning coals.

A new religion, emerging as the Roman Empire was ending and Christianity ascending, sharply condemned interest too. Islam was a curious twist of history, because it arose in the region where interest was first sanctioned by written law and where the major commercial centers of Mecca and Medina were located. The Quran composed by Muhammad (c570-632), founder of Islam, contained four passages denouncing interest. It denied that interest was a legitimate business activity and attached fiery punishment to it: "Those who devour interest stand like one whom Satan has smitten with insanity. That is so because they keep saying: The business of buying and selling is also like lending money on interest; whereas Allah has made buying and selling lawful and has made the taking of interest unlawful . . . . Remember, therefore, that he who desists because of the admonition that has come to him from his Lord, may retain what he has received in the past; and his affair is committed to Allah. But those who revert to the practice, they are the inmates of the Fire; therein shall they abide."

Later texts combined the threat of divine war against the taker of interest with assertions of the goodness of foregoing interest or even the principal: "Allah will wipe out interest and will foster charity . . . . Relinquish your claim to what remains of interest, if you are truly believers. But if you do it not, then beware of war from the side of Allah . . . . If, however, you desist you will still have your capital sums; thus you will commit no wrong, nor suffer any wrong yourselves. Should a debtor be in straitened circumstances, then grant him respite, in respect of the payment of the capital sum, till a time of ease. But if, in such a case, you remit the capital sum also as charity, it will be the better for you, if you only knew."

The final Quranic admonition on lending money took the high ground of charity toward the individual and the community. It pointedly asserted that it was money given in this spirit that truly earned incrementally. "Whatever you lay out at interest that it may foster the wealth of the people, it does not increase in the sight of Allah; but whatever you remit as *Zakat* [a communal capital levy] . . . that is multiplied manifold." *Zakat* became one of the five pillars of the Islamic religion. The Quran's implicit ideology decried interest for two reasons. One was the ancient observation that interest often abused relations among men. The other was that it was unfair, because the profit uncertainties faced by traders were difficult to reconcile with the risk-free activity of lending.

Muhammad did not get around to prescribing specific rules against interest. According to tradition, the revelation on interest was the last one before his death. Muhammad certainly was not against profit-making. He had been a merchant (though not completely successful), a calling furthered by his marriage to a rich widow with a business bent. His tribe had made Mecca a most important regional commercial center by the middle of the sixth century. The inhabitants of Mecca and Medina were no longer Bedouins living perilously. They were supported by settled agriculture and ruled by an oligarchy of merchant-princes. But as old tribal attitudes lost ground to individualistic values and the worship of money emerged, Muhammad had to shape a new economic vision. Muhammad sought to substitute the fear of God for traditional tribal shame. The common good had to be reemphasized.

Chapter 2

SIX CENTURIES

How did the moral positions of society and in particular of the three major religions fare through time? Did they remain intact? Were any absolutely rejected or partially modified? Did the evolution happen officially or virtually? Was there common principles retained and upheld? Did economic theorizing influence practical attitudes?

The Hebrews generally did not observe the no-interest rule among themselves from early times, frequently not even resorting to legal fictions. The prophet Amos in the eighth century B.C. revealed the greed of the rich and the sorry plight of farmers at the mercy of moneylenders. Debts frequently reduced these farmers to slavery. Denunciations backed by juridical penalties only appeared after a hundred years of flagrant violations of Deuteronomy. About 550 B.C., the prophet Ezekiel, disgusted with widespread transgressions, made the payment of interest not only a moral, but also a penal issue. Commanded by the Lord to pass judgment, he classified interest with such "abominations" as idolatry, homicide, adultery, and robbery. He threatened him who "takes both advance interest and accrued interest" with the supreme divine retribution: "Shall he then live? He shall not. He shall surely die; his blood shall be upon himself."

The prophet Nehemiah was as wrathful as Ezekiel at "the dishonest gain." In the Book of Nehemiah, dating from around 440 B.C., he told members of the Hebrew upper class, "You are all taking interest from your own people . . . . The thing that you are doing is not good . . . . Let us stop this taking of interest." He ordered them to return to their kinsmen "this very day" confiscated properties and the interest they had exacted on loans of money, grain, wine, and oil. He demanded an oath from the offenders to do so, shaking out the fold of his garment and threatening, "So may God shake out everyone from house and from property who does not perform this promise . . . may they be emptied." Documents from Nehemiah's time, showed the Hebrews lending among themselves at rates ranging up to 60%.

Besides material dispossession, spiritual deprivation also loomed. Ezekiel had numbered offenders among "evil men," thieves and murderers, and "shedders of blood." In the hereafter, when the poor are righteous and the rich not, the usurer (alluding to *neshek*, the Hebrew term for interest meaning a bite) would be "biting his flesh with his own teeth . . . . They will have no share in the world to come." A Talmudic dialogue may have said the last (and poetic) word on the spiritual argument against interest. Climaxing a lengthy observation that the harmony in all nature was a form of mutual lending, such as night borrowing from day and day from night, it declared: "He who exacts interest says to the Holy One, 'why do you not take payment from your world in which your creatures are'?" And the answer: "See how much I lend, yet take no interest, and how much the earth lends and takes no interest. I take only the capital I lent, even as the earth takes her capital. The dust returneth to the earth and the spirit unto God who gave it."

The normative Judaism of the rabbis as embodied in the Mishnah and the Talmud (completed early in the second century) prescribed adherence to the scriptural admonitions. The Talmud opened with the call: "Come and see how blind usurers are . . ." They "bring witnesses, a notary, pen and ink, and record and attest that [they] have rejected the God of Israel." A rabbi added: "More than rejecting God, they are guilty of heresy because they declare the Torah a fraud, and our master Moses a fool, saying, If Moses had known the profits it offers, he would not have written [the prohibition]." The rate of interest, whether high or low, and the time of payment, whether in advance or at repayment, were irrelevant. All the parties to an interest-bearing transaction (lender, borrower, witness, guarantor, agent, scribe) shared the guilt, although in varying degrees. Rarely did the Talmud hold responsible such a number of accessories to the violation of a religious commandment.

Toward the end of the second century, Talmudic jurists sought ways to evade what seemed impermissible at first hand—lending to Jews. A merchant, for instance, may sell for payment at a future date, and in a second transaction buy the same merchandise at a lower cash value. Similarly, a price increase in the payment for consigned goods after a lapse of time, hitherto forbidden, may be charged, if the price was tacitly and not expressly agreed upon. A creditor to a farmer could have land conveyed to himself, allow the debtor to remain on the land, but receive the produce as income from his property. Money could also be placed for hire like chattel, making interest a rental payment. Like the Romans, the Jews lent to non-Jews for relending to Jews. Some of these devices were considered reprehensible, sometimes for reasons not strictly based on charity or justice. Regarding non-Jewish intermediaries, for example, he "who hangs his money on a gentile and lends it on interest to a Jew" will be punished, since the biblical command was stated when God segregated the first-born of the Jews and the Egyptians.

Some jurists disapproved of lending with interest even to non-Jews, although not considering interest to be intrinsically evil. They equally conferred the praise of the psalmist for one "who does not ask interest on loans" to those who lent to foreigners without interest. A protectionist justification was offered for this pervasive righteousness. The "act of loving-kindness," *chesed*, should be granted non-Jews for the sake of peaceful coexistence. But segregationists felt, whether interest was charged or not, that Jews should not engage in lending to non-Jews to avoid assimilation. In fact, there were commentators who believed that asking interest from non-Jews was obligatory. Maimonedes (1135-1204), who abstracted all the then extant rabbinical literature, took the Hebrew word *tashikh* in the Mosaic law, which referred to taking interest from non-Jews, to mean "you shall" instead of "you may."

Eventually, the consensus formed condoning interest charges to the non-Jew. This was especially so if the practice became a necessary or only means of livelihood, or if it was undertaken by those learned in the Law who knew exactly what was licit. An influential rabbinical argument at the time said: "We live among the nations and it is impossible for us to earn a living unless we deal with them. It is, therefore, no more forbidden to lend at interest because 'one might learn from their deeds' than it is to engage in any other business." Economic survival remained a major justification for Jewish usury. Rabbi Eliezer Nathan of Mainz summarized it in the 12th century as follows: "where Jews own no fields or vineyards whereby they can live, lending money to non-Jews for their livelihood is necessary and therefore permitted." The rabbis insisted that a Jew should take alternative employment if available. Otherwise, "the unwelcome evil would be . . . tolerated."

The Jews besides were not immune from the expanding commercialization of Europe and from the resulting "conflict between law and life." By the end of the 15th century, Jewish religious leaders had pretty well rationalized interest for Jew and non-Jew alike. In 1500, Rabbi Farissol of Avignon, at a disputation with Christians, argued that if nature required that assistance be extended to every person needing it, then if anyone needed a house or horse, they should be provided him without payment. Making money from having money was no less reprehensible than from having land. Times had changed, "bringing a new situation and new obligations" involving payment.

The price system was considered to be an amenable regulator of society. In 1551, another rabbi asked why a peasant who secured grain to sow should not pay 10% to the lender after a good harvest. This seemed a normal business transaction, and he judged it to be correct. Chief Rabbi Loew of Prague declared that "certainly the truth is that interest benefits both [parties to a credit]" and that the biblical "prohibition was not intended to harm business transactions . . ."

The joint venture, the precursor of stock companies, became an important issue. Such enterprises were often undertaken. How justify those who merely provided funds? To legitimize this financing, a standard legal form was formalized called *hetter iska*, permission by partnership. First adopted in Poland and Lithuania in 1607, it is still used by orthodox Jews. The deed, *shetar iskah*, written with two witnesses, stipulated that the lender would supply money. The borrower would run the business solely and guarantee the lender's investment not only against all loss, but also with a fixed minimum profit. The lender would pay the borrower a nominal sum as wages and agree to share any loss. The loss would typically have to be proved by specific proof. The loan, plus the guaranteed gain, was due upon maturity.

The *hetter iska* became so established that the simple appending of the words *alpi hetter iska* to a note or contract sufficed. The *hetter iska* enabled Jews to participate widely in business, though it could not cover all situations where interest was construable in economic terms, such as cash discount on supplier credit paid early or compensation for inflation or currency debasement, since the rabbinic norm was to repay the nominal value of loans. Gradually the *hetter iska* was viewed as unnecessary. Already, for instance, the use of an agent to borrow or lend money with interest was judged to be permissible, since a man could not be held responsible for another's deed in the case of a criminal offense such as usury.

Despite their vagile experiences, the Jews played a paramount role in lending money during the Middle Ages. This was partly the result of circumstances that narrowed their choices of economic activity. Their agricultural land (the first Jews in Europe were principally farmers) was heavily taxed or ownership gradually denied them. They were excluded from the commercial guilds as early as 1099 in northwestern Europe. Peter Abelard (1079-1144) recognized their "sole resort is usury." The Jews charged a wide range of interest rates—from below normal to significantly high levels that courted resentment. Their rates were frequently regulated by the rulers of Western Europe.

When in 1179, the Third Lateran Council forbade all Christians from engaging in usurious transactions, the opportunity for Jewish entry into credit operations, already perceptible since the start of the 11th century, opened further. At the same time, civil authorities encouraged the Jews to become creditors in hopes of securing loans. Gradually, Jewish moneylenders owed much of their place in society to the financial services they rendered to royalty, the state, the upper classes, Church dignitaries and institutions, and even to a few caliphs in Islamic lands. Aaron of Lincoln in England, in the second half of the 12th century, loaned money to nine monasteries and helped build two cathedrals. A Jewish banker, Jacob Henriques, averred that his father helped plan the formation of the Bank of England.

By the 18th century, "court Jews" were firmly established in all the major countries of Europe, while Jewish petty lending to small traders and peasants declined in the context of periodic expulsion from villages, a rising Christian urban middle class, and competing merchants. The "court Jews" gave rise to powerful merchant bankers, like the Rothchilds, in the 19th century. Their opulent financial network soon reached North America, negotiating such diverse undertakings as the Civil War and the building of the railroads in the United States. In Italy, the prominence of the entrenched Jewish banking families slowly dwindled in the mid-16th century, partly due to competition from the *montes* and the pressure of Counter-Reformation polemics. Throughout the rest of Europe, however, Jewish bankers remained a leading force until the beginning of the 20th century.

There was less flexibility in Islam's disapproval of interest. The Arabic term for interest, *riba*, meant a fixed excess or addition. The word originated in the pre-Islamic experience of non-paying debtors seeing their debt double at each default. Early Islamic scholars supported a strict interpretation. Lending with *riba* was described as the sale of "one dinar for two." Thus, exchanges of non-monetary precious metals and of some foods that entailed unequal amounts of the same commodity were not allowed, even if the transaction was completed immediately and with items of different quality. The rule was no "sale of gold for gold, silver for silver, wheat for wheat, barley for barley, dates for dates, and salt for salt, except like for like, equal for equal, and hand to hand." *Riba* was prohibited to non-Muslims as well. Islamic jurists deemed demanding interest as equivalent to committing adultery thirty-six times. They thought it to be punishable by death.

Nonetheless, as early as the eighth century, the practice of various types of transactions that embodied interest was devised in the Arabic region, where lenient Talmudic interpretations of interest also first took shape. Islamic law and morals, gathered in the Shariah, were true to the Quran's prohibition, but the emergence of schools of legal thought lent interpretative nuances. Partnerships were permitted, whereby "profits" were shared. Or loans were split into two transactions: the borrower buys an item on credit from the lender, and the lender repurchases the item for a smaller cash price. Sometimes, a third party was introduced in this arrangement to avoid involving the same two parties. A lender may sell a good on credit for a higher than its common price. The purchaser-borrower would then raise the repayment money elsewhere. A borrower also may sell property for a limited period, while the buyer-lender would get the rent. The orthodoxy of these and other ingenious devices, *riyal*, had their supporters, but also never went unchallenged.

The sale, for example, of a certain quantity of goods and the immediate buying back of part of it by the seller was considered a usurious transaction, because, as the Hamdi jurist al-Jawziyyah (1289-1349) taught, the Shariah considers both the acts and the intentions behind them. The Mdiki scholar, al-Shab Shatibi (d1388), agreed: "anyone who seeks to obtain from the rules of the Shariah some thing which is contrary to its purpose has violated the Shariah and his actions are null and void." But this consideration of the internal motivation was not shared by two other schools, the Shafi'i is and Hanafi. They focused on the external conduct, so that for them the turnaround sale was not improper.

There were rules held by all sides. A Muslim could sell one dinar for two outside Islamic territory. No *riba* could be taken from non-Muslims, *dhimmis*, living under Islamic protection, and no *riba* could be paid them by Muslims. Several Muslim rulers countenanced financing operations involving indirect interest. A decree of al-Muqtadir (d931), caliph of Baghdad, when he began his reign in 908, allowed Christians and Jews to engage in banking. These bankers, *jahabidha*, were paid a service fee, frequently in the form of another monetary metal, that is, not gold and silver. These metals were the standard in currencies, since their value were held to remain constant. Riba was not concerned with equivalence in numerical value. A borrowed gold dinar could be paid with two dinars of a baser metal coin.

Later apologists for *riba* argued that the "excess" meaning of the word should be understood as only forbidding excessive rates. They also said that the stricture was only for consumption loans. It did not apply to certain transactions like payment of interest by governments, trade financing, penalty for defaulters, inflation indexing, and productive investments.

Recent response to evolving leniency so far has been pragmatically obedient to the Shariah, Islam's code of law. It is best exemplified by the rise of the so-called Islamic banking. Islamic financial institutions have fashioned sophisticated products not directly invoking *riba*. These bank facilities, essentially based on an equity system, cover a broad range of services from interest-free deposits to joint-venture investments, leases, mortgages, and mutual funds. Nonetheless, Islamic scholars are still divided on these banking contracts. The controversy between the modernist and rigorist schools of Islamic law on *riba* remains unsettled, so that Islamization of the financial sector in Arab countries continues to be pursued. Even Western banks are beginning to offer products complying with Shariah strictures.

The evolution of Christianity's practice of interest-taking is reflected in the studious efforts, starting with the schoolmen, to develop reasons for the moral justification of interest. Their arguments, strengthened by rational economic observations, gathered force and by the 17th century had become persuasive. The legality of interest was becoming more established in Europe. Its practice was near universal, and the Protestant Reformation boosted the growing liberalization.

Initially, Martin Luther (1483-1546) and John Calvin (1509-64) had vehement reservations about interest, taking it to be sinful. Soon enough, however, Calvinist doctrine came down to abrogating Deuteronomy's prohibitions, but left untouched its presupposition of justice and charity which admonished avoidance of injurious rates. The Golden Rule was both the norm and permit for interest. It allowed interest "neither in every case, every time, in all forms, and to everybody." A person's conscience acted as the unerring judge. "Let each one then," Calvin explained, "place himself before God's judgment seat, and not do to his neighbor what he would not have done to himself, from whence a sure and infallible decision may be come to. To exercise the trade of usury . . . [and] in what cases, and how far it may be lawful to receive usury upon loans, the law of equity will better prescribe than any lengthened discussions."

In 1547, Calvin fixed the maximum rate for interest in certain parishes around Geneva at 5%, plus penalties and fines. Two years later, he was able to say that anyone could accept in good conscience the 10% maximum of England's Henry VIII, because situations varied in different places. Ultimately, the inner word of God should guide the lender in fixing the interest rate.

In terms of economic justification, Calvin regarded money as fruitful. He assailed Aristotle's barrenness theory as of "little weight." Money could purchase a house, whose use could beget money. Money could also buy idle land, which when tilled yielded yearly revenue. "Tell me," asked Calvin, "when I buy a field, does not money breed money?" Unused money was surely infertile. But no borrower left money unemployed. A borrower was not cheated by paying interest from his gain. The lender himself could procure land or house. Why should he be blamed for choosing to earn instead income in the form of interest? From Geneva, Calvinism spread to the great merchant cities of London, Antwerp, and Amsterdam.

The Reformation did not close the debate on the morality of interest. For a century after Calvin, bitter controversies swirled through European towns, particularly in Germany and England. Traditionalists cited all the learned authorities they could muster from Plato to Luther. They disputed the exegesis of Calvin point by learned point. They also stooped to coarse invective, calling usurers drones and "Messrs Mammon, Lucre, Hoard, Gripe, Bloodhound, & Co." The nub of the debate remained the applicability of the law of Moses. Was the brotherhood of mankind universal, removing all distinctions, or not?

The logic of those who answered affirmatively was often labored, but sometimes it came close to making sense. John Jewel, an Anglican bishop, posed this *non sequitur*: "What kind of dialectic is that—it is not allowed to ask usury from the poor, ergo it is allowed to ask it from the rich? Even schoolboys know that from a negative it is not right to conclude an affirmative." Around 1590, another English preacher, Henry Smith, wielded the Mosaic prohibition like a double-edged weapon: "Of a stranger, saith God, thou mayest take usury, but thou takest usury of thy brother; therefore this condemneth thee, because thou usest thy brother like a stranger." The stranger, Smith continued, "doth signify the Jews' enemies they were commanded to destroy . . ." Usurers, he hoped, would "allege this Scripture no more."

The hold of medieval rules was tenacious. In England, "canon law," wrote an economic historian, "was nationalized, not abolished." Thus, a high ranking official "would not have . . . men altogether to be enemies to the canon lawe, and to condempne everythinge there written, because the Popes were aucthours of them, as though no good lawe could have been made by them." The Popes made "rightly godly" laws. Equally acceptable were "the statutes of holie Synodes and sayings of godlie Fathers, whiche vehemently forbid usurie." For one ecclesiastic, "by the laws of the Church of England . . . usury is simply and generally prohibited."

The English church, while now subject to the Tudor crown that was becoming more tolerant of interest, struggled to preserve its jurisdiction over the ethics of economic behavior by virtue of its prerogative on matters of conscience. The polite clash did not preclude blunt affirmations by the church, such as: "The permission of the Prince is no absolution from the authority of the Church. Supposing usury to be unlawful . . . yet the civil laws permit it, and the Church forbids it. In this case the Canons are to be preferred . . ." As late as the mid-17th century, ecclesiastical courts heard usury cases, granting absolutions or meting out excommunications, always issuing admonitions, like to one Thomas Wilkoxe, "a horrible usurer, taking 1*d*. and sometimes 2*d*. for a shilling by the week."

The defenders of interest, who were less aggressive in Germany than in England, where civil law had countenanced interest since 1545, also arrayed an assemblage of arguments of varying validity. They repeated that it was not intrinsically evil, because it would then be absurd for God to allow the Hebrews to exact it from strangers. Moreover, strangers meant aliens, not enemies. Besides, it was still wrong to mistreat enemies. Moreover, enemies meant a state of war. Normal trade relations, including credit transactions, were suspended during wartime and resumed at its conclusion when enemies became friends. Interest was appropriate among friends.

Another syllogism, raised in the late 13th century, pointed out that Deuteronomy legislated against the alien on account of the Hebrews' hardness of heart. But all men are similarly hard of heart. Therefore, rulers could permit interest in their laws, implying that Jews lent anyhow. A legalistic break between Jews and Christians was also invoked. The Law of Moses "never bound any other Nations . . . . Much less do they bind us that are the servants of Christ, so long after the dissolution of their Commonwealth." Richard Baxter, a pioneer Puritan leader, admitted that Mosaic laws, insofar "as they are a part of the law of Nature, or of any positive law of Christ . . ." bound Christians, but "not one of them as Mosaical." In America, Puritan divines in 1699 decided that the intention of the selfless counsel in Luke's gospel was merely that alms, not credit, should be given to the poor.

England, a rising trade power, witnessed a flurry of interest regulation and deregulation. The Commons under Henry VII (1457-1509) repealed statutes from the time of Edward III (1312-77) and Richard II (1367-1400) that prohibited chevisaunce (loan with profit) and usury. The Commons thought them to be too abstruse anyway. Henry VIII, who in his reign (1509-47) secured considerable six-month loans from Flemish bankers at 14%, legalized interest in 1545, asserting that the policy required only a purely secular prerogative. A maximum rate of 10% was allowed. Charging a higher rate meant triple forfeiture of the principal. But market rates existed alongside legal rates. John Shakespeare, for example, the father of William, was accused twice of violating the law by charging 20 pounds for loans of 80 and 110 pounds.

Henry's legitimization of interest soon disturbed social-reform minded members of Parliament, which was admonished for being "so voyed of Gods Holy Spirit that thei shoulde alowe for lawfull any thyng that Gods Worde forbideth . . ." Under Edward VI (1537-53), Parliament legislated the Usury Act of 1552, barring all usury as a "vyce moste odyous and detestable, as in dyvers places of the Hollie Scripture it is evydent to be seen." Imprisonment, fines, and forfeiture of the loan were again imposed on the lender. But after voluminous written debate, Elizabeth I (1533-1603) reenacted the legality of interest in 1571, which has remained till now. Elizabeth herself, noted for fiscal discipline, paid off "promptly the short-term, high-interest loans she occasionally had to raise in the Antwerp money market."

The impracticality of prohibiting interest and the growth of an influential class of financiers made the revival of usury inevitable, but its restoration still compromised with tradition. The document contained the contradictory declaration that "all usurie being forbydden by the lawe of God is synne and detestable." Contracts to pay over 10% were automatically void, and contracts to pay less than 10% could be contested by the borrower, if he so desired. The lender, while committing no crime, technically remained liable to forfeit the interest, even if small. Borrowers, however, rarely attempted to recover interest paid, if only to maintain their credit standing. The provision favoring the borrower became a dead letter of the law.

The new Usury Act of 1571 marked the formal distinction between interest and usury in England. The latter was identified with exorbitant rates. "The mischief is of the excess, not otherwise . . . ," an advocate of the legislation wrote, "it is sharp dealing which is disliked and nothing else." In this spirit, courts usually ruled for borrowers in hearing lawsuits. Consequently, astute lenders resorted to creating loopholes. For example, they tacked on additional interest to loan agreements for contingencies that were in fact certain. Thus, one borrower had to agree to pay 33 pounds in six months for a loan of 30 pounds, if his son were still alive. The court judged this contract to be usurious because of the short time frame.

Toward the end of the century, charging interest "was perfectly practiced almost by every Christian and so commonly, that he is accounted for a fool that doth lend his money for nothing." In 1586, the Anglican clergy had to study a manual that did not compromise on "oppressive contracts which grind the poor," but which also cautioned that "before interest is condemned as usury, it is necessary to consider both the terms of the loan and the position of borrower and lender." Gradually, natural law was invoked, not to restrain interest, but to assert individual freedom in economic affairs. A merchant character speaking in a book written by a Tudor official typified the changing attitude: "What man is so madde to deliver his moneye out of his own possession for naughte? or whoe is he that will not make of his owne the best he can?"

Soon, the ethical debate gave way to discussions about the right level of interest rates. The emerging capitalists of the Elizabethan era saw high interest not as "bad morals, but as bad business." They were the forebears of mercantilist economics. In 1624, James I lowered the ceiling on the interest rate to 8%, with the House of Commons striking out from the statute the phrase "that all usury was against the law of

God." Other references to divine displeasure in legal documents were replaced by economic statements like "the great abatement in the value of land and merchandise" that would ensue were interest disallowed. Almanacs, one with the modern title of *Money Manager*, appeared, listing "the necessary tables of interest, the usurer's gain, and the borrower's loss" and distinguishing between acceptable and objectionable rates.

In 1652, the maximum rate was again reduced to 6% and in 1713 under Queen Anne (1702-14) to 5%. Public debt offered a greater inducement for creditors. In 1693, the government issued an annuity yielding 14%. In general, however, the enforcement of the 5% maximum and of the previous ceilings was not so difficult, since domestic market rates were slightly lower through most of the century. The government borrowed at 3%. In the English colonies in America, the legal and market rate kept close together within a range of 6% to 8%.

English legalization encouraged efforts to justify interest. A Puritan theologian presented as the ideal loan contract for Christians one in which the creditor would share the risks with the borrower and ask only "a fair share of the profits, according to the degree in which God has blessed him by whom the money is used." Richard Baxter seconded his coreligionist in this Thomistic view of partnership, saying interest becomes unlawful when the lender refuses the borrower "such a proportion of the gain as his labour, hazard, or poverty doth require, but . . . will live at ease upon his labours; or when in spite of the borrower's misfortune, he rigorously exacts his pound of flesh . . ."

It also was not usury to invest money in commerce to generate regular income for people, like widows and orphans, who could not trade on their own. The next step in this argument was easily taken—to ask the rhetorical question why the poor could not lend with interest too, why they should give money, for instance, to a rich market speculator for free. And against the assertion that interest, being earnings from barren money, was not like rent and profit, which were not objectionable unless excessive, the retort was that if it was not criminal to purchase a rent-charge or to participate in business profits, why would it be unlawful to charge for a loan?

Like England, France, while loyal to Catholicism, saw an easing interest policy. In decrees of 1425 and 1455 under Cardinal Richelieu, the Church in France permitted lending with interest not exceeding 10%. Under Louis XI (1423-83), annuities, *rentes*, began to be issued. Their rates varied from 5% to 10%. Francis I (1494-1547) then issued perpetual annuities. Louis XIV (1638-1715) reenacted the usury regulation, extending it even to commercial loans, except in Lyons. During his reign, the conversation of the upper class in Paris easily included the rates of interest as prices, women, and civil disputes.

Subsequently, a legal rate was established. Royal and municipal bond issues paid interest between 8% and 16%. But investment in shipping ventures to the East could yield from 20% to 150%. In the last two decades of the 17th century, annuities paid from 5% to 8.3%. In 1720, the legal rate was lowered from 5% to 2% (the fiftieth penny). In 1724, it was raised to 3.5% and in 1725 was moved back to 5%. In 1766, it was reduced by Royal Edict to 4%. In 1789, the dormant usury prohibition was finally revoked and a maximum rate of 5% set. These alterations, frequently lower than market rates, were often induced by policies to ease the public debt burden. Napoleon, following English statutory policy, fixed a maximum interest rate of 6% for commercial credit and 5% for property loans. In 1800, the Banque du France was established to stabilize money conditions after the revolutionary years and to set monetary policy.

Lending with interest also prospered in Italy. The father of Francis of Assisi, for example, was reputed to be a moneylender. Living in an environment disapproving of interest, especially of high rates, many of the merchants resorted to a host of devious circumventions, which became partially acceptable as liberal scholastic theory evolved. Pawnbroking offered the easiest opportunities for practically extorting interest. The value of the object pledged was predictably more than the money lent. A certain Oderigo di Credi pawned a jacket in Florence in 1412 for 20 lire. He retrieved it six months later, paying 24 lire and 13 soldi for an annual interest of 45%.

A Cardinal Gonzaga received 3,500 ducats against 20 trays of cameo from a Medici bank in 1486. When his family tried to redeem them, it was asked to pay 4,100 ducats, an amount later raised to 5,000 ducats because the claimants objected. The family subsequently lost ownership of the jewels. While the stigma of usury dogged the pawnbrokers, they too eventually gained acceptance. When Florence imposed a yearly penalty on pawnbrokers, other cities followed, knowing that the heavy fine would be understood as the tacit grant of a license. Pawnbrokers generally charged from 23% to 37%, depending on the security.

The rising city-states in northern Italy, with their sophisticated fiscal structures, were lucrative ground for earning interest. As early as the mid-12th century, wealthy families of consular lineage lent large sums of money to the commune of Genoa at high rates of interest. This financial arrangement, at first a privilege, became practically a right, stirring up aggressive resentment from the populace by the 14th century. In Milan, in the last decade of the 12th century, controversy gripped the city over the high interest rates paid to rich communal creditors. Taxes due from merchants and noblemen were converted into interest-bearing loans.

Throughout the region, second only to land taxes, usury aggravated the division between the nobility, medium landholders, and rising entrepreneurs on one hand and commoners on the other. Like cross-border trade, the large interest-bearing loan was one of the quickest ways of amassing big profits. The funds for such credit often came from the earnings accumulated from countless small and oppressive loans. Debt piled up in the countryside on tenant farmers and petty landowners, frequently resulting in loss of home and agricultural tools. Interest rates went from 10% to 100%, clustering in the 20-40% range. In Venice, well into the 16th century, accumulated funds were used to buy an office or to extend personal loans under the guise of false property rentals to hide illegal interest.

Charging interest was a particularly explosive issue in Florence. Commerce there was intertwined with established great fortunes. Friars were banished from the city for questioning the practice. Like Luther in the north, the Dominican Girolamo Savanarola (1452-98), burnt at the stake for his reformist zeal, included usury in his sermons against the city's sociopolitical behavior. Savonarola placed usury under the general sin of avarice. He bewailed its rampant practice and denounced the dichotomy between the lawful and the unjust that men accepted: "Because of avarice neither you nor your children lead a good life: you have found many ways of making money and many exchanges, which you call lawful but which are most unjust . . . . No one can persuade you that usury is sinful, you defend it at the peril of your souls. No one is ashamed of lending at usury, nay, those who do otherwise pass for fools." Later, when engaged in reconstructing the Florentine republic, he dictated the draft of a bill for the establishment of a Monte di Pieta.

Elsewhere in Europe, the payment of interest was taken for granted. Many types of private and public annuities, which Pope Martin V had declared lawful in 1425, were circulating. They paid 6.5% to 12.5%. Around 1458, this observation was made by Pope Pius II: "The Viennese . . . who lend money for a certain period, if they should suffer any loss after the term of the agreement has expired, extort whatever sum they wish, and impose the highest penalty on the debtors. Pledges which are given for loans, if they are accepted, are not considered usurious."

Monarchs paid interest too. In September 1511, the Hapsburg Maximilian I, grandfather of Emperor Charles V, sought to be pope, expecting the death of Pope Julius. He approached the Fuggers for a 300,000-ducat loan with "reasonable interest." Additionally, he wrote that he was "willing to give . . . one hundred thousand ducats for his [Jakob Fugger's] three jewels . . . although they are not worth the said sum—but still as secret interest on the loan." In 1560, Emperor Charles V issued an ordinance allowing an annual interest rate of 12%. The rate was maintained by his son King Philip. This rate was meant for merchants experiencing difficult times. But it became a general permissive benchmark. Antwerp accepted deposits at 12%. Because the rate was more than the 6-8% allowed the nobility for its lending, some of the nobility and wealthy merchants secretly lent at higher rates. They preferred to be idle. The result was "uncultivated lands and an insufficient and high-priced supply of victuals, goods, and merchandise." In 18th-century Russia, 5% was the legal maximum, but loans were made at 8-10%.

The official doctrine of the Church lagged behind easing scholastic conclusions and economic and civic realities. The earliest extant edition published in 1566 of the catechism of the Council of Trent which was assembled in December 1545 as a counter-reformation move, passed this judgment under the heading of the seventh commandment: "Various forms of robbery. Violation against justice. Robbery is more comprehensive than theft. To this class also belong usurers, the most cruel and relentless of extortioners, who by their exorbitant rates of interest, plunder and destroy the poor. Whatever is received above the capital and principal, be it money, or anything else that may be purchased or estimated by money is usury; for it is written in Ezechiel: He hath not lent upon usury, nor taken an increase . . . and in Luke our Lord says: Lend, hoping for nothing thereby."

Several popes reinforced Trent. Sixtus V issued a bull in 1586, whose title, *Detestable Avarice*, sufficiently revealed his contempt for "the whirlpool of usury." Alexander VII and Innocent XI in 1666 and 1679, respectively, censured the external titles to interest of lapse of time and lack of money. In 1835, Rome extended to the whole Church a 1745 encyclical of Benedict XIV that reasserted the injustice of interest. But an explicit reservation on certain contracts and titles left much open to theological discussion. Benedict's encyclical was the last direct papal pronouncement on interest.

Rome, however, was becoming more susceptible to the sound economic reasoning for interest accumulated over the centuries. It was aware of people's de facto acceptance of interest. It finally decided in non-committal responses to seventeen pastoral inquiries from 1822 to 1838 that lenders generally "should not be disturbed," *non esse inquietandos*, as long as the interest was allowed by law. Rome refrained from defining the immorality of interest as a dogma. Conscience was left alone to rely on the correctness of the legal title, removing all practical doubt about interest. Nonetheless, ethical argumentation on interest persisted. The civil title had to be defended for awhile. The Church's distinction between licit and illicit contracts eventually held and debate subsided.

Leniency was creeping into the Church. Pope Pius IX himself borrowed in 1850 millions of francs at substantial interest from the Rothchild bank to remodel the basilica of Saint Peter. In 1891, Leo XIII issued an encyclical on the condition of the working classes. In it the Pope observed that "the mischief [exploitation of labor] has been increased by rapacious usury, which . . . is under a different guise, but with like injustice, still practiced by covetous and grasping men." As the meaning of these words was vague, they had little effect on lending practice or the question of morality. Pius X, pope from 1903 to 1914, again obscurely used the word "usury" when he admonished capitalists and masters "to pay a just wage to workmen; not to injure their lawful savings by violence, fraud, nor by open nor hidden usury . . ." Scholastic thinking in favor of interest increasingly assumed a syncretist form. Theologians pressed the notion that money was a fruitful good and its "possession . . . draws a value of which the creditor is deprived for a time . . ." The passage in Luke was sustained as a counsel for charity.

All this time, the straightforward condemnation of interest was still found in past compilations of the Church's statutes. A new Code of Canon Law in 1917 toned down the stricture with some ambivalence. Once more there was recourse to civil legality: "If a fungible thing is given someone, and later something of the same kind and amount is to be returned, no profit can be taken on the ground of this contract; but in lending a fungible thing it is not itself illicit to contract for payment of the profit allocated by law, unless it is clear that this is excessive, or even for a higher profit, if a just and adequate title be present."

In 1983, a revised Code of Canon Law was released. It spoke of interest indirectly, because this time it was urging its practice. It said that "all administrators are bound to fulfill their office with the diligence of a good householder. For this reason they . . . could invest the money which is left over after expenses and which can be profitably allocated for the goals of the juridic person." What was previously morally forbidden was now a recommended financial task of cleric functionaries. The latest revision of the *Catechism of the Catholic Church* published in 1992 contained no mention of usury.

In countries of other religions, interest periodically came under regulation. Rates were determined sometimes on account of economic policy (to promote agricultural production for instance), but oftener to prevent financial oppression. In 18th-century Japan, when metal had replaced rice as money, courts frequently altered contract rates, once alleging that the action was for the peace of mind of the lenders. In 1877, the Meiji passed a law restricting maximum annual rates on different loans to 12%-20%. The law was little obeyed. In India, the British unsuccessfully sought to break the monopoly of rural credit by moneylenders in 1879. This was followed by usury legislation in 1918 and the 1920s. In the 1930s, colonial boards trimmed the terms of agricultural credit.

China had a long history of lending with interest since 400 B.C. and of interest rate regulation. The dynasties successively prescribed rates and loan terms, which usually went unheeded. In 511, the accumulation of interest exceeding the principal amount was prohibited. The prohibition was maintained onward from the T'ang dynasty (618-907). Compound interest was typically illegal. The T'ang dynasty permitted from 728 relatively high rates of 4-6% per month. The Sung dynasty (960-1279) followed with 5%, and the next three dynasties with 3%.

Beginning in the eighth century, the Chinese state was a major moneylender. Invested government funds fetched around 3%, down from 8% early in the seventh century. Actual rates, especially of private loans, were 8-10% a month, but trended downward to 3-5%. Interest was assigned for funding public projects, and the rates here were high. In the 11th century, the government began lending at lower rates, such as 10-20% for farmers. In the 13th century, it loaned to merchants at 9.8%, who re-lent the money at strikingly higher rates. The legal maximums were scarcely enforced. Evasion was common and uncomplicated, such as less money actually loaned than written in the contract. Chinese pawnshops in the 18th century observed the 3% maximum, which was reduced to 2% in the next century.

The ecclesiastical teaching office of the Church was mistaken in its sustained prohibition of interest. It changed its mind, somehow belatedly. The Catholic and Protestant arguments for and against on the matter have since subsided. Christianity's present view on interest is acceptance of its morality. There is, however, an overriding and implicit norm of charity. Simplistically, this means avoidance of relatively excessive rates. Such rates are the basic rational for existing usury laws. But their prescribed maximum levels are, at best, studied calculations of fairness. They are legal thresholds, not moral absolutes. A 3% interest rate for a consumption loan to a small-salaried person with a large family may be extortionate. A 15% rate to finance an enterprise of a billionaire could be concessionary.

The "thou shalt not" of Judaism and Islam still stands. Interest must not be directly sought. Jews are free to receive interest from credit to non-Jews. They also lend to coreligionists, but they must follow prescribed procedures so as not to violate the Mosaic law. In some places, they operate free loan societies like a small parallel banking system. Jewish institutional lending to Jews observes religious rules. Muslims also are prohibited from explicitly asking interest from anyone. The transactions of Islamic financial institutions are carefully structured to be formally interest-free. Western banks operating in Muslim countries have to be Shariah-compliant.

For both religions, as in Christianity, the obligations of charity retain relevance in the conduct of monetary credit. There is always the "act of loving kindness" for the Jews and communal alms for the Muslims. And there is the Golden Rule for everyone else who charge and pay interest as a matter of course.

PART TWO

FOUNDATIONS OF THEORY

Chapter 3

THE FIRST ABSTRACTIONS

Introductory economics textbooks retain the traditional and simple definition of interest as a payment for the use of money. The interest rate is the price of using money, conventionally reckoned as a percentage of the amount used for a one-year period. Eventually, the money is returned, for it was not bought, but borrowed or, as some economists say, hired.

This functional definition of interest goes back to antiquity. Aristotle (384-322 B.C.) felt "with the greatest reason" that lending money with interest was not "the natural use of it." For the Romans, the technical term for interest, as handed down through their law of contracts, was usury, *usuria*, derived from the future participle of the Latin verb "to use." Interest was the charge for the use of a loan of money or commodities. Usurers were simply moneylenders.

There was some evolution in the word usury. In the works of the dramatist Plautus (234-184 B.C.), usury signified the mere use or enjoyment of a thing. Later, the word was applied to the use of a borrowed thing, usually money. The scholar Varro (116-27 B.C.), in accordance with legal writing, then used it to designate whatever increment was paid in excess of the principal. This meaning has persisted. But usury originally was not a reprehensible term necessarily denoting lending with excessive rates. In 1595, Shakespeare accurately rendered the Roman definition as "the rate of usance."

From this elementary understanding of interest, the history of the economic theory of interest progressed to answering two critical questions with more scientific explanations. Why is interest paid? And what is interest? The questions were interrelated. The reply to one often implicitly answered the other. Interest, for instance, was paid because of its productive nature. Chronologically, however, the first question received the early attention, since it touched on the morality of interest.

The principal task until the middle of the 15th century was to show why interest should not be paid at all. On one hand there loomed the total religious prohibitions against interest by ancient Jewish law, medieval Christianity, and Islamic doctrine. On the other, the prevalence of exorbitant interest rates, especially on consumption loans to individuals, was an economic plague. Lastly, the antipathy to interest of Greek philosophy continued to retain some of its validity.

Later, theorists, living in more permissive and rapidly commercializing economies, often took the payment of interest for granted, but they could not avoid the second question. They had to define the fundamental essence of interest. In this inquiry, they were quickly faced with a third question. What determines the rate of interest? Here too, formulating the answer sometimes either depended on what they held interest to be or showed them what it was.

Greek philosophers, living in a society that allowed interest freely, presented the first abstractions. Plato (428-347 B.C.) was firmly opposed to interest, and even to credit, as harmful to peace in the community. By multiplying their capital, usurers multiplied the number of drones (criminals and paupers) in the hive of society. But Plato consented to a form of interest when the payment of a commercial obligation was delayed beyond the agreed time. In this case, the debtor was to pay twice the amount involved and, if the payment remained overdue for a year, an additional penalty of an obol a month for each drachma owed (about 17% interest). For Plato, interest was less a payment than a penalty for delay. It was meant to discourage borrowing.

Aristotle agreed with his mentor's opposition to interest. For Aristotle, "the most hated sort" of money-making "is usury, for it makes a gain out of money itself, and not from the natural use of it." Furthermore, Aristotle improved on Plato's socio-political arguments. While he condemned usury in very descriptive language, placing those who "lend small sums and at high rates" in the same class as brothel keepers, cardsharpers, and those who steal the clothes of somebody bathing, his treatment of interest combined metaphysics and economics.

According to Aristotle, the nature of money, whether money was instituted by men, the temple, or the state, was to serve as an efficient medium for the exchange of goods. Through money, one can exchange shoes for either food or a house, and one can import and export goods. As a go-between tool and not an end in itself, money was not intended to be a source of gain or to increase on its own. To make it do so would be contrary to its nature. Lending with interest "makes a gain out of money itself, and not from the natural object of it. For money was intended to be used in exchange, but not to increase at interest . . . . Wherefore of all modes of making money this is the most unnatural."

Aristotle supported this *contra naturam* argument by his view of the two uses of all goods. A shoe is used for wear. It can also be employed for exchange or barter. The first use is proper and the second improper, because a shoe is made for the road and not for the trading place. The proper use of money was to facilitate exchange.

To emphasize the perversity of the multiplicative effect of interest, Aristotle used the word *tokos*, meaning offspring, for interest. "This term usury," he insisted, "which means the birth of money from money, is applied to the breeding of money because the offspring resembles the parent." Interest could be defined as "currency, the son of currency." The organic metaphor was in vivid contrast to the obvious barrenness of metal coins. Aristotle had a wry note for his terminology. He observed that a rich man will starve, like Midas in the fable, because he cannot eat his money. Centuries later, Shakespeare echoed Aristotle when he had Antonio in the *Merchant of Venice* ask Shylock, "When did friendship take a breed for barren metal of his friend?" Nonetheless, a few passages earlier, Shakespeare had Shylock admitting that he breeds his gold and silver as fast as "ewes and rams."

The succinct logic of Aristotle's objection to interest was persuasive for a long time. The phrase "barren money" would be repeated and expanded as a theoretical principle until the Renaissance. In fact, the notion could be extended to 1803, when the French economist, Jean Baptiste Say, implied in his famous "law" that all goods produced (supply) would be consumed (demand). Money was merely a neutral intermediary in the economic cycle. Still, barrenness was a departure from ancient Middle East thinking, which sometimes took objects as animate. The loan of "food money" (dates, olives, seeds), for instance, embodied the act of reproduction.

Aristotle's methodically correct definition of money proved to be a mental straitjacket. His observation was narrowly based on money as physical coin. He failed to abstract the power of money and the relevance of the other functions he assigned to it, holding them as secondary. Like Plato, he held that money also served as a unit of account, "a single universal standard of measurement," that made exchange easy. Unlike Plato, who thought a nation's hoard of wealth should be spiritual and not material, he further saw money as a store of value that was "useful too for future exchange," although, he correctly noted, prey to inflation. Had Aristotle probed deeper into these secondary purposes and into his perception of the use and exchange values of a commodity, his analysis could have produced fuller insights. Instead, Aristotle closed it with syllogistic simplicity: interest went against the nature of money, what is unnatural is wrong, therefore interest is wrong. From this reasoning, Aristotle implied that interest was payment for nothing. The creditor did not deserve it.

Rome's legislators and jurists, seeking for their great legal compendiums objective and lasting principles of justice for credit relationships, provided much of the thinking on interest in the Roman Republic and Empire where interest was permitted, but regulated. A maximum legal rate was set, altered periodically up or down in response to socio-economic conditions. There were several categories of Roman loans.

In the so-called *commodatum* loan (the very thing lent was returned such as an agricultural tool), Roman jurisprudence consented to a charge for the use of what was lent, since the lender retained ownership, and the contract was deemed a *locatio* that invoked the nature of a lease.

The other type of lending, the *mutuum*, was debt in its truest sense. Imbedded in a contract, it created a two-way bond in which the creditor had a right to claim and the debtor an obligation to pay. "The bond was independent of the fact whether the debtor has now the thing rendered to him or not, indeed whether he has anything at all to pay with or not."

An example of the *mutuum* was the loan of money or grain, "which is to be returned in kind only, and which may not legally be reclaimed except through some action of the borrower, since the ownership of that thing rendered has passed over from the lender completely." The word *mutuum* conveyed the sense of mine (*meum*) becoming yours (*tuum*). Unlike the *commodatum*, the claim of the *mutuum* was on a person, not on a thing, and the Romans referred to debts as names (*nomina*), a practice later banking adopted for its clients.

Interest was not allowed in the *mutuum*. Any interest was stipulated in a separate agreement, turning the loan into a *faenus*, a debt carrying interest. The *stipulatio*, being often unwritten, was difficult to enforce. The stipulation was necessary, because the *mutuum* was a gratuitous loan and assumed no risk of default for the lender. The *mutuum* specified the transfer of fungibles, which were goods whose distinct units were interchangeable, such as coins or grains of corn. Thus, the borrower really needed to return only an equal amount, even if payment was delayed. Since fungibles were almost always either destroyed or lost when used, that is, were consumables or perishables, the *mutuum* was also called a consumption loan.

The *mutuum* was no different from the Roman deposit known as the *depositum irregulare*, which was the deposit of fungible goods with another party. Restoration was explicitly restricted to only as much as was deposited originally, even though the custodian had assumed ownership in the interim. Roman jurists saw the inadequacy of the *mutuum* contract in itself as a basis for interest, so that it sought justification for interest outside of the loan in what became known as "extrinsic titles." An easy title to invoke was the purpose of a loan.

Interest was reasonable in commercial loans, such as a mortgage, since their aim was profit and the acquisition of assets. In addition, the typical circumstances of the commercial borrower indicated one who was not in dire straits. Another good reason for interest was the repair of any damage inflicted by a credit transaction. The Romans, who long held that interest could be claimed in sales involving defective merchandise or delayed payments for merchandise bought, readily made the analogy between paying late for goods and repaying borrowed money past the due date. They recognized why the passing of time could be damaging.

In directing the payment of an amount equal to the prevailing rate of interest to an aggrieved supplier-creditor, Roman law declared that delay imposed a loss of potential profit on the lender. The Romans identified the gap between what the lender received and what he should have received as *quod interest*, meaning that which lay in between or that which constituted a difference. Soon, interest shifted from possibility to actuality. Interest became restitution for gain automatically foregone. This punitive reasoning was amplified repeatedly.

Domitius Ulpianus (170-228), a prominent jurist, considering a buyer who is behind in his payment, noted that it was fair to pay the seller interest, since the buyer was enjoying "the fruits" of possessing the good. Another jurist, this time arguing on the buyer's side, more than supported Ulpianus. He wrote that the non-delivery of a sold slave should entitle the buyer to compensation that equals his lost gain, plus any gain earned in the interval by the seller from the slave he was withholding. To prevent abuse, the jurist set a rate cap of 100% in computing this combination of potential and actual loss. Nonetheless, there was legal disagreement on the matter. Julius Paulus, a contemporary of Ulpianus, rejected the validity of exacting interest from a non-performing seller of consumable goods to offset any potential gain lost by the buyer. Paulus apparently dissented, because he did not consider money to be an example of a consumable, which was a significant departure from the common view. Money could not be lost.

Another business transaction that normally allowed interest was the sea loan, *faenus nauticum*. It involved the pooling of money, commodities, or labor resources. The sea loan was technically considered as part loan and part partnership, *societas*. However, it did not apportion the risk equally. The debtor was not responsible for any loss at sea. Only when he landed did he incur risk and the obligation to repay the loan. But he had to pay the creditor for the absence of any liability while at sea. For this, Roman legislation allowed a charge of twice the legal rate of interest, calling this "the price of peril." Thus, interest also became payment for risk.

As the Roman Empire waned, its experience with money and with interest notably diverged. Rome watched its currency retrogress to debased coins amidst bursts of hyperinflation. This led to draconian and ineffectual price-fixing by the state. In contrast, its juridical treatment of interest saw the early emergence of directional ideas with a filial potential. First, there were external grounds that legitimized interest. Second, the loan's purpose and the type of goods lent were pertinent. Third, the notion of time was relevant. Fourth, the example of a good producing a stream of income as embodied in the slave working in one of Rome's landed estates was important. Lastly, risk had to be covered. These concepts, particularly of time and a capital good, were primal building blocks. They would never disappear from the sequential formation of interest theory.

Chapter 4

THE SCHOOLMEN'S TURN

The ancient and early-medieval definition of interest was quite generic—*quodcumque sorti accedit,* whatever is over and above the principal. This plain generalization induced intellectual dormancy on the subject. Thirteen centuries had to pass before the philosophical probing of interest by the Greeks was assiduously resumed. Besides the rediscovery of Aristotle's *Ethics* and *Politics* when they were completely translated into Latin around 1250, moral and economic forces spurred the study. Christianity, paralleling the stern prohibitions of the Jewish and Arab religions, had attached to interest the notion of sin. It was a crime against canon law that was subject to Church courts. At the same time, commercial growth was reshaping Europe with metropolitan centers where fortunes were amassed. The economic expansion of the Roman Empire was being repeated, only on a grander scale.

The volume of European business from the 13th to the 15th century, a period that has been called "the commercial revolution," grew to be so great and complicated that the prohibition of interest became impractical, honored more in the breach than in the observance. Recourse to obvious subterfuges abated as loans were structured to fit complex market situations, and new ideas about money appeared. The bulk of interest rates fluctuated between 10% and 50%, sustained by capital scarcity and imperfect financial markets. By the 16th century, interest was prevalent.

Given this dynamism of the age, the tracts of the so-called schoolmen or scholastics, who dominated the academic world from roughly the seventh to the 16th century, understandably produced the first organized and sustained analysis of interest and the beginnings of a positive theory. Intending to rationalize the Church's doctrine against usury, scholastic philosophers and theologians began to differ from the lawyers of canon law. The immorality of interest had to be grounded not only on human legislation, but also on natural law. They gradually realized that the extreme positions of no interest under any circumstance and interest at any level stood against reason. The canonists, chiefly concerned with directing the conduct of people toward saving their souls, based their objections mainly on the greed of the lender or the exploitation of the borrower. The scholastics, while intent on the moral aspect, inevitably crossed over to more economic arguments.

In his discussion of interest, three traditions—Aristotelian logic, the permissive Roman law, and the prohibitive Bible and its patristic interpreters—guided Thomas Aquinas (1225-1274), the most renowned and authoritative of the scholastics. His *Summa Theologica*, written from 1265 to 1273, began the thesis entitled *Of the Sin of Usury, which is Committed in Loans* by posing four questions, two of which contained seeds of theory.

Aquinas asked "whether it is sinful to receive money as a price for money lent, that is, to receive usury; [and] whether it is lawful to borrow money upon usury. The first question referred to the lender and the latter to the borrower. Responding to the first question on the basis of natural law, Aquinas wrote that interest was "in itself, unjust, since it is a sale of what does not exist; whereby inequality obviously results, which is contrary to justice." Interest was paying for nothing, because the use of money as a medium of exchange was its own consumption. The concrete use of money meant its loss. "It should be noted," Aquinas said, treading on the grounds of the Roman *mutuum* loan and of bequests, "that there are some things the use of which is the consumption of the things themselves; as we consume wine by using it to drink, and consume wheat by using it for food. Hence, in the case of such things, the use should not be reckoned apart from the thing itself."

The grant of use meant the grant of the thing itself "and therefore . . . the act of lending involves a transfer of ownership." Alienation at the first exchange was proven by the fact that the coins lent disappeared, and other coins were returned in payment. "Therefore if a man wished to sell wine and the use of wine separately, he would be selling the same thing twice, or selling what does not exist; hence he would obviously be guilty of a sin of injustice . . . . A man commits injustice who lends wine or wheat, expecting to receive two compensations, one as the restitution of an equivalent thing, the other as a price for the use, which is called usury." In another passage harking back to Plato's prohibition of a seller in the marketplace from asking two prices, Aquinas wrote: "The use of money . . . is not other than its substance: whence either he sells that which is not, or he sells the same thing twice, to wit, the money itself, whose use is consumption; and this is manifestly against the nature of natural justice."

In furthering his consumptibility argument, Aquinas contrasted money and food with a house or a field. "There are some things," he argued, "the use of which is not the consumption of the thing itself; thus the use of a house is living in it, not destroying it. Therefore a man may lawfully receive a price for the use of a house, and in addition expect to receive back the house lent, as happens in leasing and letting a house." Civil law recognized usufruct in this case, but ruled that "things which are consumed in use do not receive a usufruct." Accordingly, Aquinas took the secondary use of coined silver for show, *ad pompam*, and for bailment also to be licit.

An earlier passage from another work, where Aquinas took money as a measure, again stressed the nothingness in the use of money, that is, in interest. It retraced Aristotle: "All other things have some utility from themselves . . . money, however, has not but is the measure of the utility of other things . . ." The utility in the use of money, therefore, does not come from the money itself, "but from the things which are measured by money according to the different persons who exchange money for goods."

The notion of equivalence in exchange was behind this argument. What was borrowed was exactly repaid. A money loan was a contractual claim expressing an immutable measure in fungible terms. If utility was ascribed to money itself, the measurement became incorrect. The value of money in itself was independent and unchangeable—an abstraction that did not refer to the face value of money. Thus, "to receive more money for less seems nothing other than to diversify the measure in giving and receiving, which manifestly contains inequity." Interest therefore created an unfair price. It was not paying for any utility. Aquinas was implying with the modern economist "that the price of any commodity that is chosen for the standard of value is unity by definition."

Aquinas' position was tightly formulated logic. Intrinsically, the use of money was self-destructive and therefore no positive value could be attached to it. The union of use and substance, plus the fixed value of money, rendered money fundamentally barren. Aquinas' final words on usury were that the usurer "sold what did not exist." His reasoning proved durable for almost two centuries, until later scholastic thought migrated from Aquinas' mind-set on personal consumption loans to commercial lending. The issue was subtly shifted to "pure" interest, that is, the price not of the use of money, but of money itself as related to the prices of goods. Unfortunately, the word "utility," pregnant with economic meaning, failed to nudge Aquinas toward further avenues of analytical thought. He was busy with less mundane subjects. Six centuries had to intervene before the word was taken up again.

Interest assumed great importance for the scholastics in the immediate post-Aquinas period. They began to write tracts on the subject that began the mixed rejection and acceptance of interest. Their disagreement on several counts with Aquinas and other anti-interest advocates harbored the perception that interest was really a payment for something. Joannes Andreae (1270-1348), a renowned canonist, criticized the tenet that ownership passes in a loan. The lender loses ownership in terms of substance (the very same money is not returned), but he retains it in terms of value and can ask for profit "according to the mode in which it pertains to him . . ." Andreae also believed that time could be sold, "since many licit contracts occur in which is interposed a delay of time, and yet it is not said on this account that time is sold." Aquinas thought that time should not be sold, being God-given.

A Franciscan friar, Gerald Odonis (d1349) was next on the scene. He was one of a triumvirate of friars deemed to have reached the apogee of medieval economic thought. Their manuscripts on trade and credit became the grit of sermons and the material for subsequent scholarship. Odonis threw a wide net over the subject of interest, courting controversy. He held that use and ownership could be separated, that a loan and a lease were distinct in terms of the burden of risk, that the creditor sold the right to use and not use itself, and that a lender, instead of benefiting from someone else's labor, was in fact losing the opportunity for the use of his own industry and time.

The second friar, an Augustinian named Gerardo of Siena (d1336), sided with Aquinas on consumptibility He offered a "corrected" rendition: "A thing having always a given value cannot increase in value with use; use and substance are one value and the sum must remain constant." The use value of money was taken as zero. However, Gerardo affirmed vendible time against Aquinas. He distinguished between common time and time "applicable to something, which duration and use are conceded to someone for him to use." This time "is the property of someone, just as the year for which a horse is lent to me is said to be mine: and this kind of time can be sold." In addition, Gerardo did not admit barrenness merely because a thing was man-made. Employing Aristotle's procreation terminology, he wrote: "A house can be seen to be an artificial thing, and yet within a certain period of time someone might profit from a house as much as another house is worth, and thus a house would give birth to a house."

The third friar, the Franciscan theologian Bernardino of Siena (1380-1444), came like Gerardo from Tuscany, a region thriving with commerce. He quickly gained with his treatises on money and interest the reputation of being among the world's first bona fide economists. Intent on condemning interest, he preached its material and spiritual evils as much as explaining its economic nature. Like Aquinas, he thought the loaned thing became the property of the borrower. But he attached the loan's duration to the transfer of ownership. This led him to admit the sale of the opportunity to use money and the sale of time as when a debtor reduces the amount of his loan by repaying earlier than the contracted term. The anticipating debtor sold what he owned. Bernardino revised this view afterwards, saying that the debtor in this instance was selling the chance of using money and not time.

Bernardino must have recognized a relation between time and gain and how these factors rendered money to be "capital." He was among the first scholastics to elaborate on this term. He conceded that one could sell at the present moment, for instance, corn, at the higher price expected in the future, because the owner's preconceived gain contained "something of the seminal character of profitability, which we commonly call capital." Profit was the offspring of capital. Borrowed money somehow brought a yield that justified interest.

While views remained conflicted, there was a less controverted side to the scholastic coin. Most of the early scholastics objected to interest on intrinsic grounds (usurers were "worthy of eternal death") or proposed hair-splitting qualifications. But practically all of them accepted payment exceeding the principal on the basis of "extrinsic titles" or factors external to a loan. Such titles could be traced back to the Roman law that compensated damages. Around 1150, a jurist in Bologna surnamed Azzo may have substituted the infinitive form *interesse* for the Roman juridical phrase *quod interest*. Both literally meant "to be in between." The latter was understood as that which was between the lender's current state of loss and what would have been his uninjured condition. The former, from which the noun "interest" was derived, became standard by 1220 to mean the gap between what the lender was paid (the original sum) and the total of what he should receive, given that damage was inflicted by the debtor's failure to fulfill obligations.

Subsequent usage, often influenced by the idea of damage inflicted, tended to mention interest in connection with commercial loans. The term usury became increasingly confined to advances for personal purposes where arbitrary abuse was likely to occur. As a result, business cases provided the impetus for the growing approval of interest as opposed to usury. An early high-profile case involving guarantees was typical, if somewhat convoluted. Guarantors first had to repay a debt in default by borrowing money with interest. Then, Lucius III, pope from 1181 to 1185, ordered the debtors to reimburse the guarantors, including the interest paid and other losses incurred.

Parties to a loan could agree to a penalty for damage beforehand. The lender, however, had to set the penalty to induce the borrower merely to repay on the due date and not to circumvent the usury prohibition. The latter intention was presumed if the penalty was not a fixed sum, but varied relative to the length of the delay, or if the lender was a known usurer. Throughout the 13th century, notarial records show the penalty was frequently outlandish, amounting to twice the principal. Churchmen lent money with penalties, construing them as just punishment, *poena*, and not interest. The scholastics therefore insisted that the penalty should be proportionate to the costs of recovery, as was the practice of the Roman jurists. This prior estimation of damage formally tied penalty to delay, since it came into force only after the actual incidence of damage, *damnum emergens*. Such interest was licit "because it is sought for the sake of avoiding loss not taking gain." Aquinas agreed with this interpretation.

Eventually, the distinction between penalty and delay was completely blurred, and the preset interest was payable upon a delay whether there was damage or not. This practice developed from the question that delay had quickly raised: does delay cover only actual damage or also injury presumably to be incurred, that is, potential profit lost, *lucrum cessans*? To this question Aquinas had answered yes. Speaking of a thief who stole seeds and of a creditor faced with a default, he wrote: "One is held to give some compensation . . . . The sower of the seed in the field has the harvest not actually but virtually. In like manner, he that has money has the profit not actually, but only virtually; and both may be hindered in many ways." In this combination of seed and money, Aquinas apparently sensed the fecundity of money that signified an increase in value.

Toward the end of the 14th century, the claim to lost potential profit was generally accepted, but strictly in the context of delay. Most scholastics initially rejected calculating the lost profit as equivalent to the profit made by the borrower. They still regarded money not as the principal or the equally principal cause of gain, but the industry of the borrower. Aquinas, still skeptical about the potency of money, explained this view in treating of restitution: "The money . . . is not related as a root to the profit which is made from it, but only as matter. For a root has . . . the power of an active cause, inasmuch as it ministers food to the whole plant . . . this, however, is not necessary in that which is matter."

In scholastic metaphysics, matter, *materia*, is inert, awaiting an activating form, *forma*. Hence, Aquinas carefully pointed out that measuring the amount of foregone profit was correctly done in terms of the lender's productive occupation, for example, as a merchant continuously engaged in trade.

The recognition of forsaken profit naturally led to another issue. Did the lender have a right to compensation right from the start of a loan, in effect even without the debtor delaying payment or defaulting? The extrinsic titles were becoming intrinsic factors, imperiling the gratuitous loan. Solid resistance to this advanced interest lasted for more than a century. Aquinas favored profit foregone, siding with another's justification for interest that "each one may licitly keep himself indemnified," by writing: "A lender may without sin enter into an agreement with the borrower for compensation for the loss he incurs of something he ought to have, for this is not to sell the use of money, but to avoid a loss." Aquinas, however, did not explicitly say that the compensation had to be advanced: "One ought not to sell what one does not yet have and may be prevented from having in many ways." The claim to compensation could be exercised only in the case of actual delay or default.

Aquinas endowed this final position of his with a sarcastic double-sided caveat. In the first place, "he who lent the money ought to beware lest he incur damage for himself. Nor ought he who receives the loan incur loss from the stupidity of the lender." Duns Scotus (c1266-1308), whose theology differed from Aquinas on certain major issues, repeated this admonition: "If he [the lender] does not wish to be injured, let him keep back the money . . . because no one forces him to do a merciful deed for his neighbor."

Enrico Bartolomei Hostiensis (c1200-1271), a cardinal and canonist who liked to sing and play the viol, provided in 1270 the first indication that an a priori claim to lost profit could be licit. But he attached a strict condition, namely, that charity motivated the lending and that the lender was not a repetitive creditor. "If some merchant," he wrote, "has, out of charity to me, who needs it badly . . . lent money with which he would have done business, I remain obliged from this to his interesse . . ." In 1312, Astesanus de Ast (dc1330), a Franciscan moral canonist who resided in usury-infested Lombardy, quantified the same opinion, citing the example of a man, who, about to buy land, lends the money instead to a pleading borrower. The lender was entitled to charge what he would have reaped from the land. At the time, Astesanus had already approved of interest for damage incurred, applying this to the notorious debt of the cities of northern Italy sold with interest to the public under compulsion.

Toward the end of the 15th century, the objection to prearranged interest for lost profit, based primarily on the argument that there was no certainty of profit being gained prospectively, started to lose ground. The impetus for the change came from civil action. Seeking funds, the governments of the major cities in northern Italy began borrowing money through the formation of the so-called *mons*, a fund in which lenders were given, more accurately levied, shares. The shares had no fixed maturity, but the city could redeem them anytime, albeit rarely, at a 28% value. Payments were made to the shareholders annually "as gift and interest," which were not subject to restitution. Florence paid 15% in the 13th century, later 10%, and finally down to 5%.

The defenders of this fiscal practice, largely Franciscan scholastics as opposed to the Dominicans and Augustinians, sought justification of the interest payments in the compulsory nature of the scheme and the meager rate of interest. Justice demanded compensation not only for hardships forced on the lenders, but also for missed future profit, since the majority of the bondholders were merchants. Moreover, the interest was merely an average and not proportionately variable, since it was practically impossible to determine each lender's financial circumstances. Interest could be paid at the start, because the cities set no date for redemption (no obligation to repay in effect) and could be considered to be in perpetual delay. If citizens were to remain uncompensated in advance, they "would . . . be driven to desperation and would plot against the republic to the serious loss of body and soul and danger to the republic."

Bernardino of Siena, mindful of money as capital, took another tack in favoring the receipt of interest from the start. It was still compensation for actual damage, given that the *mons* lender suffered deprivation from the outset. But he granted lost profit only in the case of the merchant, because he "gives not money in its simple character, but he also gives his capital." Lest this opinion admitted that money could fructify, Bernardino was careful to explain that "money has value not from itself, but from its owner's industry, and therefore the receiver of the money not only deprives the owner of his money, but also of all the use and fruit of exercising his industry in it and through it." However, while recognizing the external title of lost profit, Bernardino avoided immediately inferring that a lender out of charity had the same initial right to interest as the lender induced by force. Bernardino was backed by Antonino Pierozzi (1389-1459), another theologian from Tuscany and reputed economist, who stated that the money of a businessman had "the nature of capital."

When Bernardino and Antonino spoke of capital, they were unaware of nurturing a topic that would grow immensely with time. Capital had ancient roots. It was the plural form of the Latin word *caput*, meaning head. It alluded to the practice, which antedated the Romans, of counting heads, *capita*, of cattle when men figured out their assets and transactional accounts in terms of livestock. The Latin term for money, *pecunia*, derived from a word that meant a herd, because pasture lands were the sole public revenue for a long time and fines were imposed by the paying of so many sheep or oxen. The earliest Roman coins had the image of a bullock or sheep's head. The English word "fee" corresponded to the German *Vieh*, meaning cattle. The Sumerians' word for interest was *mas*, which meant a young animal. Eventually, the precious metals with their high value and portability gained preeminence as the embodiment of wealth.

Bernardino and Antonino were aware that the transfer of precious capital carried the risk of a loss. Risk featured in two major forms of investment of the age, namely, partnerships and the census. What did the scholastics say about risk-sharing partnerships? Medieval thought generally held from the beginning that interest did not arise where the financier shared all the risks with his partner. In fact, the creditor was deemed to be an investor, not a lender, and exercised ownership. The issue thus devolved on the burden of risk, if any, borne by the capitalist. Hostiensis denied the partnership nature of the sea loan, as the total risk was not shared in common as in a brotherhood. Hence he accepted interest here as licit on the basis of Roman law, citing analogous arrangements that assigned partial risk to one of the parties or did not differentiate the profit arising from the use of money from the profit realized by the use of a borrowed non-consumptible such as a workhorse.

Differing from Hostiensis, Bernardino and Antonino, attempting to preserve the intrinsic stricture on interest, judged that the risk of defaulting on a simple loan was similar to the risk involved in a partnership venture. They therefore did not excuse the notion that a lender should be able to ask interest beforehand for the risk of a partner's default, *periculum mutui*. Bernardino held that "the risk of this case is nothing different from the character and act of lending . . . . Therefore to profit from this risk is to profit from the act of lending alone." Or as Antonino put it tersely: "By reason of doubt in a loan, which is implicit in it, one may not licitly hope profit."

Aquinas, in contrast, was forthright in regarding partnerships as a lawful source of interest income. His opinion, centered on the issue of retained ownership, was concise: "He who commits his money to a merchant or craftsman by means of some kind of partnership does not transfer the ownership of his money to him but it remains his; so that at his risk the merchant trades, or the craftsman works with it; and therefore he can licitly seek part of the profit thence coming as from his own property." This defense of partnerships was respected for nearly two centuries, even though it harbored three reversals of the author's previous principles against interest. Aquinas may have tolerated these inconsistencies, because he (and many others) instinctively thought this analysis of partnerships to be patently fair. Firstly, Aquinas said in effect that the use and ownership of money were not indistinct, for the use alone was handed over to the partner. Secondly, ownership did not go with the use of a consumable, but was established by the incidence of risk. Thirdly, money was implied to be fecund.

The authority of Aquinas did not suffice to settle the issue of partnerships definitively. There remained scholastics who, while aware of the reasonableness of the risk-taking argument, strove to keep the usury doctrine intact. Several claimed partnerships sold time. Some simply denied that risk justified earning a profit. Others maintained the sterility of money by assigning profit to the labor of the working partner or to the goods bought by the money. Interest as payment for risk in a partnership remained a conflicted belief.

The other investment tool that the scholastics could not avoid treating was the census. This was the sale of a contract that obliged the issuer to pay an annual return. People, usually the nobility, raised money this way against their land assets. States sold the census against their land, monopolies, and tax revenue. Was investment in a census, which originated in feudal economics and initially paid in actual agricultural produce, usurious? There was no immorality in buying fruit, even over a period of time, unless the price was unjust. But when the fruit was cash, the matter became debatable. Money and interest were obviously playing a central role in the census transactions.

Henry of Hesse (1325-97), a theologian and an early specialist on justice and money lending, took a favorable view. He believed that the creditor bought an interest in the property and was part owner. He had a right to an annual return. His contemporary, a Henry of Eutin, simply denied the direct involvement of interest. He declared that the lender purchased solely the right to the money. The right and the actual return were distinguishable. A number of scholastics agreed with Henry of Eutin, including Bernardino and Antonino. But the problem of the just price immediately surfaced. Pope Innocent IV had a ready reply to the objection that the census return would eventually exceed the cost. He pointed out that property purchased would likely appreciate in value. Appreciation did not make trade unlawful.

More important, Henry of Eutin had an argument that explicitly invoked a concept critical in the development of interest theory in the 20th century. He declared that the census exchange was one for one, money and the right, and that the money and the right were to be valued as to their present utility. He wrote: "There may also be considered the circumstances of the seller as to industry and other things of this sort according to which, it may be weighed how much the money he receives is worth to him." Thus, the census issuer could set the price in terms of his present valuation of money. In the same vein, Giles of Lessine (c1235-1304), a Dominican philosopher and scientist, a pupil of Aquinas, and author around 1280 of the most complete study on usury in the Middle Ages, held that the just price was what parties to an exchange think it to be. "Future things over a period," he wrote, "are not estimated to be of such value as the same things collected in an instant nor do they bear such a great possible utility."

Securities pricing proved to be more of a distraction than an impediment to the interest earnings of the census. A few prominent scholastics abstained from treating the census, including Aquinas. Silence may have been consent. The census was already a widespread practice in Europe. The scholastics generally approved a secondary market where the census right to money was sold to a third party at a discount, particularly in the case of the state censuses. The *mons* right was similarly sold and also personal debt in positive danger of default. In these cases, interest accounting was incorporated.

The scholastics examined banking too, but not rigorously at first. Only at the start of the 15th century was serious discussion about banking practices undertaken. Deposit-taking by banks and trading companies began marked growth in the late 13th century and was a large operation by the 15th century. The great banking families of Florence flourished. They initially paid an interest of 20% for a four-month deposit and later 5-10% for demand deposits. They netted 14-20% in the first decades of the 14th century. Companies paid 10% for demand deposits. Both the banks and the companies, working on fractional reserves of around 30%, created credit, largely for investment in partnerships, which would be considered licit. Wards of the state and widows accounted for a significant share of the deposits. The interest earned by widows was justified on the basis of gain foregone. Wards were excused in that the interest (usually 5%) was deemed as penalty for the carelessness of the guardians.

Thinking on the morality of fixed bank deposit interest was divided. Bernardino and Antonino thought it was reprehensible usury. Even the widow depositor was committing wrong. But Antonino elaborated by describing inconsistent liabilities. He believed that "a true deposit stands to the peril of the depositor, not to that of the depositary . . . nor does the depositor intend to have gain from the depositary." Yet, he said that money in deposit banks "stands . . . to the peril of the recipient in every eventuality, and the depositor receives profit . . ." He further observed that the risk of the usual turnaround loan by the bank was borne by the borrower, "in which peril the depositor did not wish to be a participant." The puzzling conclusion apparently was that interest paid for bank deposits was unjustified. It was payment neither for risk nor for a sharing of profit. The same reprimand was directed at the discounting of pending bank disbursements, for bank credits were treated as virtually cash in hand.

Some forms of exchange banking aroused suspicions of error as well from the moralists. Early in the 12th century, credit was combined with currency conversion in a transaction known as *cambium nauticum*, a sea loan payable in foreign currency. The cross-border bill of exchange became a standard instrument for conveying credit. Three cardinals frowned on the bills of exchange negotiated at the merchant fairs of Europe. One of them, Hostiensis, said that a 100% annual rate was realized in these arrangements. The denial that the bill of exchange was a loan, but a simple sale in reality, was dismissed as "verbal defense." Albert the Great (1196-1280), who pioneered the teaching of Aristotle in the Middle Ages and taught Aquinas, viewed the exchange dealers as creditors. Aquinas himself was more derogatory. He applied the fifth verse of Psalm 5 to them, which used the words boastful and evildoers. Albert and Aquinas were both commenting on Aristotle's dislike of traders.

Those siding with the money changers presented their position by mainly defining the resulting monetary difference between two places and two points of time as entitlement to *interesse* for expenses and services rendered. They proposed that the value of money could be different "through diversity of place," with the relative strength of one currency explained by the locality's supply of and demand for money. Here too, however, the matter of intention was introduced. The future value of money must be truly doubted. Otherwise, the desire to profit was present, time was sold, and usury committed.

Bernardino and Antonino, although accepting pure money changing and bill-of-exchange charges for safekeeping, transport fees, and expected devaluation, came down hard on the exchange dealers, not even sparing the bills practices of the papal curia. Despite the scrutiny, exchange banking flourished. Its complicated contracts eluded the identification of straight lending. The bankers, whom society respected, were growing in the belief that interest from commercial credit was not objectionable. Money was emerging as a commodity. It had the characteristic of an investable and not solely of a consumptible, It had established market pricing and therefore deserved a legitimate claim to business profit. Interest was excused as a service charge. But more significantly, the ideas of time, place, and capital were increasing their relevance in the explanation of interest.

The late scholastic period—the 15th to the mid-16th centuries—opened the door, which was left ajar by preceding analysis, wider to licit interest. Coupled with pressure from expansive and inventive commerce, the disunity in the views on partnerships, the census, and the banking and exchange operations eased the way for the next instruments of finance to meet with favor. Laymen were joined by clerics, and together they adopted lenient attitudes and new analytical viewpoints. Insurance next came up for scrutiny.

Insurance markedly developed in the 14th century to protect against risk in the growing Mediterranean trade. By the turn of the century, insurance had expanded to cover property on land as well as financial guarantees. Previously, insurance was judged as selling risk unconnected to the existence of a loan. Bernardino considered it as the hire for or price of a service. But Antonino disagreed. Guaranteeing a loan, which entailed a fee (2% was mentioned by Bernardino), may not be insurance, but was like selling the credit of the guarantor which was tantamount to the price of a loan. Meantime, in 1485, the vicar-general of the Franciscans, Angelus de Clavasio, wrote that the capital invested in a partnership could be insured, but by a third party, with the working partner reducing the profit he has to share to compensate for any insurance cost he assumed. An insurance guarantee then served as some form of interest income.

Johann Eck (1486-1543), a theologian living near Augsburg, then the financial center of Germany, trusting that the insurance practice would be generally confined to knowledgeable merchants, flatly proclaimed in 1514 that the guaranteed contract was lawful. Theologians in Mainz, consulted in the disturbing aftermath of this statement, judged the issue an open one. The next year, Eck journeyed to Bologna, seat of canon law learning, and successfully debated his thesis. It became popularly known as the 5% contract in reference to the rate of return usually earned by its German investors. He explained the agreement as comprised of three contracts, instead of two. The first contract was the partnership agreement; the second was insurance on the investment contract. The third was the sale of an uncertain future gain for a certain lesser gain. For getting his capital guaranteed, the investor might agree to receive a fixed 5% profit, though he knew that his guarantor partner would probably realize at least a 10-12% gain from the partnership.

This "safe" transaction became known as the triple contract. In defending the contract, Eck denied the scholastic tenet that "the good perishes to the owner." The 5% was payment for "the advantage of the money," and the investor was entitled to profit sharing from giving "the commodity of his capital." Eck received conditional support from Tommaso Gaetani Cajetan, (1469-1534) a cardinal, General of the Dominicans, and esteemed as the most competent follower of Aquinas. Cajetan thought Eck's second and third contracts, if executed independently of the partnership agreement and intended exclusively to protect the capitalist "from care and fear of fraud," were licit. But Cajetan also surmised that the removal of the equality of risk for both parties and the presence of the invariable 5% rate were circumstances that could invalidate the arrangement. Nevertheless, faced with the realities of the marketplace, he admitted that this could be tolerated and be preferred to overt usurious loans.

Scruples about the triple contract continued to bother the business community and resulted in the involvement of the powerful Jesuits. In 1560, the Jesuit Peter Canisius (1521-1597), later to be a cardinal and doctor of the Church, began refusing absolution to practitioners of the 5% contract in Augsburg. "Real usury," he wrote to his Father-General, Francis Borgia, a former duke and viceroy whose paternal great grandfather was Pope Alexander VI and maternal grandfather was King Ferdinand the Catholic, "is here openly committed . . . whatever objections are made by certain men skilled in law." Borgia replied that some of the contracts were probably excusable, and in 1567 notified Canisius that Pope Pius V had privately expressed the licitness of the triple contract with the 5% return. A year later, Borgia repeated the acceptability of the triple contract, though advising the Jesuits to dissuade people in the confessional from taking the 5% rate.

In 1573, a congregation of Jesuits in Rome, the second convened to rule on the triple contract, decided that a simple loan at 5% was illicit, but that the triple contract was not. The back and forth between Augsburg and Rome continued, prompted by the House of Fugger. The Jesuits adhered to their second congregation's pronouncement, persuaded of its justice. The Pope advised Duke William of Bavaria in 1581 that widespread use of the 5% contract was wrong, but that supplemental contract forms could be utilized to justify it. Another Jesuit cardinal and doctor of the Church, Robert Bellarmine (1542-1621), who presided at the trial of Galileo, wisely refused to be drawn into these uncertain waters. He detested the idea of "preaching courses in Italian to the merchants of his own country trafficking in Antwerp . . . guessing that they would besiege his confessional and confront him with all sorts of problems arising out of the swift development of capitalism and investment about which the moral theologians were still at sixes and sevens. The old legislation of the Church on the subject of interest was breaking down before the onslaught of bankers and big business, and no new guidance had come from the popes to replace it."

The triple contract showed how far acceptance of interest had gone. The contract protected the investor with an insurance cover. In addition, it guaranteed a return, in effect interest, under the guise of profit sharing. It was a riskless transaction. It granted capital a right to profit and renewed recognition of the external title of profit foregone. Konrad Summenhart (1455-1502), a professor at the Universities of Tubingen and of Paris, who wrote on human rights and a treatise on licit and illicit contracts in 1484, realized all this. He had taken *interesse* to mean "the losing of some temporal good now held, or the not seeking of some temporal good obtainable." The loss of interest was a specific case of profit foregone. It was like depriving a landowner of his field and thus inflicting lost potential fruits, or a worker of his tools. Summenhart concluded that money was not sterile.

Cajetan pursued Summenhart's positive argument. He first objected to profit foregone, saying with Aquinas that it would overturn the interest prohibition if admitted outside of delay. But then he added qualifications that liberalized his view. He distinguished the power of money to produce profit. First was its absolute power. This referred to its being a medium of exchange, consumed in the process of purchasing goods, as wheat is eaten instead of being sown. Second was money's power "subject to industry." This feature was not common to all money, but was "in relation to some person" and was "susceptible of being greater or less . . ." The variable rate of return on the loan was determined, as later economics would do, by "its proximity to profit and the quantity of the business, of labor, and other [factors]."

Cajetan went on: "About this [second] power are not to be understood the sayings of the doctors. Rather to sell this beyond the principal, or, to put it better, to redeem this, is licit . . ." It is licit, in fact, not only if one was forced to lend or to lend for the sake of charity, but also if the loan was sourced from funds intended for business and lent for business purposes. In the latter case, the lender voluntarily transferred his money to a state as equally valuable as when it was with him. That original state had profit value to which he was entitled. The economist in Cajetan was unshackling commercial loans from the usury charge.

Martin Azplicueta, called Navarrus, (1493-1560), a Spanish theologian and counselor to two kings and three popes, thought alike with Cajetan. He began his treatise on interest by flatly denying that profit foregone was usury. Usury was gain procured by force of the loan itself, but profit foregone was sought under the just title of compensation. He dismissed the relevance of intention and willingness, for justice in contracts was independent of these. His sole requirement was that the money loaned was originally intended for business pursuits, so that the loss was truly incurred. He never minded if the creditor had in addition a cash reserve to meet necessities.

Two Spanish Jesuit theologians supported Navarrus—Louis Molina (1536-1600) and John de Lugo (1593-1660). Molina reasoned that money has a special value to business people and this value could be estimated and fetch a higher price. He considered profit foregone as the justification for the triple contract and the personal census. But he prescribed a difficult reservation. The title of profit foregone could not be claimed if the lender's business did not experience a decline on account of the loan. Lugo, a professor at the Jesuit college in Rome, said that profit foregone was "the general title for purging usury" and that this was the common opinion. He maintained that the demand or need for money caused the loss of profit, so that creditors committed no wrong preparing their funds to meet its future incidence. He exemplified this opinion by referring to their preparing to meet oncoming royal credit needs.

On the other hand, Lugo restricted his permissiveness by giving the borrower the right to calculate the lost profit. The borrower could base it on the earnings of businesses similar to that of the lender, or, more typically, he could set the loss beforehand using his past business performance, with a reduction established for a possible unsuccessful venture. Lugo restated the business orientation of his teaching when he attributed some importance to the criterion of intention. The lender must not prefer lending to business activity, which clearly indicates that he expects more from the loan than what he could actually make on his own. At the same time, Lugo did not object to this preference of the lender if "that way of making money is more according to his talents and character, and he avoids some inconvenience . . ."

A third Jesuit theologian, Leonard Lessius (1554-1623) discarded the doctrinal hesitancies of the scholastics. Lessius was the leading figure in a small band of progressive Jesuits during the brief brilliant revival of scholasticism in the 16th century. He was born and lived near Antwerp, the commercial hub of the region that was northern Europe's counterpart to northern Italy's financial and trade centers. Familiar with the mercantile outlook, he was careful to point out at the beginning of his economic writings that the foundation of his analysis was the *negotiator diligens*, the careful and astute businessman who foreshadowed the classic abstract "economic man" formulated in the 19th century.

Lessius' monetary insights explained the righteousness of interest as forcefully as the biblical texts had denied it. He fleshed out the liberal intuitions of his predecessors. Reasoning that the accepted concept of profit foregone meant that the seeds of gain existed in money, he identified the importance of money balances, particularly those held by merchants. Anticipating 20th century economics, especially John

Maynard Keynes, he broke down these cash holdings according to the motives of the owners. They were held for transactions, speculation, and for precautionary purposes. Interest could be fairly charged for the use of the first two types of holdings.

Transaction and speculative balances were earmarked for meeting consumption needs and for direct investments. Title to interest on the basis of gain foregone was evident in this case. But could the same be said for the precautionary balances that included money kept for lending? Lessius answered yes, bringing in another rudimentary concept that would become vital in modern macroeconomics and finance. He said that the lack of money in hand, *carentia pecuniae*, meant a loss of liquidity, a sacrifice of convenience and freedom from risk, and a deprivation of "some power or advantage." He advanced a pivotal point to be held by future economists—the advantageous value of cash on hand. Present money, Lessius observed, "furnished control over many things," in contrast to claims of future money. In other words, present money was worth more than future money. It was right to compensate for this difference.

Lessius explicitly drew the conclusion from what Bernardino had recognized. Bernardino, writing of risk, had rendered more precise the statement of Peter Olivi, (1248-98) a Franciscan friar, that the possession of a thing in the present was more valuable than a future right of possession by observing that possession was "more secure" than just a right of possession. Thus, Lessius allowed merchants to withdraw funds from their business to ready it for lending and to "charge for having reduced money from a fecund to a sterile state." The analysis did not have to be confined to an individual act. The accumulation of loanable funds could be collectively taken as the cause of profit foregone and "the burden of compensation for this profit can be distributed to single loans, according to the proportion of each." Money lending could become a profession.

Lessius' demand for cash balances was strengthened by the historical environment. The social conditions he knew were not those of the limited polities of Greece or of structured medieval feudalism at its height, but those of the burgeoning Renaissance. Lessius drew two critical observations from his surroundings. First, a formal market for the intertemporal transfer of money existed. Given this institutionalized mechanism, profit foregone ceased to be hypothetical, even for the non-merchant money holder. Second, the market freely produced a price for the deprivation of money. As Lessius described the process, merchants would gather daily in the bourse in Antwerp, look at "the abundance and shortage of money," examine the demand for money as to quantity required, the duration of the loan, and the commercial purpose weighed against the background of prevailing business conditions, and finally arrive at an interest rate that usually ranged from 6% to the 12% ceiling imposed by Charles V in 1540.

The consensus rate was important for Lessius. Though dubbed a reactionary by some of his critics, Lessius was known for his piety. He believed in the doctrine of the natural or just price and went to great lengths explaining how it was set. Lessius saw that he had a just price in the money market's interest rate. The rate was estimated by the community "in good faith, for the sake of the common good, in view of all the circumstances . . ." This interaction between economics and ethics was a capstone for the interest theory of Lessius. Even granting that the act of lending caused no risk-taking or loss of profit to the creditor, Lessius saw nothing wrong in any lender demanding the payment of interest, simply because interest was an objective price, fixed on reasonable business grounds, for the loss of the power of present money.

Finally, Lessius denied that the value of the labor the lender would have undertaken if he chose to work should be subtracted from the interest. This totally safeguarded the title of profit foregone. Lessius also supported the census, following a mild renewal of its controversy. Two features had been allowed the census, namely, an "insurance" of payment despite the loss of the census base and mutual redeemability. These additions and other qualifications, such as the creation of a census based on a census or a wider range for pricing the issue, brought the census not only very close to being a loan, but also often rendered it more advantageous for the investor.

Summenhart, while maintaining the basic distinction long held between a census and a loan in that the former was a sale (money is exchanged for another kind of good, a right), mentioned the expected excuse that any lender could then assert: "I do not give this money, obliging you to give me a good of the same genus . . . but for the right of demanding such an amount from you in money, even beyond the principal given you by me." In effect, the granting of debt was likened to a purchase of either a temporary or a personal census, as both involved the purchase of a right. The purchase price was determined by market forces, as in the case of merchandise, and it represented the estimation, mainly of the buyer, of the difference between what is had on hand and in the future.

Summenhart, cautious, prudent, and refusing to give ground, imposed a condition on the escapist mental generalization. Usury, he said, depended on intention. The lender's conscience was the final court. Was he truly thinking of buying a right or not? Pope Pius V in 1569 invalidated the seller-guaranteed, mutually redeemable, and personal censuses. A census could only be instituted based on a fruitful, immobile, and dedicated base. His bull, considered in the words of Lessius as having "many conditions not the least required by the natural law," was taken to be non-binding by Western Europe. In Bavaria, imperial laws prohibiting the buyer's redemption of a census were abrogated.

In 1581, another Jesuit Congregation allowed its Order's members to counsel in favor of the censuses deemed usurious by Pope Pius V. Lessius enunciated the theoretical principle applicable to this permissive attitude. The profit from the purchase of a census was acceptable only where interest was also acceptable. This meant the extrinsic titles to interest. Again Lessius referred to risks and contrasted present and future valuations: "A personal right is almost always joined with dangers and difficulties, and with money in hand fruitful goods can be bought or business executed with great profit." The same holds for the purchase of debt, as there is "some power which present money gives, which a note of debt does not have." But Lessius was careful to insist that the census form be used, because "one and the same thing is differently estimated according to the different contracts employed."

By the next century, Alphonsus Liguori (1696-1787), a lawyer, moral theologian, and saint, could give the subject a routine epilogue. He accepted the census, whether the theory stipulated the purchase of a right to money or of the fruit of work. The personal census did not violate natural law, save where it was based "on an unfruitful thing or person, for there no real good or usufruct is purchased." Intrinsically, the buyer incurred the risk, but a guarantee contract could be executed. Liguori likewise endorsed the lender's claim to profit foregone, "since the loan is the true and efficacious cause that gain from businesses ceases for him." Liguori's conclusion was made easy by the lengthy reasoning of Lessius. Lessius tried to prove that interest was not only payment for forsaken gain, but also for deprivation of money on hand. The latter designation held true for both the merchant and the ordinary individual creditor.

The proliferation of various types of credit transactions and their growing legitimacy gave rise to arguments acknowledging the so-called implicit contracts, which were becoming more common. Many contracts couched in a simple loan form were judged to be readily reducible to being lawful instruments upon examination, such as the triple contract, census, and *mons*. "Nothing," wrote Franz Zech (1692-1772), a German Jesuit canonist, "is more certain than the same effect, the same profit, can be sought through different contracts and interpreted differently. Profit on a loan can be illicit, the same profit on a census will be licit." The structure of the loan formula did not have to be explicitly detailed. The implicit contract sufficiently signified the honest intention of the parties involved, particularly the lender, to seek a just title to interest.

How was the existence of an intended implicit contract known? It was "an immemorial custom," said Navarrus. Investing the money of widows and wards at 4%, for instance, was a de facto widespread confirmation of the unsaid understanding. Good faith in the implicit contract could be taken for granted and conceded, especially if the yield was low. The implicit contract "virtually existed," to use the terminology of the 1581 Jesuit Congregation. Lessius undertook the psychological proof for its existence, writing that if the investor "is so disposed in act, that if he were asked by what title, or what form of contract, he intends to gain those 6 per 100, he would reply, 'By every good means I can'—a clause the notaries are generally accustomed to add to instruments . . ." The implicit contract thus rendered the requirement of right intention from the lender superfluous.

Widespread recognition of morally licit (and legal) contracts fostered the reassessment of a most crucial title to interest, namely, the simple risk of lending. Allowable risk had been confined to partnership risk, *periculum sortis*, because to permit it elsewhere seemed to reject the principle of the gratuitous loan and usury itself. The sole exemption was granted to merchants selling on credit who feared incurring collection costs. They could seek payment for anticipated expenses. Summenhart thought such costs were extrinsic to lending and recompense could be estimated from the merchant's entire customer base.

It was a Spanish theology professor, John Medina (1419-1516) who first attempted to formally justify an interest charge due to the exposure of the lender to risk and to extend it to both credit sales and to all loans. In the case of credit sales, he argued "that a man throw away his own property for another, or expose it to risk of being lost, is sellable, and purchasable at a price, nor is it among those things which are to be done gratuitously." A guarantor's fee was here allowed, he pointed out, when the debtor offered neither a pledge nor a guarantee. Why could not an ordinary lender do the same? A lender's peril was incurred, even if the principal was repaid. The fear of a default was as real as the fear of expenses for recovery. Medina went farther. He stated that the risk was imposed on the lender by the borrower, if the latter solicited the loan. But in these cases, the interest was to be reckoned on the basis of the individual debtor. Complete freedom in interest-taking was still withheld.

Jesuit moralists overcame the scanty opposition to Medina's position. Molina declared: "No one denies that, if what is given is exposed to danger, either of being not repaid, or of being repaid only with labor and annoyance to the lender, it is right to accept a price for that peril . . . to which the lender exposes himself. For a good given in a loan, provided it is exposed to a morally probable peril . . . is worth so much the less, the greater or more likely the risk." Molina implied that the risk title went deeper than the risk itself. Risk affected value.

Lessius also amplified Medina's arguments. Using the analogy of a bailor, he asserted that the transfer of ownership in a loan and the complete responsibility of the borrower were no hindrance to demanding interest. However, the lender must give the borrower a choice of providing security or paying the charge, which should not exceed the fee of a third-party insurer. Lessius additionally backed Molina's allusion to purchases of debt at a discount. He emphasized the common risk involved: "a personal right is almost always joined with some difficulties and dangers."

Lugo pushed this proposition of Lessius a step farther. The lender may charge for mental anguish and fear, even imaginary fear. Suffering was part of lending. He asked a rhetorical question: "Where today is there to be found a debt so placed in safety that in security it equals ready cash?" Lugo, unwittingly or not, was suggesting that the title to risk could be universally applied.

The role of the Jesuits on the interest debate transcended Europe's borders. Their missionaries in China sought the opinion of a Roman Congregation in 1645, asking if their Chinese converts could continue the practice of charging 30% interest for likely default, delay, or court proceedings. With the approval of Pope Innocent X, the Congregation, while warning against charging "by reason of the loan, immediately and precisely," responded: "If indeed, they receive something by reason of a probably imminent danger . . . they are not to be disturbed . . . provided that there is kept a proportion between the danger and what is received." Although the non-observance of this instruction carried the penalty of excommunication, the favorable conclusion was clear. The only uncertainty in Rome's platitudinal "not to be disturbed" was whether it was adopted to avoid alienating its new religious adherents or to express a now widely permitted aspect of interest.

Though much of later scholastic analysis gravitated toward commercial credit, personal consumption loans, in which the notion of unjust interest was originally rooted, were not overlooked. The prevalence of the 32-43% interest charged by public usurers prodded churchmen to find some public means of making cheap loans available to the poor. In 1461, Hermolaus Barbarus (1454-93), a member of a prominent Venetian family of humanists, diplomats, and churchmen, established for the purpose a "mount of piety," *mons pietatis*. It was a variant of the fiscal *mons*. The initiative was quickly repeated throughout Italy. The *mons* was a pawnshop, funded by charitable donations, directed by one or two ecclesiastical representatives and a few respected merchants. It charged a low fee to meet its administrative expenses. The fee was usually 6%. In 1467, Pope Paul II approved the charter of the first *mons* in Perugia. His successors did the same for the other *montes* in the country.

The Franciscans understandably supported the charitable movement. Some of the *montes* they founded lent money gratuitously, until capital shortages revealed the impracticality of the policy. There were 80 *montes* in Italy by the end of the 15th century. To end the continuing debate (from the Dominicans) that the *montes* were usurious, the Fifth Lateran Council in 1515 released a papal bull that praised the *montes* "in which for their expenses and indemnity something moderate is received beyond the principal, not for the profit of the same *montes*, but for the salaries of their employees and other things necessary to their conservation . . ." The charges were not usurious; anyone who deemed otherwise incurred excommunication.

However, interest as payment in the form of a fixed fee from the *montes* proved to be short-lived. To maintain funds, Lugo asserted that the interest charge on loans could vary with their term, since the longer the loan the more expenses were incurred and the less opportunity for new lending. The preservation and growth of capital was crucial for the *montes*, since gifts were insufficient. Consequently, a number of popes in the 16th century authorized the acceptance of interest-bearing deposits on the basis of the profit-foregone title.

With their dual source of funding, the *montes* soon resembled savings banks. They paid 5% to depositors and charged their borrowers, by then including businessmen, 8-10%. This development virtually broke the pawnbroker-like shell of the *montes* and expanded the potential horizon of institutional lending. Belgium heeded Lessius' recommendation. In 1618, it outlawed public usurers and organized a string of *montes* in the country with the approval of the Belgian bishops. The Lombards, who had frowned on a 22% interest, were forced to offer loans at 15%. The *montes* existed until the French Revolution in 1789. Henceforth, their viability was slowly undermined by mismanagement and by levies and takeovers by the state.

The charges of the *montes* brought to mind the analogous fees for professional services allowed the exchange dealers. Exchange banking generated sizable profits, especially in Antwerp and Lyons. Profits ranged from 10% per fair to 30% a year to ten times the original capital. The task of legitimizing exchange banking was to explain how profit was earned and that the monetary transaction involved was not a loan. Further rationalization of the dealers' right to profit brought together three concepts previously argued separately. First was service.

Gabriel Biel (c1410-1495), a theologian and Rector of the University of Tubingen, said that profit was made from the charges for "virtual transportation." This likened the banker's movement of funds to the physical transport of specie with all its expenses and perils, for which a fee was unquestioned. Besides service, the second reason adduced was that the worth of contracted money was already reduced at a distance compared to the money at hand. Cajetan called the latter money "expendable" and the former "non-expendable." To exchange "expendable" money for "non-expendable" money was not to lend. It did not postulate an immutable amount, and "notable" profit from this was licit. The pricing practices of the exchange market were not questioned. Cajetan acknowledged the merchants' expertise on estimating the proper fees.

Cajetan offered a third reason by continuing his differing valuation of absent and present money. He looked at the basis of the charges and concluded that the value of money (purchasing power and not worth in gold) changed in response to current and future money demand and supply in a particular location just like any good. He regarded distant money as a commodity at the same time as it was a measure. Hence, distant money could be worth less and transactional equality was lost. Cajetan used the word "distant" not only geographically, but also temporally in affecting supply and demand in the credit market, forces that Navarrus identified as "the voice of God and nature." In this regard, Molina tried to salvage the usury doctrine with a locational distinction. But in the end he repeated Cajetan. He wrote that the (legal) value of money was invariable within a state, but outside the country, it became subject to supply and demand and assumed an extrinsic value.

Summenhart in 1499 wanted to extend to exchange dealers a right to interest, writing that the bill of exchange was comprised of both an exchange and a loan. Navarrus gave two reasons to uphold this position: profit foregone and the public obligation to operate exchanges. Lugo expanded the latter reason, citing the professional skill entailed, especially when large amounts were involved. Lessius candidly said that exchanges were loans, because payment of the bill was usually set longer than the transit period to the other location. Interest was allowable.

A contract that Lessius was consulted well illustrated his assertion. Merchants would give the equivalent of 94,000 ducats in Antwerp to the king of Spain to meet military expenditures. They were to receive 100,000 ducats in Spain two months later. This prolonged period of time precisely entitled the dealer to interest under the title of "lack of money" in addition to the service charge and value adjustment. The lack of money also explained why absent money was worth less than present with "its greater facility and convenience." The price of money in the exchange market determined by supply and demand mirrored the price of the lack of money. Lessius likewise accepted the profit-foregone title and the risk of nonpayment, although in these cases, absent the equilibrium of a structured market, individual calculation of the rate was necessary.

While interest under the appropriate titles was approved in principle for exchange banking, suspicions of usurious agreements persisted. In 1571, Pope Pius V, cognizant of the abuses, issued a bull against the so-called dry exchanges. These were arrangements that did not dispatch bills of exchange to another place or did not pay them there, but returned them to the originating party. The bull additionally ordered a standardization of the interest rates and shortened the term of bills to the next fair. A Roman Congregation in 1631 repeated the 1571 edict, detailing when a dry exchange occurred. These condemnations mainly served to spur exchange bankers to sharpen their practices to either reconcile with or evade the rules. For instance, they sought partial reliance on deposits as a source of funds by offering an interest-related feature. Dealers sometimes credited their clients' accounts with 20-50% more money for settling debts at the fairs in hopes of getting more deposits from them. The utilization of this created credit naturally generated more occasions for charging interest under one or two relevant titles.

The roughly five centuries of extensive scholastic investigation of interest left the application of its prohibition tightly constrained. The biblical authority had been found inadequate. The text in the Gospel of Luke urging the lender not to expect a return, even of the principal, ceased, after much dispute in the second century, to be taken as prescriptive, but as a counsel of charity. Christ had not renewed the Old Testament directives and in a parable upbraided a steward for not even earning interest on entrusted money. The intrinsic violation of natural law had been whittled down to a single, extremely narrowly construed argument, that of Aquinas' consumptibility. This liberal trend was clearly reflected in the point-by-point criticism of early medieval interest theory written by Summenhart. He listed 23 typical natural law reasons against usury grouped under five headings.

First, Aristotle's insistence that a thing be used for its proper end, he found "absurd." Sin is not committed if a shoe is utilized as storage space for money, or if wine is used to douse a fire. Such acts are not against natural law. Second, to say that the lender gains without risk is untrue. The borrower can become bankrupt or earn less than what the creditor could have made on his own. Third, to make profit from what is barren (metal) is not wrong. Grain that is lent grows and multiplies. A sterile house earns rent. Money, if used, produces fruit. Fourth, that fungibles possess an unchangeable value is misleading. Value derives not purely from quantity, but from human determination and external circumstances. The value of a fungible could differ at the grant of the loan and at its liquidation. On the fifth, Aquinas' consumptibility argument, Summenhart compromised.

Summenhart faulted the Aquinas principle that the ownership and use of a consumptible are inseparable. A servant may hold and use money on behalf of his master, yet he does not own it. However, he admitted the validity of the statement of Aquinas, not expressed absolutely, but in relation to a loan. A borrower received both ownership and use of money and these did comprise one value. But Summenhart then denied that the lender fully shared this view. The lender charged for something else other than the substance and use of the money. "For the good conceded for the use of an intervening time with the renunciation, or lack, of his own use of it, [the lender] demands this other whole aggregate, to wit, the principal and increment."

In other words, Summenhart argued that the interest-free repayment of a loan did not return all that was given. The use of the money during the term of the loan was not restored "for that intervening time, because that passes irrevocably into the past." Hence, the lender did not sell the same thing twice or sold time. He endowed his sacrificial lack of money during a certain time with a monetary value and charged for it. It was a distinct value from the integrated ownership and use of money. Summenhart displayed a broader claim to interest than actual damage incurred or profit foregone. He reinforced Lessius' lack-of-money argument by citing the sacrifice endured by the lender. Such an extra cost held for every loan and deserved payment.

Charles Molinaeus (1500-1566), an expert French jurist on contracts, similarly objected to Aquinas' consumptibility argument. He contested the meaning of the word "use." He argued that "the use and fruition of money does not consist only in its first momentary spending, but also in the succeeding use of the goods or things purchased with the money." Money use, he said, was not like consuming food. It was a process toward producing a fruit, and he totally agreed with Aquinas that "money likewise yields a product through the industry of man." But Aquinas, in discussing restitution, while accepting man's industry to be the cause of any profit resulting from the use of money, ruled that typically the industry belonged to the borrower and so was the resulting gain. On the other hand, the creditor, according to Molinaeus, deserved his due. Molinaeus regarded the lender in the case of commercial loans as "the near and efficacious cause . . . the sine qua non" of the borrower's profit and therefore was owed a share. This value-laden participation was embodied in the utility, hinted at by previous writers, offered by the lender's money.

Molinaeus objected to calculating the interest rate on an individual basis. Instead he wanted determination by "common estimation," that is, market rates. In the beginning of his 1546 tract on contracts and usury, Molinaeus reviewed the prohibitions in Scripture and judged them to be misinterpretations. Interest was not forbidden in general, but only specifically where it was levied against "the laws of charity and brotherly love." Hence, the core of any opposition to interest found in Molinaeus was the excessive rates (18%, for example, in Lyons) charged on the premise of profit foregone. Molinaeus saw nothing unjust in interest. In every loan, he perceived the right to *interesse*. In fact, interest favored the borrower, since the payment of a moderate rate meant an opportunity to earn a larger sum. As for the concept of barren money, he pointedly argued that even land did not bear fruit without the tending of man. In these arguments, Molinaeus made an important theoretical point. Interest looked beyond the pure use of money to its purchasing power, which incorporated utility.

Summary of the schoolmen. Many scholastics hesitated to confront the consumptibility argument of Aquinas with a prompt and head-on denial. After all, a substantial number of them, being churchmen, were engaged in moralizing. Instead, the scholastics who were rationalizing interest skirted Aquinas by expanding on the extrinsic titles to interest, acknowledging new forms of finance, and taking into account attenuating economic and civil circumstances attending individual cases. The repeated invocation of the principles of indemnity and duress made money to appear as possessing earning power. Money as an investable emerged as a companion, if not dominating, idea to money's traditional notion as a consumable. The scholastics developed two major points of departure for differing with Aristotle and recognizing fertility in money. These were human industry and time, with the first understood to include not only pure labor but entrepreneurship as well. Industry applied over time resulted in the multiplication of money.

Up to the middle of the 17th century, papal statements (Alexander VII in 1666, Innocent XI in 1679) continued to resist the growing latitude given non-gratuitous loans. The proscriptions went mostly unheeded, interpreted as not explicitly stating the intrinsic error of interest or being too general for application to particular concrete contracts. Clearly, the fundamental question of should interest be paid, which opened the scholastic period, had ceased to be answered that no one should pay it. Extrinsic titles to interest, like profit foregone and risk, were gradually being strengthened or transformed into intrinsic ones.

The equality required by Aquinas and his followers between the amount loaned and repaid was challenged by the purported change in value caused by the lapse of time, geographical distance, lack of ready money, or market supply-demand conditions. The lender's loss of ownership of the money lent grew less convincing as an argument against interest. Money was recognized as capital, that is, potentially productive with the input of human endeavor. Capital assumed the nature of a commodity, creating its own nascent market. Importantly, the formation of capital entailed personal financial hardship that came down to an economic loss.

Some arguments for the payment of interest were stronger than others, like compensation for risk or loans granted under duress. In these cases, a measure of agreement among the scholastics was reached. Nevertheless, no formal, definitive universal consensus on one or two viewpoints was reached, except that the trend toward interest as a legitimate payment for a real value embedded in money or at the very least traceable to it, was gaining momentum. Canon law clung to a core disapproval of interest, even as Church thinkers discovered a multitude of reasons for it. They sought to establish its rationality and reconcile it with natural law. For what was interest paid?

Besides the use of money, the scholastics found that interest was payment for service, insurance, risk of default, passage of time, delay, purchase of a right, lost gainful opportunities, damage incurred, deprivation of cash on hand, transferred utility, personal sacrifice, and profit share. Did any or all of these determinations indicate the metaphysical nature of interest? The scholastics did not probe this deeper question. They may have thought that they had already answered it affirmatively. Their findings sufficed for their age. But when accelerating economic progress demanded more sophisticated responses, their extensive insights, such as those of Bernardino and Lessius, found legitimate places in the future development of a positive theory of interest.

PART THREE
ECONOMISTS AT WORK

Chapter 5

POLITICAL ECONOMY

The scholastics had progressively, although laboriously, loosed usury from its morality-based prohibitions. The majority of them had, among others, contested Aquinas' tight understanding of the consumptive use of money, accepted the profit-foregone title and later even divorced it from the required delayed payment proviso. They also ascribed yield to money by the application of human industry, and established differences in the value of present and distant money. In their wake, the Protestant reformers quickly pushed this liberalizing trend to the point of accepting the routine payment of interest.

At first, ambivalence marked the attitudes of Martin Luther (1483-1546) who was trained in Thomistic doctrine, of Philip Melanchthon (1497-1560), a close collaborator of Luther, and even of John Calvin (1509-1564), the second pillar of the Protestant Reformation. Luther was virulent in some of his condemnations of interest. Money lending was a calling "that generated parasitic profit . . . from which the stream of abomination, injustice, treachery and guile flows far and wide . . ." Interest-taking was like lending a goose to a peasant and demanding not only the goose, but also the eggs. Melanchthon believed that the Mosaic prohibition of interest applied to both Jew and Gentile.

All three reformers sensed some validity in the old anti-interest arguments. Their minds bore the traces of the lifeless money concept.

More important, they respected Christian justice and charity. Moreover, with their emphasis on Scripture, they had to wrestle with the dilemma of the double standard in *Deuteronomy*. Finally, they shared, sometimes with greater intensity, the dislike of the Church for a materialistic conception of the universe. When the last reformers finally approved interest in the late 16th century, they attached conditions to it. Many viewed their consent as an unavoidable concession of the ideal to the imperfections of mankind. Taking interest from the poor was still absolutely wrong. Throwing a wider net, the Diet of Nuremberg, which marked the rise of the Reformation, legislated in 1522 that money should not be loaned at excessive rates.

In light of the eventual general permissions for interest, Luther admitted that usury could be demanded for late payment that caused additional expenses or a lost profit opportunity to the lender. In 1587, five Protestant ministers were dismissed for questioning the 5% rate of the German triple contract. But Luther derided interest in the form of annuities and census contracts, *Zinskauf.* They were "the greatest misfortune of the German nation . . ." And in his sermon published in 1520, he agreed with Aristotle that money was lifeless and interest was exploitation by the rich. For his part, Melanchthon allowed interest for money invested freely in a partnership with merchants. The fact that the loans extended for a long or indefinite time meant that the lender suffered some damage. Justice required that he receive recompense, but not exceeding 5%.

Calvin, rooted in the disciplined bourgeois economy thriving around him, insisted that where the rich was concerned, "usury is freely permitted." He likened interest to profit made on the sale of a good. Calvin assailed Aristotle's theory of barrenness as of "little weight" and stated that money could be made to bear fruit. Money could purchase a house, whose use could beget money. Money could also buy idle land, which when tilled yielded yearly revenue. "Tell me," asked Calvin, "when I buy a field, does not money breed money?" Only unused money was infertile. But no borrower left money unemployed. A borrower was not cheated by paying interest from his gain. The lender himself could procure land or house as well. Why should he be blamed for choosing to earn income instead in the form of interest? Calvin had a particular distaste for the licit external titles of the scholastics, although he adhered to their doctrine of business gain from borrowed money. The titles were false pretenses, he said, as "always will there be a place for compensation, since no creditor gives his money to another without loss."

The first Protestant scholar of note favoring interest was the German lawyer Christoph Besold (1577-1638). In 1598, and again around 1623, he maintained that money was no longer barren if situated in commerce. Since in trade, any man was allowed to pursue his gain, short of inflicting injury on others, interest was permissible. Besold analogized interest with hire. In addition, the amount of loan interest should be allowed to rise in tandem with any increase in profit. However, a contemporary of Besold, the Dutchman Hugo Grotius (1583-1645), known as the father of international law and a moderate Calvinist, observed the indecisiveness still persisting on the subject of interest. Grotius indeed found the barren argument unpersuasive, for "houses also, and other things barren by nature, the skill of man has made productive." He also reckoned the natural law argument "not of a kind to compel assent." Despite these denials, Grotius took the prohibition of Scripture as binding without doubt. To offset this stricture of conscience, he finally accepted the taking of interest under the titles proposed by the scholastics. In fact, in 1654, following local laws, German imperial legislation approved the claim to *interesse* stipulated in advance, which virtually tolerated all interest.

A prolific, Calvinist classical scholar, Claude Salmasius (1588-1653), finally swept aside all moral reservations with the rapid publication of three dissertations from 1638 to 1640. Salmasius recognized the usual definition of interest as payment for the use of money. He affirmed its legitimacy by invoking the legal classification of the Romans of loan transactions. In the loan of fungibles, *mutuum*, whose use was its single consumption, he demurred at the inseparability of use and consumption, since to assert it would make it impossible to transfer something (use) whose very existence is denied. Therefore, all interest-free loans have to be negated. Interest was further justified in the *mutuum* precisely because what was loaned perished, so that the lender suffered anxiety, delay, and loss. For the rest of his point-by-point rebuttal of the traditionalists, Salmasius drew principally from Molinaeus.

Legalization of interest by Henry VII (1457-1509), by Henry VIII in 1545, and finally by Elizabeth I in 1571 increased efforts to attach justice and charity to interest-taking in England. A Puritan theologian presented as the ideal loan contract for Christians one in which the creditor would share the risks with the borrower and ask only "a fair share of the profits, according to the degree in which God has blessed him by whom the money is used." Richard Baxter seconded his coreligionist in this Thomistic view of partnership, saying interest became unlawful when the lender refuses the borrower "such a proportion of the gain as his labour, hazard, or poverty doth require, but . . . will live at ease upon his labours; or when in spite of the borrower's misfortune, he rigorously exacts his pound of flesh . . ." It also was not immoral to invest money in commerce to generate regular income for people, like widows and orphans, who could not trade on their own.

The next step in this argument was easily taken—to ask the rhetorical question why the poor could not lend with interest too, why they should give money, for instance, to a rich market speculator for free. And against the claim that interest, being earnings from barren money, was not like rent and profit, which were not objectionable unless excessive, the retort was that if it was not criminal to purchase a rent-charge or to participate in business profits, why would it be unlawful to charge for a loan? With the morality of interest settled by the Protestants, at least in doctrine, the history of interest theory now moved squarely to the sphere of economics.

England, riding the wave of mercantilism, assumed a leading position in economic theorizing that would endure for over three centuries. The first wave of English economists consisted of philosophers, civil servants, and merchants. The outcrop of commercial policies drove them to think in terms of "political economy." As a result, these men-of-affairs chiefly directed their inquiry to the rates of interest instead of to the nature of interest. What was the correct level of rates? How were they determined? Should they be mandated by law?

Francis Bacon (1561-1626), the philosopher, wrote a chapter on usury in his famous *Essays* that reflected the growing attention to the interest rate. After enumerating the many "witty invectives" of his time against usury (the usurer, for example, "breaketh the first law . . . made for mankind after the fall," because he eats his bread by the sweat of the brow of another), Bacon proceeded to weigh its disadvantages and benefits "since there must be borrowing and lending, and men are so hard of heart, as they will not lend freely, usury must be permitted." Bacon listed seven "discommodities" of usury, basically all variants of a single argument. Usury concentrates and sterilizes wealth, contracts economic activity, and lowers the selling price of land. Usury is a "lazy trade." It "doth dull and damp all industries, improvements, and new inventions, wherein money would be stirring, if it were not for this slug." For benefits, Bacon named three, two of which contradicted his stated disadvantages. He admitted that usury efficiently advances trade and prevents bankruptcies and that its abolition would dry up lending altogether.

Bacon ended by writing the safe prescription for an ambivalent situation: minimize the negatives (grind the tooth of usury, he wrote, "that it bite not too much"), and retain the beneficial effects of usury. He proposed a reduced rate of 5% for general lending, which would be tax-free to induce lenders to offer a constant supply of credit. This rate was low enough to keep the value of land and of alternative forms of enterprise attractive. Bacon calculated that land yielded a 6% return, while business earned much more. Bacon wanted the state to license a number of individual lenders involved in purely commercial loans, who would be allowed to charge 9%. Their operations would be restricted to a few principal mercantile centers to prevent monopolies. With fixed locations, they "will not suck away the current rate of five; for no man will send his moneys far off, nor put them into unknown hands."

Like most men, Bacon mistrusted institutional lenders. Part of his policy proposal was: "Let it be no bank or common stock, but every man be master of his own money. Not that I altogether mislike banks, but they will hardly be brooked, in regard of certain suspicions." Like Aquinas' practical tolerance of civil laws permitting interest, the closing paragraph of Bacon's "civil and moral counsel" displayed the attitude prevailing in Europe at the time toward interest as an unavoidable evil. "If it be objected that this doth in a sort authorize usury, which before, was in some places but permissive; the answer is, that it is better to mitigate usury, by declaration, than to suffer it to rage, by connivance."

The half-dozen or so prominent economists during the 17th century shared the same yes and no mentality of Bacon on interest. They were non-committal regarding the morality of interest. They concerned themselves with the practical issues of taxation, money, and international trade. They analyzed the control and appropriate level of interest rates. The English merchant class, envious of the success of their competitors in Holland with its lower interest rates, was urging the "abatement of interest." One side argued for rates lower than the maximum allowed, using most of Bacon's disadvantages of usury as their reasons—makes "Land sell so cheape" and "men grow lazie in their [mercantile] professions." They pointed out that businesses promising to yield less than the maximum rate would not be pursued and that low rates would improve agriculture and revive manufacturing. That low rates led to high prosperity became a central doctrine of mercantilism, a school of economic thought lasting approximately from 1500 to 1750.

Those who favored a freer money market recognized the validity of some of these mercantilist conclusions. But they also claimed, using Holland itself as an example, that cause and effect run the other way and that "the natural lowness of interest to be the effects of riches." Prosperity, because it meant more lenders, lowered rates. High rates also would bring out hoarded wealth, increasing the supply of money for trade. A richer nation would induce more traders to emerge "who want Stock to manage." Thomas Mun (1571-1641), a wealthy director of the East India Company and a leader among the first mercantilists, saw a simpler type of this association between business conditions and the interest rate, namely, a unilateral movement. Rising trade could be accompanied by high rates. He wrote: "We might conclude contrary to those who affirm that Trade decreaseth as Usury encreaseth, for they rise and fall together." Mun favored the payment of interest, as it gave the "opportunity to the younger and poorer merchants to rise in the world and to enlarge their dealings . . . and made possible the advantageous employment in trade of the funds of widows, orphans, and gentlemen."

After Mun came Thomas Culpeper (1578-1662), a knighted member of Parliament, and Josiah Child (1630-99), a wealthy businessman. Both favored low rates. Culpeper expressed his stand against interest in general and a high rate in particular (identified in terms of percent) in severe moral language couched in the Hebrew allusion to the bite of interest: "It is agreed by all the Divines . . . without exception of any; yea, and by the Usurers themselves, that biting Usury is unlawful: Now since it hath been proved that ten in the hundred doth bite the Landed man, doth bite the Poor, doth bite Trade, doth bite the King in his Customs, doth bite the Fruits of the Land, and most of all the Land itself: doth bite all works of Piety, of Virtue, and Glory to the State; no man can deny but ten in the hundred is absolutely unlawful, howsoever happily a lesser rate may be otherwise." Beneath this sweeping denunciation lay Culpeper's awareness that English traders faced Dutch rivals, who borrowed at only 6%.

Child, chairman of the East India Company, also aimed to put his countrymen on a par with the Dutch. He advocated lower maximum rates, but not the abolition of interest, in the belief that "Nature must and will have its course." He named two good results from cheap money. It would foster industry by attracting merchants, who would not be "prohibited" by the prospect of making less than 10%. It would encourage frugality by yielding smaller lending profits. In contrast, a high rate made money scarce, because any little saving would be consigned to a goldsmith immediately.

Repeating Culpeper's view that 10% made "men grow lazie in their professions, and become Usurers," Child saw a high rate bringing unemployment, because merchants, "when they have gotten great wealth, leave trading" to lend money, "the gain thereof being so easy, certain and great; whereas in other countries, where interest is at a lower rate, they continue merchants from generation to generation, and enrich themselves and the state." Child appended a third modification to the relationship between rates and economic progress invoked by his predecessors. He envisioned a circular causality. Prosperity, induced by a low rate, could further depress rates and drive further prosperity, since "the egg was the cause of the hen, and the hen the cause of the egg."

The mercantilist intramural controversy seesawed. The factors behind interest rate levels were studied, such as the incipient demand-supply ideas hidden in Bacon's policy proposals. Like some of the scholastics, both sides of the mercantilist school considered interest as a purely monetary variable. The price of money's use was low or high if money was abundant or scarce. John Law (1671-1729), famed paper-money advocate, financier, and speculator, unreservedly accepted this proposition. He even said that one could unambiguously infer the level of money existing in a country from the prevailing interest rate.

Interest was the price for the use of money. Law therefore advocated low rates to stimulate business.

Another prominent figure in the debate was William Petty (1623-87). A man of many abilities (physician, engineer, businessman, parliamentarian), he pioneered the statistical approach to economics, calling it Political Arithmetick. Petty claimed that the rate of interest responded to the quantity of money. "As to Mony," he wrote, "the Interest thereof was within this fifty years at 10 1. per Cent, forty years ago at 8 1., and now at 6 1., no thanks to any Laws which have been made to that purpose, forasmuch as those who can give security, may now have it at less: But the natural fall of interest is the effect of the increase of Mony." Inevitably, subsequent discussion broadened to include some rationale for paying interest, which had an underlying "natural" or standard rate as opposed to the legal rate.

Petty, schooled by the Jesuits, disapproved of interest on call loans, but he found nothing wrong with term loans. His essay, *Of Usury*, in 1662, opened with this statement: "What reason there is for taking or giving Interest or Usury for any thing which we may certainly have again whensoever we call for it, I see not; nor why Usury should be scrupled, where money or other necessaries valued by it, is lent to be paid at such a time and place as the Borrower chuseth, so as the Lender cannot have his money paid him back where and when himself pleaseth, I also see not. Wherefore when a man giveth out his money upon condition that he may not demand it back until a certain time to come . . . he certainly may take a compensation . . ." The lapse of time justified interest. Petty downplayed interest as a charge for the use of money. Anticipating economic theory yet to come, he defined it as "a reward for forebearing the use of your own Money for a Term of Time agreed upon, whatsoever need you self may have of it in the mean while." This reward for the "inconvenience which [the lender] admits against himself "was similar to the premium paid "when one man furnisheth another with money at some distant place, and engages under great Penalties to pay him there, and at a certain date besides . . ."

This added notion of geographical exchange buttressed Petty's argument, for such exchange involved labor and hazards and indicated the "emergent uses for money more in one place than another" at different points of time. Thus, Petty named exchange "local usury" or, as a contemporary called it, the "usury of location." Together with time and geography, Petty included risk in treating of the basic rate of interest or what he called "the natural standard of usury." He said: "the least that can be, is the Rent of so much land as the money lent will buy, where the security is undoubted; but where the security is casual, then a kinde of ensurance must be enterwoven with the simple natural Interest, which may advance the Usury very conscionably unto any height below the principal itself [that is, not exceeding 100%]."

Petty saw the temporal behind land rent, "the use of fruit per year." He valued land accordingly. On the average, he figured land to be worth the equivalent of rent for 21 years, because this period was then typically held as covering three generations. Petty calculated that "Grandfather, Father, and Childe are but three in a continual line of descent usually coexisting together . . ." that will be able with some certainty to enjoy the purchased land. The calculation of the rate of interest paralleled this valuation, which was influenced by location (proximity to "populous places") and type of crop (corn). Advocating flexibility, Petty criticized another determinant of the interest rate, namely, legislation. In exchange, he explained, given all the unavoidable hazards and troubles it entailed besides the labor, the rate of interest was not limited by "the practice of the world." There was "no reason for endeavoring to limit [by decree] Usury upon time, any more than that upon place . . ." He described such attempts as "the vanity and fruitlessness of making Civil Positive Laws against the Laws of Nature."

Like Petty, the philosopher and high-ranking civil servant John Locke (1632-1704) perceived many interest rate determinants and wanted the interest rate left alone. Locke made his mark in economics by writing tracts on money, and he published the best one of them in 1692 to bolster opposition (unsuccessfully) to a bill to lower rates being considered by Parliament. Locke said that interest was paid for the use of money which had two values. First, its value in exchange "and in this it has the Nature of a Commodity," with its value "depending only on the Plenty or Scarcity of Money in proportion to the Plenty or Scarcity of those things [commodities] . . ." In other words, this value was measured by the amount of goods money could buy in the market. Second, "its value in use "and in this it has the Nature of Land, the Income of one being called Rent, of the other Use [interest]." The use value of money derived from its service as productive capital. The borrower-producer needed capital to pay wages and material costs over a (short) period of time. However, since capital was essentially circulating money, Locke did not explicitly relate the rate of interest to the rate of profit.

Locke considered demand for money to be more or less constant. Men will borrow and pay for it as long as profit can be made: "no man borrows money, or pays use, out of mere pleasure; 'tis the want of money drives men to that trouble . . . and proportionably to this want, so will everyone have it, whatever price it cost him." In contrast, the supply of money for hire (Locke leaned toward capital as a stock of loanable funds) was changeable, affected by the level of the interest rate and lending risk. Thus, the value of money emerging from this demand and supply "depended on the whole quantity of the then passing money of the kingdom in proportion to the whole trade of the kingdom." Locke thought that the more money was available, the greater volume of trade resulted. But he stopped short of saying that increased money lowered interest rates or that low rates brought prosperity. Locke also denied that changes in interest rates affected the prices of commodities.

Locke established two types of interest rates besides the legal rate. The legal rate, fixed by Parliament as a fair rate for debts without agreed-upon contracts, would approximate the market rate. The latter rate was set by the demand from borrowers, given the amount of money in the country. The third rate was the natural rate. This was "that rate of money which the present scarcity of it makes it naturally at, upon an equal distribution of it." An even distribution of money throughout the kingdom meant a perfectly competitive structure. In this environment, all rates—the natural, the market, and the legal—should tend to be equal. Locke thought that if money in England totaled one million and "two millions were necessary to carry on the trade, there would be a million wanting, and the price of money would be raised." A monopoly on money by "bankers and scriveners, and other such expert brokers . . . skilled in the arts of putting out money," would similarly drive the rate over what was natural and also above the market rate reached by parties bargaining equally.

Locke believed that the legal rate should adhere to this consensus price reached by the market. An attempt by Parliament to lower the legal rate below the market rate would not only "put . . . affairs out of order," but was ultimately impossible: "Tis in vain . . . to go about effectually to reduce the price of interest by law; and you may as rationally hope to set a fixed rate upon the hire of houses, or ships, as of money . . . . Experience will show that the price of things will not be regulated by laws . . . . The skillful . . . will always so manage it, as to avoid the prohibition of your law, and keep out of its penalty . . . . Your act, at best, will serve only to increase the arts of lending, but not at all lessen the charge of the borrower."

Besides its futility, Locke argued that legislating lower rates would have negative economic effects. Given the lower return, individual lenders would tend to minimize risks and not lend directly "in the country." They would consign their money to bankers, bringing about a concentration of funds and consequently a higher market rate. The same result would be achieved by the related possibility that the supply of money would be reduced because the rich would lend less or be altogether discouraged from lending due to "such a disproportion of profit to risque." In addition, a reduced rate would "transfer a third part of the monied man's estate, who has nothing else to live on into the merchant's pocket; and that without merit in the one, or transgression in the other." Wealth would be redistributed, penalizing "widows, orphans, and all those who have their estates in money." This segment of society would contract the quantity of money, offsetting the expansionary gains of the enriched merchant. There would be no net benefit for the country's economy.

Locke further denied that a lower rate would increase the value of land as some claimed. First, there was no historical evidence that land values and interest rates were closely associated. Lands differed among themselves, while money was homogenous. Second, land values could not be expected to rise, if the entire economy were languishing under the influence of less money around and higher interest rates. The prices of agricultural produce would fall, so would rents. The demand for land, along with that for other goods, would decline. Knowing the landed interests of the parliamentarians proposing to lower rates, Locke emphasized that a decreased rate did not favor the landholder, but "him that ceases to be so."

Locke also provided purely political arguments against the regulation of interest. Like Plato, Locke described how usury laws may lead to increased perjury in the nation as people create false contracts to cover up lending at illegitimately high rates. Locke criticized the state for passing bad laws, which force basically honest men to become criminals in order to conduct their business. Thus, he was against price controls. Natural law determined prices, and natural economic laws take precedence over civil economic laws just as natural law over civil law. The same obedience to natural law made interest moral. It was as natural "as the tenant pays rent for your land." What Petty strongly hinted before, Locke made explicit. Interest was a rightful fee for the use of another's property. As one who owned more land than he could till can take in a tenant, so one who had more money than he could use can accommodate a borrower. Interest, like rent, found its ultimate cause in the unequal distribution of economic resources.

The analogy to land gave Locke more insight when probing for the source of interest. He wrote: "Money is a barren thing, and produces nothing; but by compact transfers that profit, that was the reward of one man's labor, into another man's pocket." Interest derived not from the owner of funds, but from the borrower or, in this case, the cultivator of land. Its payment was "equitable and lawful," because commercial borrowers earned more gains than tenants. Locke attributed all production to man's labor with this proposition: "For it is labour indeed that put the difference of value on everything." He proved this by showing the great difference between "land planted with tobacco and sugar . . . and land lying in common without any husbandry . . ." He continued that "if we rightly estimate things [used by man] and cast up the several expenses about them, what is owing to nature and to labour, we shall find that in most of them ninety-nine hundredths are wholly to be put on the account of labor." Hence, interest was largely the fruit of labor. Locke's labor-based and money-use analyses, set against a macroeconomic background, presaged the next steps in the theory of interest decades later.

While Locke was writing his well-reasoned essays, the English analysis of interest took a major theoretical turn. The emphasis on money that had chiefly characterized it was discarded by Nicholas Barbon (1640-98), a little known English physician turned businessman, who invented fire insurance after the Great Fire of London. An opponent of mercantilism and metallic monetary standards (he helped plan the land-banks that issued paper legal tender against land), Barbon's "real" analysis underlined Locke's treatment of productive activity and intimated a lasting feature of future theorizing. In his 1690 *Discourse on Trade*, Barbon declared in an astute and deceptively brief sentence: "Interest is commonly reckoned for Money . . . but this is a mistake; for the Interest is paid for Stock." Interest is "the Rent of Stock, and is the same as the Rent of Land; the First is the Rent of the Wrought or Artificial Stock; the Latter, of the Unwrought or Natural Stock."

Locke and others before him, including the scholastics, had compared interest to rent. Barbon pushed the similarity forward to ultimate uses. He reasserted the obvious fact that money is borrowed for what it can buy. He identified interest with the thing bought, specifically, physical capital. He disassociated interest with money taken absolutely. To say otherwise was as roundabout as asserting that the payment for eyeglasses is really payment for the book to be read or, as a 20th-century critic put it in noting the incompleteness of Barbon's comparison, that "the price we pay for the knife [to cut food] is really paid for the food." Barbon had business loans in mind. Stock meant producer, not consumption, goods. It was either owned or purchased by the manufacturer or merchant and not by the lender.

However, while the capitalist may not be lending goods, he did so, Barbon admitted, by imputation. Thus, although it was the entrepreneur who earned the return on these goods by using them, his profit could be construed as the lender's interest or, equivalently, his interest was the lender's profit. This notional interchangeability indicated that Barbon was still aware of the monetary aspect of interest. He seemingly placed interest in the price (or rent) of the capital goods purchased. Unlike Locke, he did not directly refer interest to the productive yield of those goods. Profit was money gain and not an increased quantity of commodities. In Barbon's mind, the lender lent money, not goods. But by linking interest and stock, he guided the inquiry on interest away from the "monetary veil" and toward the concepts of capital, production, and income distribution that later economists would clarify.

Dudley North (1641-91) was a customs commissioner, and, like Barbon, a merchant who struck it rich (in Turkey). As a free-trader, he saw no reason for government "to prohibit the taking more than 4l per Cent Interest for Money lent or to leave the Borrower and Lender to make their own Bargains." In his *Discourses upon Trade* in 1691, he too grasped the idea of capital as "heaps of Goods," apparently the first to call it stock ahead of Barbon. North's stock was more comprehensive. It was a combination of physical capital and metallic money and "any thing valuable." Lending this mixed stock was equivalent to letting out land. Interest was rent for stock.

North reasoned as follows: "Now as there are more Men to Till the Ground than have Land to Till, so also there will be many who want Stock to manage; and also (when a Nation is grown rich) there will be Stock for Trade in many hands, who either have not the skill, or care not for the trouble of managing it in Trade. But as the Landed Man letts his Land, so these still lett their Stock; this latter is call'd Interest, but is only Rent for Stock, as the other is for Land. And in several Languages, hiring of Money, and Lands, are Terms of common use; and it is so also in some counties in England. Thus to be a Landlord, or a Stock-lord is the same thing." North went on to say that stock should earn more than land, because the "Tenant cannot carry away the Land, as the tenant of the other may the Stock. Stock involved "the greater hazard."

With the idea of stock that included money, North handily concluded his views, which was drafted to oppose the "abatement of interest," by repeating the dominant role of the existing amount of credit, fueled by prosperity, in setting rates. "As plenty makes cheapness in other things, as Corn, Wool . . . when they come to Market in greater Quantities than there are Buyers to deal for, the price will fall; so if there be more Lenders than Borrowers, Interest will also fall; wherefore it is not low Interest makes Trade, but Trade increasing, the Stock of the Nation makes Interest low. It is said, that in Holland Interest is lower than in England. I answer; It is, because their Stock is greater than ours. I cannot hear that they ever made a Law to restrain Interest, but am certainly informed, that at this day, the Current Interest between Merchant and Merchant . . . is 6 per Cent and the Law justifies it."

Looking at the supply side of credit, North reversed the negative relationship between increased trade (stock) and lower interest rates, unknowingly harking back to Mun, who died in the year North was born. The amount of stock will tend to increase with a rise in the interest rate, he declared, because "high Interest will certainly bring Money out from Hoards, Plate, et cetera, into Trade, when low interest will keep it back . . ." As one of the first free-trade advocates, North was against the mercantilist hoarding of treasure. Wealth had to bear fruit constantly by being put in trade or lent out. With many loans made out to buy luxuries, North saw no reason for subsidizing such sterile expenditure with a low rate. He dismissed the moral stand against interest in a pithy sentence: "I will not say any thing to the Theological Arguments against Interest of Moneys; but their 3 per Cent is no more lawful than 4 or 12."

The attitude on interest of Sir James Steuart (1712-80), lawyer-scion of a prominent Scottish family, resembled Locke's recognition of business profitability sourced in productive labor. Around 1767, Steuart promoted the primacy of labor in creating not only value, but, importantly, also excess value: "The interest they [workers] pay for the money borrowed is inconsiderable when compared with the value created (as it were) by the proper employment of their time and talents. If it be said that this is a vague suggestion, supported by no proof, I answer that the value of a man's work may be estimated by the proportion between the manufacture when brought to market and the first matter." Loan interest precisely originated from this increased production.

Going farther than Locke, Steuart derived the rate of interest from the rate of profit: "In proportion, therefore, to the advantages to be reaped from borrowed money, the borrowers offer more or less for the use of it." The rate of profit in Steuart's time likely exceeded 3%, since Daniel Defoe, the author of *Robinson Crusoe*, wrote in 1701 that 3% was being paid for deposits. Steuart also emphasized money supply as an additional determinant of the interest rate. He thought the amount of money, which statesmen could increase or decrease, "greatly influenced the rate of interest [which] . . . falls in proportion to the redundancy of money to be lent."

David Hume (1711-76), a Scot utilitarian philosopher and economist, closed the main post-mercantilist period of economic thought. His stature as an economist matched Locke's, and he equally grasped the diverse macroeconomic factors shaping interest. His writings, principally dealing with trade and money, launched a strong case against interest as a purely monetary phenomenon. In 1752, he wrote an essay, *Of Interest*, which discussed the level of rates. It began by quoting the popular monetary belief that a large quantity of money caused low interest rates and by quickly knocking it down. "Nothing is esteemed a more certain sign of the flourishing condition of any nation than the lowness of interest . . . . [which] is generally ascribed to plenty of money. If money became plentiful, it could raise the rate, but only temporarily by "exciting industry" borrowing. Silver is more common than gold; and therefore you receive a greater quantity of it for the same commodities. But do you pay less interest for it?"

Hume then mentioned Batavia, Jamaica, and Portugal. In these places, interest rates were higher than in London and Amsterdam which had less of the precious metals. He also pointed out that prices had gone up nearly four times since the discovery of the Indies and that money supply multiplied much more, "but interest has not fallen much above half." It was the supply of goods and services that determined the interest rate, for "it is evident that the greater or less stock of labour and commodities must have a great influence; since we really in effect borrow these, when we take money upon interest." Augmentation of the money stock merely "heightened the price of labour and commodities . . ." The observation that expansive money growth raised commodity prices would be repeated until the 20th century when its correctness would be definitively verified.

Hume presented alternative "all connected together" determinants of interest. "High interest," he said, "arises from three circumstances: a great demand for borrowing, little riches to supply that demand, and great profits arising from commerce. Low interest, on the other hand, proceeds from the three opposite circumstances." High interest, for instance, reflected not merely a scarcity of gold and silver, but a primitive (agricultural) stage of economic development, characterized by an unequal distribution of income. "In a state . . . where there is nothing but a landed interest, as there is little frugality, the borrowers must be very numerous . . . . The difference depends not on the quantity of money, but on the habits and manners which prevail." Prodigals would outnumber the misers, remarked Hume, so that this would retard the existence of a great number of lenders, since "property, or command of that quantity . . . should be collected in particular hands, so as to form considerable sums, or compose a great monied interest." The "increase of industry and frugality, of arts and commerce," meaning the arrival of merchants, "one of the most useful races of men, who serve as agents between those parts of the state that are wholly unacquainted . . . of each other's necessities" would result in such a pool of loanable funds and depress interest rates.

Trade produced "an overplus of misers." The crucial saver was the seeker of profit: "But if the employment you give him be lucrative, especially if the profit be attached to every particular exertion of industry, he has gain so often in his eye, that he acquires, by degrees, a passion for it, and knows no such pleasure as that of seeing the daily increase of his fortune." Hume made the fine distinction, hinted by Locke, between the supply of money and the supply of savings, since the demand for money is different from the demand for loans. He transferred the monetary supply-demand equation from money to "the proportion between the borrowers and lenders in any state." The discovery of the West Indies, for instance, increased not so much the amount of money in Spain as the number of savers and lenders.

Along with Barbon, Hume contributed to the de-linking of money from interest by calling attention to the dynamic element in economic development. But he did not go as far as Barbon in bringing physical goods to the forefront of his discussion. Hume's attention was nuanced more toward traders than entrepreneurs. He eyed commercial profit more than industrial earnings. The end result, Hume continued, "when commerce has become extensive, and employs large stocks . . . is rivalships among the merchants, which diminish the profits of trade . . . . The low profits . . . induce the merchants to accept more willingly of a low interest . . . . It is needless to enquire which of these circumstances, to wit, low interest or low profits, is the cause, and which the effect. They both arise from an extensive commerce, and mutually forward each other. No man will accept of low profits, where he can have high interest; and no man will accept of low interest, where he can have high profits."

This reciprocal relationship rendered interest to be "the barometer of the state." With North, Hume concluded as he began:" Those who have asserted that the plenty of money was the cause of low interest, seem to have taken a collateral effect for a cause . . . . But it is evident, that the greater or less stock of labour and commodities must have a great influence; since we really . . . borrow these, when we take money upon interest." Hume granted that "the most industrious nations always abound most with the precious metals: So that low interest and plenty of money are in fact almost inseparable. But still it is of consequence to know the principle whence any phenomenon arises . . ." With this admonition, Hume steered the next group of economists to investigate interest in real terms. He had indicated that the amount of real stocks and the business results they generated were what determined the interest rate.

One such economist was Joseph Massie (d1784), a prolific writer on trade and finance. In his *Essay on the Governing Causes of the Natural Rate of Interest* in 1750, he repeated the views of Barbon and Hume and refuted Petty and Locke. The quantity of money did not set the interest rate. The rate was determined by the amount of disposable capital (loanable funds) on one hand, and on the other the demand of borrowers and the rate of profit. His views would be repeated one way or another by succeeding generations of economists.

Summary of the political economists. After the mercantilists, Locke and Hume, with their extended work on money and interest, set the next stage for further theorizing. The scrutiny of the correct (high or low) levels of interest rates had progressed from identifying their varying effects on an economy (stimulative or dampening) to explaining their causes. The quantity of money was seen as largely behind the behavior of rates, explained in common-sense supply and demand terms. More money available led to lower rates and vice-versa.

This money supply causation was strongly denied by some, such as Hume, who substituted for it either the number of lenders and borrowers, or the profit made by the latter, or people's saving habits. These represented magnitudes of credit, productivity, and thrift. The exclusive currency framework of interest subsequently evolved toward larger parameters, like the volume of commerce or the development of industry or general prosperity. This broadening was stimulated by the insight, perceived less emphatically before by a few scholastics, that demand was not really for money but for business stock.

The goods that money could buy really drove borrowing. The employment of the stock of labor and producer goods resulted in more goods and therefore in profit, so that interest became associated with labor and the resulting profit. Money was capital, and capital could be abundant or scarce, impacting rates. The demand for loans was distinct from the demand for money. In addition, the concept, mentioned by Lessius, of a natural rate of interest to which all rates tended, was acknowledged in relation to the market rate. Ideally, they should converge. Both were superior levels to the legislated rate.

All the propositions presented during this period explored new ground. But they did not result in a unified view of the desirable level of rates and of their determination. Juridical measures for or against rate control and for or against low or high rates were recommended. Most of them favored deregulation.

The redirection by Barbon and Hume of interest to the purchase of physical stock raised the intelligibility of the intrinsic value behind interest. Nonetheless, interest was still predominantly perceived as monetary. The analysis of money as stock was rudimentary, so that interest remained possessed of diverse definitions, including a few of the scholastic external titles. It was use of money, rent, a time or location premium, risk protection, compensation for lack of liquidity, the fruit of labor, and (with some forcefulness) business profit. Intent on reaching conclusiveness and narrowing the definitional spectrum, the next group of economists, emulating the lengthy works of Locke and Hume, undertook encyclopedic exposition that has earned the designation of "classical." Their efforts were made easier by the fact that the fertility of money was no longer controverted and that this Aristotelian argument was a thing of the past. Furthermore, time was no longer a free and valueless good. Individuals had a claim on it.

Chapter 6

CLASSICAL ECONOMICS

The transition from the assessment of the morality of interest to its rate was an analytical benchmark, but it was a digression. The persuasive discovery of the fundamental economic nature of interest was still wanting. To remedy this failing, the period of "classical economics" that lasted up to the late 19th century had to lift the "veil of money" from interest. This changed focus easily fitted into the preoccupation of classical economics. Its economists scrutinized the whole gamut of wealth, production, consumption, and the distribution of income.

Their broad approach explored the gradated genesis of profit from productive activity. How interest was related to capital, land, and labor was addressed. Capital or stock was increasingly viewed as real or physical goods. The mental image had changed from the moneylender with his moneybags to a provider of machines. As a result, the concept of interest spanned both real and monetary dimensions. It assumed greater complexity than in scholastic doctrines, which was referenced to the contractual money loan. The origin of real interest had to be explained in addition to its derivative, that is, nominal or market interest.

Again, English economists led the endeavor. Adam Smith (1723-90), a Scotsman and a close friend of Hume, ushered in classical economics. Smith was a professor par excellence, taught literature in Edinburgh and philosophy in the University of Glasgow. In 1776, he published *An Inquiry Into The Nature And Causes Of The Wealth Of*

Nations, a two-volume presentation of economics unprecedented for its comprehensiveness. Smith tidied up the looseness of the centuries, sharpening reasonability. With Smith, economics became a scientific field of study in its own right, apart from ethics and politics. He became an intellectual patriarch.

Smith did not break much new ground in the theory of interest, but his synthesis of income distribution prepared the bed for the seeding of future major ideas. First of all, Smith did not discuss the ethics of interest at length. Feeling that interest-taking no longer required belabored moral justification, he simply took it as a given, whose nature was to be analyzed purely in economic terms. Noting, for instance, that "in some countries the interest of money has been prohibited by law," he went on to say that the prohibition "instead of preventing, has been found from experience to increase the evil of usury." Why? Because the borrower had to pay more interest. He paid not only for the use of money, but also for insuring the creditor against the risk of penalties for violating the law.

Smith's primary objection to the prohibition of interest was its unfairness. "But as something can everywhere be made by the use of money," he argued, "something ought everywhere to be paid for the use of it." Smith saw that purchasing power gave money value. Its use therefore had value. "By means of the loan, the lender, as it were, assigns to the borrower his right to a certain portion of the annual produce of the land and labour of the country to be employed as the borrower pleases . . . . The borrower in return shall, during the continuance of the loan, annually assign to the lender a smaller portion, called the interest . . ." Because of the productivity of land and labor, Smith regarded interest from the payee's viewpoint as "revenue" or income, subject to tax. He repeatedly likened it to rent, "the price paid for the use of the land."

Smith even interchanged terminology to show the commonality of land and money. "The stock which is lent at interest is always considered as a capital by the lender. He expects that in due time it is to be restored to him, and that in the meantime the borrower is to pay him a certain annual rent for the use of it . . . . The rent of land, it may be thought, is frequently no more than a reasonable profit or interest for the stock laid out by the landlord for its improvement." The same commonality was noted in the economics of public finance. Smith identified the chief sources of government revenue as interest and land rentals. Interest as a form of income rested on Smith's division of the annual produce of an economy "into three parts: the rent of land, the wages of labour, and the profits of stock . . ." These payments for the three fundamental sources of production resulted in earnings for "three great, original, and constituent orders of every civilised society, from whose revenue that of every other order is ultimately derived."

When economic time began, Smith saw only the presence of labor. Later came the appropriation of land (agricultural, then mineral). Lastly, the accumulation of stock from net productive activity began. Part of this stock was productive wealth (capital), either fixed (machines) or circulating (money and goods inventory). Like labor and land, capital deserved proportionate compensation. "Interest," Smith declared, "derived from the income claimed by this third productive agent." He insisted that "something must be given for the profits of the undertaker of the work, who hazards his stock in the adventure [because] he could have no interest to employ them unless he expected from the sale of their work something more than what was sufficient to replace his stock to him; and he could have no interest to employ a great stock rather than a small one unless his profits were to bear some proportion to the extent of his stock."

Smith assigned interest its clear locus in the economy's structure. It was subsumed under profits, a "derivative revenue." The causes of profits were also the source of interest. Profit was interest (or vice versa) for the totally self-financed entrepreneur. But interest in the strict sense was the return for any borrowed funds, and Smith recognized the possible distinction between the claim of the owner and of the creditor. Interest was a transfer from the earnings of an enterprise. Smith explained the origin of profit, defined as proceeds minus cost. Profit either came out of the purchaser by way of a price for the product higher than its labor value or out of a deduction from the share due the laborer. Smith wrote: "The value which the workman adds to the material . . . resolves itself . . . into two parts, of which one pays the wages, the other the profits of the employer upon the whole stock of materials and wages which he advanced."

Smith admitted that the claim of profit (and interest) came from increased prices, if wages were not to be curtailed. This sympathetic note for labor was discernible when he first declared that rent and profit were subtractions from a product that seemed to result wholly from labor. But given his threefold distribution of income, Smith was uneasy about applying value exclusively to labor. Thus, a page later he noted that the labor employed in producing any commodity was not "the only circumstance that can regulate the quantity it could exchange for," but that "an additional quantity . . . must be due for the profits of the stock . . ." A product must "always be sufficient to purchase or command a much greater quantity of labour than was employed raising, preparing, and bringing that produce to market."

Smith hesitated to specify an average rate of profit on which to hang the rate of interest. He was aware of the great variability in individual profits. For him, the rate of profits determined the interest rate in accordance with the maxim "that wherever a great deal can be made by the use of money, a great deal will commonly be given for the use of it," and vice-versa. But Smith also suggested that interest on loans could provide a clue to the rate of profits from capital goods. The former reflected the latter. Hence Smith tentatively judged the typical average profit rate to be about twice the interest rate on highly secured loans, indicating the difference as due to the risk inherent in a business enterprise. The creditor supposedly ran no risk.

However, instead of proceeding to the logical description of the free-market pricing of interest, Smith, who favored laissez faire, approved the prevailing restriction of the maximum rate to 5%. He thought the rate induced sound investment. If it were higher, he wrote that "the greater part of the money which was to be lent, would be lent to prodigals and projectors, who alone would be willing to give this high interest . . . . A great part of the capital of the country would thus be kept out of the hands which were most likely to make a profitable and advantageous use of it, and thrown into those which were most likely to waste and destroy it."

The availability of abundant capital was vital for Smith's income and growth theories, since the demand for it was unceasing as "in all arts and manufactures . . . the workmen stand in need of a master to advance them the materials of their work, and their wages and maintenance till it be completed." Saving drove the formation of capital. Smith said that "parsimony, and not industry is the immediate cause of the increase of capital," and that "every frugal man appears to be a public benefactor." Saving did not directly depend on the quantity of money in an economy. He reiterated Hume's emphasis on human behavior. Capital was stock (fixed or circulating) withheld from immediate consumption.

Smith, like many of his fellow theorists, did not completely separate the capitalist-saver from the businessman. Profit often stemmed from the stock supplied by the businessman. In Smith's time, such single-sourced income was known as "double interest" and was considered fair. Profit depended strictly on the "size of capital." The capitalist's share of the value produced by labor after wages and the compensation of the entrepreneur's "labour of inspection and direction" was "regulated altogether by the value of the stock employed, and are greater or smaller in proportion to the extent of this stock."

Smith did not omit compensation due to the "risk and trouble" of the Businessman. But he regarded it as a secondary element. It was a supplement to interest, even as "the lowest ordinary rate of interest must be something more than is sufficient to compensate the occasional losses to which lending, even with tolerable prudence, is exposed." As capital increased and productive activity developed and became more competitive, profits and interest rates would decline. The rate of profit, itself determined by the amount of capital employed, determined the rate of interest.

Smith recapitulated the several conclusions on interest reached in the past. Interest was payment for the use of money and for risk. Interest could also be understood as a rental. Interest was not directly or exclusively the fruit of labor. Lastly, interest was a share in profit. Smith gave intrinsic import to this last definition. Interest, by nature, originated from profit. This essential observation was Smith's principal contribution to interest theory.

Jeremy Bentham (1748-1832), famed utilitarian philosopher, in his *Defense of Usury* written in 1787, corrected Smith for supporting the public regulation of interest. Bentham advocated a naturally free market system. There is "no more reason for fixing the price of the use of money than the price of goods," Bentham contended. He went on to say that "no legislator can judge, so well as each individual for himself, whether money is worth to him anything, and how much, beyond the ordinary interest."

Moreover, the laws were defective, since many people became unable to borrow at all. Some were coerced to borrow under unfavorable terms (even under "the very way forbidden"), entrepreneurs suffered undeserved disgrace, and "treachery and ingratitude "were induced. Bentham considered the second reason the most important, concluding that the result of usury laws was to hike interest rates due to the risk of being caught. He went to the extent of campaigning for the repeal of the maximum legal rate. Government should not interfere in business, and "every man should be free to make his contracts as he will . . ." Lending money should be treated like any other trade. He made the exceptional comment that "usurers are men as honest as other tradesmen . . ." They were abstemious and had no "worldly love of present pleasure."

On the theoretical level, Bentham suggested interest as provision for frugality and risk. He suspected a connection between interest and savings and investment, but he doubted whether interest served an equilibrating function. He did recognize the important seminal point that "putting money out at interest, is exchanging present money for future," and those who did were the envy of those "who have sacrificed the future to the present."

David Ricardo (1772-1823) was a giant figure in the history of economic theory. Landowner, stockbroker, multimillionaire, member of Parliament with the help of a 20,000-pound, interest-free loan to an Irish borough holder, Ricardo expanded the themes of Smith. Like Smith, he took interest for granted and did not deeply probe the subject. His references to interest in his *Principles of Political Economy and Taxation* published in 1817 were confined to the interest rate. However, his analysis foreshadowed at least three later principal theories of interest, namely, the so-called abstinence, profit residual, and labor theories. Following Smith, he established the origin of interest in man's self-interest and desire for wealth: "For no one accumulates [capital] but . . . to make his accumulation productive, and it is only when so employed that it operates on profits. Without a motive there could be no accumulation . . ."

Ricardo disagreed with the mercantilists who held that the interest rate depended on the quantity of money. He went along with Smith. The "alterations in the rate of interest" was a consequence of the "permanent variations in the rate of profit," which in turn was caused by the trend of wages. "The rate of interest," wrote Ricardo, is "ultimately and permanently governed by the rate of profit . . ." In the long run, profit stabilized, and the credit market had to adjust the rate to equal profit. In effect, there would tend to be a single equilibrium interest rate, much like the natural rate.

Ricardo stressed this profit-oriented belief: "The interest of money is not regulated by the rate at which the Bank [of England] will lend, whether it be 5, 3 or 2 per cent, but by the rate of profit which can be made by the employment of capital, and which is totally independent of the quantity or of the value of money. Whether the Bank lent one million, ten millions, or a hundred millions, they would not permanently alter the market rate of interest; they would alter only the value [purchasing power] of the money which they thus issued. In one case, ten or twenty times more money might be required to carry on the same business than what may be required in the other. The applications to the Bank for money, then, depend on the comparison between the rate of profits that may be made by the employment of it, and the rate at which they are willing to lend it. If they charge less than the market rate of interest, there is no amount of money which they might not lend; if they charge more than that rate, none but the spendthrift and prodigals would be found to borrow of them."

Ricardo analyzed what was increasingly perceived by the economists. Expanded money supply caused inflation in the long run, cheapening the real value of money. For the short run, later economics would usually repeat Ricardo when he wrote: "If . . . the quantity of money be greatly increased, its ultimate effect is to raise the . . . prices of commodities [proportionately]; but there is probably always an interval during which some effect is produced on the rate of interest." Ricardo regularly granted that the rate of interest could be affected in the short run by the supply of money. This would happen, for instance, when the Bank of England issued loan notes, "which would be sent to every market, and . . . raise the prices of commodities, till they were absorbed in the general circulation. It is only during the interval of the issues of the Bank, and their effect on prices . . . [that] interest would, during the interval, be under its natural level . . ." Interest would also rise briefly when the government withdrew huge sums to pay public debt. Ricardo minimized these transitory effects.

The long-run view guided Ricardo in assessing the behavior of the interest rate. Real economic forces ("amount of capital and the means of employing it") governed the rate. Citing the authority of Smith and Hume, he repeated that "the rate of interest for money is totally independent of the nominal amount (abundance or scarcity) of the circulating medium. It is regulated solely by the competition of capital, not consisting of money." He quoted Smith's statement that "the rate of interest depends on the rate of profits," and characterized this one-way relationship as "ultimately and permanently" true. The individual rates of return may be unequal and high at first, for example when tillable land was abundant. Eventually, as production grew and competition intensified, such as when less land became available or less fertile, they would all sink to the same marginal level, that is, "the profit obtainable in the least remunerative employment of capital."

While competitive output would stay the same or decrease, the value of the products would not remain unchanged, because more and more labor would be needed. The rising value of labor (wages) in this situation would squeeze the profit share of capital toward zero. At some point before capital accumulation ceased, wages would have to adjust downward. Ricardo alleviated this wage pressure on profits by guardedly assigning an added value to products resulting from the employment of capital in which postponement of present enjoyment was imbedded. Profit or interest from capital therefore additionally arose, first, from the abstention from consumption by the capitalist and, second, the extended life of producer goods and their operation. Ricardo pointed out, as would happen about half-a-century later, that goods taking longer to produce had a higher value than goods requiring a shorter period, given the same amount of labor. "The difference in value," Ricardo said, "is only a just compensation for the time that the profits were withheld" or reduced.

Profits, which were the amount left after the subtraction of wages for Ricardo's main economic agent, the farmer-businessman, were the price of waiting. Like Petty's view, interest was the recompense for the element of time. Ricardo accordingly expressed some reservations to the assertion that all value was regulated by labor. Ricardo saw a hindrance to this rule in capital's unique capabilities: "The principle . . . suffers a considerable modification by the employment of machinery and other fixed and durable capital . . . . and on account of the unequal durability of capital, and of the unequal rapidity with which it is returned to its owner." Production that utilized much durable capital or involved a longer payback time created extra value, which could be rightfully labeled as profit. But for the long run, Ricardo, living in a time of great national stress caused by the Napoleonic wars, was unavoidably pessimistic. His macro-view foresaw falling profits and an economy ending in a stationary state.

James Maitland, Earl of Lauderdale (1759-1839), continued the analysis of profit. He broached the so-called productivity theory of interest in 1804, the first in England to do so since its formulation in France a year before. Stating with Smith that capital was a third original source of wealth, he set about to solve, as his avowed task, the question of the nature and origin of profit, specifically, "by what means capital or stock contributes towards wealth . . ." He rejected the thinking of Locke and Smith that put much store on labor value. Interest was profit or capital value. He began with the contribution of capital in the production process: "In every instance where capital is so employed as to produce a profit, it uniformly arises either from its supplanting a portion of labour, which would otherwise be performed by the hand of man, or from its performing a portion of labor, which is beyond the reach of the personal exertion of man to accomplish."

Lauderdale discerned that the substitutability of labor and capital goods gave rise to additional profits. With this physical productivity of capital, the capitalist was able to acquire wholly or partially the wages of the displaced workers. Enhanced profit was realized from the same prices charged the consumer on goods whose cost had been lowered by the improved efficiency. Thus, the dynamics of consumer market demand and supply intertwined with the shifting capital-wage relationship.

Supply and demand likewise ruled the capital goods market: "The actual profit drawn for the use of any machine . . . must be regulated on the same principle with the hire of a field . . . or the price of any commodity; that is, the proportion betwixt the quantity of machines that can be easily procured, and the demand for them."

Lauderdale's productivity model was far-sighted, but not enough. He and the other classical economists had so far failed to see that a straightforward reading of some of their unqualified statements on profit could mean equating profit with gross return. This was a critical problem soon to arise. Interest has to be linked to net return, that is, to gross return minus depreciation or capital replacement. Otherwise, interest has no extra value. It earns nothing. To say that it is an income would be questionable.

Thomas Malthus (1766-1834), a professor curate famed for his treatise on population and a warm friend of Ricardo, maintained the affinity to profit of Lauderdale's analysis. He probed additional insights. Publishing in 1820, he recognized the role of market prices in generating profit, since "the prices of commodities do not depend upon their intrinsic utility, but upon the supply and the demand." Capital would be advanced as long as the commodities produced could be brought to market. The existence of remuneration was a necessary condition for such advances. Part of that return, Malthus seemed to imply, did not emanate exclusively from the productive power of capital. It came partly from the price paid by the consumer.

Malthus understood profit from capital as a proper constituent part of production costs like wages. He therefore saw no cause for grievance from workers as a result of increased physical productivity. "With regards to the labourers employed," he wrote, "as neither their exertions nor their skill would necessarily be much greater than if they had worked unassisted, their remuneration would be nearly the same as before . . . . It is not therefore . . . correct to represent, as Adam Smith does, the profits of capital as a deduction from the produce of labour. They are only a fair remuneration for that part of the production contributed by the capitalist, estimated exactly in the same way as the contribution of the labourer."

Malthus summarized the findings on interest in his time in four statements. Capital had its own productivity and the right to profit (interest) without detriment to labor. The origin of profit partially derived from market pricing and the consumer in accordance with Smith. Profit also depended on the scarcity of capital, that is, on the relative labor-capital supplies, so that "when capital is really abundant compared with labour, profits must be low, and no facility of production can occasion high profits, unless capital is scarce." Finally, interest was the required price for the very act of accumulating capital and advancing it, whether profit was made or not.

Henry Thornton (1760-1815), banker and a member of Parliament, briefly departed from the "real" focus of his predecessors. True to his financial profession, he considered interest within the monetary process, specifically, its relation with money and prices. His analysis, considered amazing and admirable by later economists, because it anticipated the principles of central bank policy by a century, pioneered several points. Among them were that a high Bank of England discount rate would attract gold from other countries and that the rate of interest influenced the public's holding of idle cash.

Thornton, like Ricardo, did not believe that the interest rate was determined by the amount of money. Instead, he offered a fuller model of the market for loanable funds, with the loan rate equaling the marginal rate of investment profits. A below-equilibrium loan rate would tend to expand lending, which, if resulting in an above-equilibrium amount of credit would cause inflation. If the interest rate was kept constant, more borrowing would continue, more credit expansion would follow, and the cycle would repeat itself unless the monetary authority adopted restrictive measures. Thornton's mechanism for the determination of interest rates was indeed far advanced from that of the mercantilists.

Thornton was also known, though not widely, as a doctrinal forerunner of the association of market or nominal and real interest rates. He lived in an inflationary period (2-3% in 1800-10) due to the suspension of the convertible gold standard and the subsequent easy issue of paper currency. He was convinced that prices impacted the interest rate. The nominal rate minus the rate of inflation equaled the real rate. The higher nominal rates, however, did not come about because people were aware or expected the price increases. They were instead caused by businessmen's reaction to unforeseen inflation, which lowered their real cost of borrowed financing in relation to their real profits. These windfall gains (windfall losses to lenders) would then encourage expectations of continued strong business yields, spurring loan demand in the face of receding loan supply as prices ate up people's cash balances. As a result, nominal rates would rise until the gap with real rates was fully eliminated. Thornton gave an example of his analysis: "Thus . . . at Petersburgh, at this time, the current interest was 20 or 25 percent, which [was] conceived to be partly compensation for an expected increase of depreciation of the currency."

Nassau William Senior (1790-1864), was the holder of the first economics professorship at Oxford in 1825. He wrote on a wide range of economic subjects. He tied psychology to Smith's treatment of capital. He was best known for formally introducing the abstinence theory of interest that gained a large following. This theory, an idea roughly alluded to by several authors in the past, derived from Senior's negation of capital as one of the three original factors of production. Since Locke, capital at times was claimed as a result of labor, forcing Senior to posit an anterior substitute. He wrote: "Although Human Labour and the Agency of Nature [land] independently of that of man, are the Primary Productive Powers, they require the concurrence of a Third Productive Principle to give to them complete efficiency. The most laborious population, inhabiting the most fertile territory, if they devoted all their labour to the production of immediate results, and consumed its produce as it arose, would soon find their utmost exertions insufficient to produce even the mere necessaries of existence. To the Third Principle . . . we shall give the name of Abstinence . . . . By the word Abstinence, we wish to express that agent, distinct from labour and the agency of nature, the concurrence of which is necessary to the existence of Capital, and which stands in the same relation to Profit as Labour does to Wages."

Aware of the psychic cost of labor (disutility), Senior deemed abstinence a necessary factor of production, although a secondary one. The economic implication of abstinence was that the capitalist had as much right to interest as the worker to wages. The issue became how to slice the profit pie. The claim to profit was conventionally framed in terms of production cost and final value. The cost was the total of labor and of abstinence. Since costs affected the value of goods, the value should be sufficiently high to allow a reward for abstinence. Again invoking psychology, Senior lightened this obligatory condition. He granted that the capitalist could "soon regard the increase of his capital as the great business of his life," thus easing the "pain" of abstinence.

Echoing Lessius, Senior minimized the negativity of abstinence with the positive quality of sacrifice: "To abstain from the enjoyment which is in our power, or to seek distant rather than immediate results, are among the most painful exertions of the human will . . ." Postponement moreover was not purely subjective. Abstinence had a real link with time. Senior declared that the process of production involved the passage of time—a delay he considered of typically two years. Hence, he described abstinence with a two-pronged statement as "the conduct of a person who either abstains from the unproductive use of what he can command, or designedly prefers the production of remote to that of immediate results."

Instantaneous abstinence meant saving or the transformation of income into capital. Capital, according to Senior, was "an article of wealth, the result of human exertion employed in the production or distribution of wealth." The human exertion consisted "of labour, abstinence, and the agency of nature." This abstinence corresponded to Smith's parsimony or frugality. On the other hand, futuristic abstinence was waiting. It involved a reconfiguration of the structure of capital. Various capital goods were seen as possessing different turnover rates or making products that need different spans of time to become available. This commonly involved the employment of additional labor, often in making "products as the means of further production," which increased efficiency and manufacturing returns. Such temporal extensions, while they could add value, were costs of production that had to be paid. Interest was the compensation for both subjective choice and objective time encapsulated in the idea of abstinence.

Meantime, the causative role of labor in interest theory was not forgotten. By 1825, the function of labor had taken deeper root. John Ramsay McCulloch (1789-1864), journalist, teacher, and civil servant, pushed the claim of labor to the extreme. He sourced all the value of goods in the amount of human labor used for their production. Labor comprised the total cost of production. However, in a contradictory concession, he went on to include in that cost of production "the common and average rate of net profit at the time . . .." Such profit was realized in the marketing price. Profit was a surplus "after all the produce expended by them [the capitalists] is fully replaced." Thus, McCulloch was the first, along with an economist in Germany surnamed Riedel, to speak of net profit and surplus.

To remain consistent to his labor-oriented position, McCulloch modified profits as "only another name for the wages of accumulated labor." Interest was the wage of the labor originally applied in the formation of the capital stock or, the "wages of anterior labor." To illustrate this, McCulloch cited the maturing of wine in the cellar with its resulting appreciation in value. McCulloch went to the extent of declaring the laborer a machine and his wages a profit of capital in addition to an amount for depreciation of this "machine called man." The idea that interest was aged labor was relatively new. But newer still, and more critical, was McCulloch's advertence to net profit in relation to interest.

Debate on the status of labor continued. Samuel Read, an economist, writing in 1829, at first forcefully objected to Ricardo's primacy of labor, then compromised. Initially, he emphasized the independent productive power of capital by saying: "How absurd . . . to contend that labour produces all, and is the only source of wealth, as if capital produced nothing, and was not a real and distinct source of wealth also." He proved this by illustrations of various productive operations, concluding that all that remained after wage payments "may fairly be claimed as the produce and reward of capital."

Later on, however, Read declared that capital was formed through labor and saving, explaining this idea in the manner of Senior's abstinence. "The person who has laboured before," wrote Read, "and not consumed but saved the produce of his labour, and which produce is now applied to assist another labourer in the work of production, is entitled to his profit or interest (which is the reward for labour that is past, and for saving and preserving the fruits of that labor) as much as the present labourer is entitled to his wages, which is the reward for his more recent labour." This McCulloch-type reasoning accorded with Read's denying the distinction between profit and wages, although in another passage, Read corrected himself and rejected the validity of valuing past labor. Still, Read's fundamental view was that the capitalist, before being anything else, was a laborer.

Franz Joseph Gerstner (1756-1832), a mathematics professor in Prague, closely followed Read's ambivalent views. A stalwart believer in the separate productivity of capital, he claimed that "rent in the total profit that is due to capital" can be exactly mathematically calculated. Yet, Gerstner also described the tools of production as "a kind of anticipation of labour" and went on to name "the rent of capital that falls to the instruments of production the supplementary wage for previously performed labour." Past labor became the ultimate source of interest. Interest was rent for labor residing in capital. And interest for abstinence entailed labor too, since abstinence was labor.

As it began, classical economics came to a close with another all encompassing economist. While not as well known as Smith's *Wealth of Nations*, the two-volume *Principles of Political Economy* of John Stuart Mill (1806-73), coming nearly 75 years later in 1848, was no less impressive as a refined omnibus of economics. The book helped set the stage for the development of 20th century economics. Like its predecessors, its treatment of usury and related laws was not ethical at all. Mill thought the Church's objections to be wrong. For Mill, interest was the reward of abstinence. He labeled this term of Senior a "well chosen expression." Abstinence was what "a person is enabled to get by merely abstaining from the immediate consumption of his capital, and allowing it to be used for productive purposes by others."

How much was the reward for this abstinence? According to Mill, the remuneration was "measured by the current rate of interest on the best security." The best security was one that practically precluded the loss of the principal. Risk was important, because Mill went beyond the simple interchangeability of profit and interest described by his classical predecessors. He broke up profit into components and capital into owned and borrowed. The gains of the business class, the capitalists, were "resolvable into three parts." They provided an equivalent for abstinence, risk, and management or "superintendence." These "different compensations may be paid either to the same or to different persons.

The capital . . . may belong to someone who does not undertake the risks or the trouble of business. In that case, the lender, or owner, is the person who practices the abstinence; and is remunerated for it by the interest paid to him, while the difference between the interest and the gross profit remunerates the exertions and risks of the undertaker."

Mill interpreted abstinence positively. The reverse of "forebearing to consume" was "the effective desire of accumulation" which "differs widely in different states of society and civilization." That desire must afford such an equivalent to the owner of the capital for refraining to consume it, so that there is a sufficient motive for him to persist in his abstinence. The strength of this desire depended "on the comparative value placed, in the given society, upon the present and the future." The interest rate was based on the abstainer's estimation of the value of money now and money later. On the future valuation of money, Mill, unaware of Thornton's treatment of the same subject, noted that interest rates were raised to cover expected depreciation caused by inflation that would reduce the real value of both interest and principal payments. In addition, Mill appended the old common generalities that the rate of interest fluctuated "from variations either in demand for loans, or in the supply," and also remotely and temporarily in the changes of the "quantity or value of money in circulation."

The formation of capital had led Mill to trace interest back to labor, which built existing real capital. However, while categorized as an adherent of the labor theory of interest, Mill tried to fine-tune the impression that labor was the sole cost of production and source of value. He pictured profit from capital as an indirect wage: "Why must profits be paid? To this there is no answer but one, that they are the remuneration for labour, labour not applied immediately to the commodity in question, but applied to it through the medium of other commodities," for example, machines that labor had produced and which the capitalist owned or borrowed. There existed secondary labor which embodied the gain of the capitalist or the lender. Mill had to account why this profit was higher than the value of the recent labor. He attempted two solutions.

First, he returned to Senior. "In our analysis . . . of production, there is another necessary element in it besides labour. There is also capital; and this being the result of abstinence, the produce or its value must be sufficient to remunerate not only all the labor required, but the abstinence of all the persons by whom the remuneration of the different classes of labourers was advanced. The return for abstinence is profit." Sufficient pay must be awarded multiple abstinence.

Second, Mill reasoned: "The cause of profit is that labour produces more than is required for its support . . . . The reason why capital yields a profit is because food, clothing, materials and tools last longer than the time which was required to produce them; so that if a capitalist supplies a party of laborers with these things, on condition of receiving all they produce, they will, in addition to reproducing their own necessaries and instruments, have a portion of their time remaining to work for the capitalist." Mill believed that profit did not arise from a productivity inherent in capital, but from an excess or surplus value created by labor. As Mill had stipulated, the excess value covered not only abstinence embodied in capital and business "skill and assiduity," both of which incidentally were given a labor characteristic, but also non-labor risk. Mill's risk, which required indemnification, included both the combined risk of the lender and of the entrepreneur.

Mill did hedge his Ricardian framework further by saying that labor was the chief, but not sole, source of all value. He had acknowledged the emergence of profit and noted that the cost of production influenced value too. Profit and interest were costs that had to be paid, although labor had "so much the principal element as to be nearly the whole." Capital was a distinct factor of production. It was distinct, but subject to the qualification that capital was the product of labor. The only productive powers were labor and natural agents. He repeated his assertion that "the cause of profit is that labour produces more than is required for its support . . ." It had "time remaining to work for the capitalist."

Mill more fully differed from Ricardo on another point. He was an optimist. Every addition to capital, meaning every abstinence, would increase work opportunities, and the economy would tend toward full employment. Mill's sanguine outlook was evident in his interpretation of abstinence. He went beyond the "parsimony" of Ricardo and the "abstinence" of Senior by making them active practices. His phrase, "the effective desire for accumulation," meant a reasoned willingness and persistency in restricting present consumption to achieve future prosperity. Mill foresaw the number of this type of savers growing to a universal proportion. Thus, when identifying the "real" costs of production, he named two together, namely, the disutility ("irksomeness") of the laborer and the abstinence of the saver.

Summary of the classical economists. Starting on the ground floor of an economy, the classical economists established a triad of independent productive factors. Capital was one of them. It was artificial as opposed to land and labor, which were the natural agents of production. More fixedly than scholastic declarations, money was construed as capital or productive wealth. But money was not all of capital. Following Barbon and North, capital was also given a technical interpretation. It included what money secured—a stock of physical goods with durability varying from variable to fixed. In a narrow sense, capital meant manufactured goods used for further production. In a broader application, capital included inventories, goods (even consumption goods) required for the upkeep of labor, and sometimes land utilized.

Invested money or advances was conceived as the fixed stocks they purchased, such as machinery, tools, buildings, and raw material. If land and labor garnered earnings, capital, whether owned or borrowed, similarly deserved income. The utilization of capital in business activity yielded profit. Interest as proceeds from capital was essentially synonymous with profit. Consequently, variations in the rate of profit, not changes in the quantity of money, induced alterations in the rate of interest. Demand for capital, not the supply of money, was a more key determinant of interest rates.

Profit was secured through either product pricing in the market or, to improve output, by substituting machinery for labor or by extending the period of production. Although profit was defined as the residual after costs, costs were mainly estimated as the wages of workers, so that the movement of wages principally impacted the magnitude of profit.

Interest was often simply equated with profit. The unqualified identification later created a problem that classical economists had overlooked. Depreciation or replacement costs could absorb all of gross profit, especially if the cost of capital goods rose. In loan terminology, this was tantamount to saying that profit replaced merely the principal amount lent. There was no room for interest properly speaking, so it had to be accommodated separately, payable to various parties. Previous rationalization was employed. Interest was payment for the multifaceted task of capital accumulation (now developed into a full-blown theory of abstinence), the financier's risk, and the entrepreneur's risk and industry. But to squeeze these additional absolute entitlements into the profit category postulated the introduction of net profit, an issue that was left largely unaddressed.

The abstinence theory looked at the formation, not operation, of capital. The accumulation of capital required the postponement of the immediate enjoyment of goods for the sake of greater consumption in the future. This conversion of the definition of interest from a use to a non-use payment had the advantage of being applicable to non-commercial loans as well. On the other hand, it shifted value to a subjective origin. Interest was the reward for waiting.

As intensively taken up as the abstinence theory was the labor factor in production. The labor theory of interest reasserted that labor (current and past) was the sole origin of productivity. The existence of profit was not negated, but its final sourcing to capital was. Labor injected all value in goods, including capital goods. Even monetary capital was formed by the labor of saving. The more labor used meant the more value produced. Labor was the total cost of production. That cost included profit, which was partly met by the pricing for the consumer. Essentially, there was no distinction between wages and profit. Profit was a rental of labor power, even though such income did not go to the laborers. Profit was an indirect wage or the embodiment of secondary labor. Interest was deviated wages.

Classical economics roughly marked the midway point in the evolution of interest theory. Analysis had moved from finding reasons for the payment of interest to shaping them into bases for ascertaining the intrinsic nature of interest. Where did interest come from? The source evidently had to be an entity that produced value. Besides labor, three other principal explanations emerged out of the various strands of past thinking, competing for recognition as a true, if not unique, explanation of interest. The residual theory, which could be merged with the productivity theory, accepted the reality of increased output coming out of the capital input. The output minus costs almost always resulted in a margin. Hope for this residual motivated borrowing. Interest was realized in the resulting profit. For the non-entrepreneur lender, interest was a share in the profit, gained by his abstinence. It was an assured share, not fundamentally different from the insurance-guaranteed partnership meticulously crafted by the scholastics.

PART FOUR

THE REST OF EUROPE

Chapter 7

ACROSS THE CHANNEL

On the Continent, French scholars probed the subject of interest as carefully and as variedly as their English counterparts. They restated arguments and added fresh and critical viewpoints in the incremental process. Two of them still supported the severe canons of Rome, the last ones of significant repute to do so. Robert Joseph Pothier (1699-1772), a celebrated jurist, whose major writing was on Roman law and on contracts, gathered all the arguments already made against interest, then wove together those he considered most plausible. He reprised two major points stressed by early scholasticism.

First, interest was unjust: "It is a fair claim that the values given in the case of a contract which is not gratuitous should be equal on either side, and that no party should give more than he has received, or receive more than he has given. Everything, therefore, that the lender may demand from the borrower over and above the principal sum, he demands over and above what he has given."

Second, this unfair exchange rested on the definition of interest as the charge for the use of money. Money belonged to that class "of objects that are known to lawyers as fungible goods—things that are consumed in the using." Hence, "it is impossible in regard to them to imagine a use of the thing as distinct from the thing itself, and as having a price distinct from the thing itself . . . . One cannot make over to another the using of a thing without making over to him wholly and entirely the thing itself, and transferring to him the property in it." In contrast, "for things that can be used without being destroyed a hire may be certainly demanded, because, this use being separable at any moment (in thought at least) from the things themselves, it can be priced." In this case, what was handed over remained the property of the lender. Pothier wrote very much like Aquinas.

Victor Riquetti, the Marquis de Mirabeau (1715-89) agreed with Pothier, drawing from the past as well. His book in 1764, harking back to Aristotle, ruled that interest was wrong, because money was barren. Money was merely a tool for exchange. It has no other value, and "to obtain a profit from this representative character is to seek in a glass for the figure it represents." To obtain income rightfully, Mirabeau contended that the owner of money should convert it to other goods that would fetch a rental, without apparently being aware of the similar refinements developed in England, especially by Barbon and North. In fact, Mirabeau conceded finely defined exceptions to his anti-interest stand. For instance, gains earned in business, reckoned not so much from capital as from the commercial activity, "*de la profession,*" of the businessman, were acceptable.

Still, Mirabeau saw injustice in interest. Equality could not be reached between the interest amount and the gain, *emploi*, of the borrower. The yield from farming, which was Mirabeau's example, was uncertain, so that the borrower by this fact already has incurred a loss and the very payment of interest was a loss. By citing the uncertainty of profit, Mirabeau unknowingly questioned the positive assumption of the residual theory of the classical economists.

In sharp contrast to Pothier and Mirabeau, Richard Cantillon (1680-1734), an Irish financier who at 22 already displayed exceptional acumen for banking, lived many years in Paris, and grew rich from speculative investments, had no objection to interest. Cantillon has been credited with the first systematic exposition of the general interdependence among all sectors of the economy, His *Essai sur la Nature du Commerce en General* in 1755, which was his only written work, was undoubtedly buttressed by experience.

Cantillon's first written words regarding "the interest of money and its causes" chose to highlight, not the mercantilist quantity of money, but the amount of funds strictly available for credit to explain the interest rate: "As the prices of things are determined in the altercations of the markets by the quantity of things offered for sale in proportion to the amount of money offered for them, or, what is the same thing, by the numerical proportion between the Sellers & the Buyers; similarly the interest of money in a State is determined by the numerical proportion between the Lenders & the Borrowers." In other words, "If the abundance of money . . . comes from the hands of money lenders it will doubtless bring down the current rate of interest by increasing the number of money lenders: but if it comes from . . . spenders it will have just the opposite effect . . . by increasing the number of Undertakers who . . . will need to borrow to equip their business . . ." Cantillon was the main harbinger of the loanable funds theory, which would attain prominence in the 20th century.

After this generalization about the interest rate, Cantillon sought the origin of interest. In contrast to Mirabeau, he found it squarely in profit. Admitting the barren nature of money in itself, yet recognizing its potential profitability, he said: "Although money passes as a pledge in exchange, yet it does not multiply, and does not produce any interest by merely circulating. The necessities of Men seem to have introduced the practice of interest. A Man who lends his money . . . runs the risk of losing all . . . . Men in need must have at first tempted the Lenders by the attraction of a profit; and this profit must have been in proportion to the needs of the Borrowers and to the fear and the avarice of the Lenders. This . . . was the original source of interest. But its constant practice in States appears to be founded upon the profits which entrepreneurs can make out of it."

Cantillon continued: "If there were in a State no Undertakers who could make a profit on the money or goods which they borrow, the use of interest would probably be less frequent than it is." He calculated profit not only as the residual of production costs, but also of the living expenses of the borrower-entrepreneur. The lender clearly had to take these expenditures into account before figuring out not only his interest charge, but also his decision to lend. He was just observing the same rule followed in merchandising: "All the Merchants . . . make a regular practice of entrusting . . . commodities to Retailers on credit, and they adjust their rate of profit, or their interest to the risk they run." But in the long run, the honest and industrious entrepreneur, sustained by trusting creditors, could slowly get out of debt and "the profit will all remain to him, and he will grow rich." Once solvent, such a person could borrow at the zero-risk rate of a loan secured by land. Cantillon did not forget to incorporate risk in the pricing of interest.

Cantillon was keenly aware of the practical aspect of interest. Besides profit, the security of a loan, meaning the integrity of the borrower, equally gave rise not only to interest, but also to its rate. Cantillon developed this point with the common example of land use. A farmer, who had to borrow either land or money, would willingly give up a third of the produce to the lender. The amount was generally equivalent to the farmer's net profit, which handily met the 20-30% rate asked by lenders to cover the risk of default. The farmer well modeled the fact that profit depended on the industry and the level of subsistence expenditures of the borrower. The frugal borrower was a good credit risk.

In another borrower example, Cantillon commented that "a Lender of money will prefer to lend a thousand ounces of silver to a Hatter at twenty per cent interest, rather than to lend a thousand ounces to a thousand water carriers at five hundred per cent interest. While the carriers stood to earn a "five thousand per cent" rate of return, since, "all the capital he will need will be the price of two buckets," they also were likely to "soon spend on their subsistence not only the money they earn by their daily work, but all that is lent to them."

Other Frenchmen in the 18th century pursued economic theorizing as basic and path-breaking as that achieved by the English. A school of economics emerged in France, with whose thinking Mirabeau and Cantillon were associated. Its tightly knit members called themselves *Les Economistes*, but were later known as Physiocrats on account of their doctrine's general physical premise, namely, that nature, as the sole source of productivity and therefore also of a natural law or order, underpinned the economic process. Francois Quesnay (1694-1774), the court physician of Louis XV, was its founder. His best known writing, *Tableau Economique*, first formulated in 1758 and explained in detail by Mirabeau, earned him the distinction of being the founder of macroeconomics. In his GNP-like presentation of the flow of goods and services in an economy, Quesnay also laid down a basis for the theory of capital.

Quesnay did not systematically draw out the idea of interest from capital. Interest on money was more of a given, needing neither justification nor explanation. He classified it as a sterile, as opposed to a productive, expenditure. In his table of the transactions originating from the production of large-scale agriculture and subsequently circulating among the various classes of society, Quesnay predicated production on three types of advances. The first, land advances, *avances foncieres*, was needed for initial, more or less fixed, expenditure to prepare the land and to build structures. The second, *avances primitives*, was used to secure equipment and livestock.

The third, *avances annuelles,* met current spending, such as on seed and labor. These advances were monetary. Quesnay had in mind wealth accumulated beforehand, standing ready at the starting point of the flow of transactions in his table. In the single instance that he used the word capital instead of advances, he wrote money capital, *capital d'argent*. Nonetheless, Quesnay knew that goods and services were what the landowner and the tenant farmer ultimately required, so he accorded accumulated value, *valeurs accumulees*, to advances.

Interest was paid for the advances. Quesnay thought that the natural rate of interest could not go higher than the rate of return from cultivating land, and he was amenable to the government fixing a maximum. Quesnay considered that it "should amount to at least 10 per 100. For the products of agriculture are exposed to ruinous accidents, which in ten years destroy the value of at least one year's crop. These advances demand, moreover, much up-keep and renewals . . ." Interest was derived from the annual returns of the cultivators, society's sole productive class. It served to maintain wealth, the result of rents accumulated by the proprietary class. Such wealth "requires to be replenished without end."

Quesnay knew the importance of capital formation and regarded the nature of interest more as an ever increasing revolving fund to constantly handle losses and depreciation than as revenue or income. He stipulated that production would increase as more advances were utilized. His subsequent scrutiny of the methods of agricultural production yielded an important circumstance raised by past analysts, namely, the idea of a time gap between the purchase of inputs and the sale of the final product. Advances coming from the landowners, the distributive class, were demanded precisely to bridge this period. That interest could be a payment for time could therefore also be attributed to Quesnay. Notably, Quesnay hardly used the term "profit" for the return from farming and the funding of interest.

Jacques Turgot (1727-81) was the most eminent Physiocrat after Quesnay. He was a baron and an unbelievably effective reformist Minister of Finance and Commerce under Louis XVI. He was the quintessential civil servant—schooled in scientific theory which he implemented in policies. Turgot's extensive insights on interest were to prevail well into the 19th century and serve as a springboard for theories in the 20th century.

Turgot rightly broadened the scope of Quesnay's advances, writing that "all kinds of work, whether in agriculture or in industry, require advances." The owners of these advances, called "capitals or accumulated moveable values, *valeurs mobiliaires*, expected back "not only all his advances, but also a profit sufficient to recompense him for what he could have earned on his money." And borrowers themselves "do not find it hard to resolve to give the owners of capitals or money . . . a share of the profits they expect to obtain in addition to recovering their advances." The total returns on the produce depended on its sale, and Turgot postulated that "it is always the needs and the means of the consumer that determine selling prices."

Turgot detailed this transactional nature of interest. It was akin to land management: "For we should make no mistake about it; lending at interest is simply a kind of trading, in which the Lender . . . sells the *use* of his money, and the Borrower . . . buys it, just as the Proprietor of an estate and his Farmer sell and buy respectively the use of leased property." Turgot, for whom capital was "moveable wealth," that is, transferable command over real resources, did not think that the creditor relinquished ownership of money. He defined interest not as the price of money, but as "the price given for the use of a certain quantity of value, *masse de valeurs*, during a certain time."

Aristotle 384-322 B.C. "Money was intended to be used in exchange, but not to increase at interest. Wherefore of all modes of making money this is the most unnatural."

Thomas Aquinas 1225-74. Interest is "in itself, unjust, since it is a sale of what does not exist; whereby inequality obviously results, which is contrary to justice."

Bernardino of Siena 1380-1444. The lender's preconceived gain contains "something of the seminal character of profitability, which we commonly call capital."

Leonard Lessius 1554-1623. Nothing is wrong in demanding interest; it is the objective price fixed on reasonable business grounds "for the loss of the power of present money."

William Petty 1623-87. "When a man giveth out his money upon condition that he may not demand it back until a certain time to come, he certainly may take a compensation."

David Hume 1711-76. "High interest arises from three circumstances: great demand for borrowing, little riches to supply that demand, and great profits arising from commerce."

Adam Smith 1723-90. "But as something can everywhere be made by the use of money, something ought everywhere to be paid for the use of it, a certain annual rent for stock lent."

Jacques Turgot 1727-81. Interest is not the price of money but of the use of a quantity of value during a certain time, equivalent to real objects, indispensable to all productive works.

David Ricardo 1772-1832. "Interest is not regulated by the Bank of England but by the rate of profit made by the employment of capital, independent of money quantity or value."

Karl Marx 1815-83. "Though it may be impossible to determine precisely the average profits of capital, some notion may be formed of them from the interest of money."

Carl Menger 1840-1921. "Interest is an economic phenomenon, the exchange of one good (capital use) for another (money); its legal or moral character is beyond our science."

Eugen von Bohm-Bawerk 1851-1914. A loan "is a real exchange of present goods against future goods; present goods possess a greater value than similar future goods."

Alfred Marshall 1842-1924. "Interest on capital is the reward of the sacrifice involved in the waiting for the enjoyment of material resources; few people would save without reward.

John Maynard Keynes 1883-1946. "Interest is not derived from net return from capital goods, but is reward for parting with liquidity," a percent excess of a sum for future delivery.

Irving Fisher 1867-1947. "The rate of interest is the common market rate of preference for present over future income" set by borrowers, spenders, lenders, savers, and investors.

Bertil Ohlin 1899-1979. The interest rate is not set by equal supply of and demand for savings; it is simply the price of credit, governed by the supply of and demand for credit.

Throughout his work, he recognized the real aspect of money, that money "is equivalent to real objects and . . . in this sense is indispensable to all productive works." In addition to nature's bounty, "personal wealth amassed in advance" was an "indispensable antecedent" to all production. Turgot repeatedly stressed that capital made production possible, not only in agriculture as Quesnay held, but also in industry and commerce as Cantillon indicated, and that capital sifted economic activity toward profitable lines. Turgot virtually admitted that capital was an independent factor of production in the same footing as land, since "the capitalist lender of money should be regarded as a dealer in a commodity absolutely necessary for the production of riches, and which cannot bear too low a price."

Turgot's pragmatic approach to interest was behind his opposition to French usury laws, Determining the interest rate rested on his premise that money "was a genuine commodity, Its price depended on agreement, and varied, like that of all other commodities, that is, according to the ratio between offer and demand. Interest being the price of loanable funds, it rises when there are more borrowers than lenders; it falls . . . when there is more money offered than is demanded for borrowing. It is in this way that the normal rate of interest is established, but this normal rate is not the only rule which is followed, nor should it be allowed to fix the rate of interest for individual transactions. The risks which the capital may run in the hands of the borrower, the needs of the latter, and the profit which he hopes to draw from the money . . . are the circumstances which, when combined in different ways, and with the normal rate of interest, will often carry the rate to a higher level than it is in the ordinary course of trade."

The only and important difference between credit and commodity transactions according to Turgot was the former's lack of immediacy. The lender exchanges an amount of money in the present for a promised sum in the future. Lending was analogical to a foreign exchange trade. It involved a time dimension, whereas the latter entailed a spatial dimension. Likewise, lending carried a change of values. It was proverbial that future money was worth less than present money. If the lender "receives less, why should this difference not be compensated by the assurance of an increase in the sum proportioned to the delay? This compensation is precisely the rate of interest." With these perceptions, Turgot was looking both backward to insights of as far back as the medieval centuries and ahead to those of the 20th century.

Turgot named three motives for borrowing. Demand for capital was fueled by spending for personal consumption, purchasing property, or undertaking an enterprise. With regard to the third motive, Turgot stated that each industry competed for the available credit without recourse to the interest rate. The quantity of money did not determine "interest on money to rise or fall, or which causes more money to be offered for lending; it is solely . . . accumulated savings that are offered to borrowers . . ." (Turgot actually suspected that more money, because it inflated commodity prices, could push up rates.) The quantity of savings was what mattered. When done by entrepreneurs, the saving immediately, *sur-le-champ*, became capital, and the quantity of capital set the rate of interest in an inverse correlation.

There was negligible savings leakage or, in Turgot's language, "hoarding." The price of money already contained an increment, not only because the effort to save funds was made, but also because the funds were advances required to bridge the time gap from start-up until the completion of production. This was in effect a substitution of future for present goods. The passage of time, required by new methods of production resulting from the division of labor, created a difference in the value of money. Turgot asked: "If these gentlemen suppose that a sum of 1000 francs and the promise of 1000 francs possess exactly the same value, they put forward a still more absurd supposition; for if these two things were of equal value, why should any one borrow at all?" Borrowers obviously realized the potential gain that money could bring.

The interest rate decided the utilization and the allocation of capital resources. Above a certain level, the price will cause "all work, all farming, all industry, all commerce to cease." At a rate of 5%, for example, agriculture will stop if its produce does not bring in 5% above "the replacement of advances and the compensation of the toil of the cultivator," and "all manufacture and commerce that do not yield 5% above the reward of the pains and risks of the entrepreneur will not exist." Turgot regarded the interest rate "as a kind of level below which all labor, all cultivation, all industry, all commerce cease. It is like a sea spread over a vast territory."

Turgot continued his water metaphor. He held that "different employments of capital . . . yield very unequal returns: but this inequality does not prevent them from exercising a mutual influence . . . and from establishing a kind of equilibrium among themselves . . ." It was evident that "the yearly returns that could be derived from capital placed in various endeavors were influenced by each other, and all were related to the rate of interest." The rate was the "thermometer of the abundance or scarcity of capitals in a Nation, and of the extent of the enterprises of all kinds in which it may engage." The ability of capital owners to shift among investment opportunities would eventually cause interest rates to cluster.

Turgot in 1776 brought up another argument less to justify than to establish more fully the natural existence of interest. It centered on the customary link to land, the original natural source of productivity and income. Land commanded rent. The use of movable goods generated rent as well. The values of land and goods could therefore be compared, and one priced in terms of the other. Capital could always secure permanent income from its use to buy land. The capitalist could expect the employment of his money in other types of enterprise to yield gain at least equal to land rent. "Those who had much movable wealth could employ it not only in the cultivation of land, but also in the different departments of industry. The facility of accumulating this movable wealth, and of making a use of it quite independent of land, had the effect that one could value the pieces of land, and compare their value with that of movable wealth."

The purchase price of land, determined at a particular point of time by demand and supply, was a multiple of the annual rent as calculated by Petty. This rental should correspond to a certain percentage of capital that the borrower must be willing to pay, if he wants to prevent the capitalist from buying land instead. Turgot did write that the opposite was true too, that the price of land could be reckoned on the basis of the rate of interest: "It is evident that the lower the interest of money is, the greater is the value of landed estates."

The morality of interest was an issue still current enough to invite Turgot's attention. He wrestled with Aristotle's barrenness of money, and his response was ruled by his notions of capital and value. Interest was justified, because money was property. The owner could dispose of it in any way. He had the "inviolable" right to set lending terms. Turgot did not think that money was consumed when used by the borrower. He believed that one "can separate . . . the use of a thing from the thing itself." Opposition to this view was incomprehensible: "What! That some one should be able to make me pay for the petty use that I make of a piece of furniture or a trinket, and that it should be a crime to charge me anything for the immense advantage that I get from the use of a sum of money for the same time . . . . It is really too ridiculous."

Turgot's explanation of interest was manifold. Reducing it to definitions would evoke ideas seen before. For the lender, interest was payment for the sale of the use of money, for the use of the value behind money, recompense for earnings given up, reward for the effort of saving, and coverage for elapsing time. But underpinning these definitions was a substantially original handling of capital, saving, and investment. Like Smith, his exact contemporary with whose stature he has been compared, Turgot aimed to emphasize the fruitfulness of capital, whose price was set by demand and supply as in the commodity market.

In Turgot's doctrine, profit was implicit. It was realized a priori in the final prices set for produce and funded interest. The essential fertility of capital was proven in its ability to be used alternatively to purchase land. As the landowner could derive a permanent rental from the land without any labor, so was it natural that a lender could seek interest. Turgot made a strong case for this comparison, so that he was credited with introducing a fructification theory of interest a century later. Unfortunately, textbook summaries of the theory have diluted or ignored his more original and acute detailing of capital and interest rates.

Jean Baptiste Say (1767-1832), businessman, professor of political economy, and expounder of Smith, advanced the theory of interest in 1803 by reemphasizing the productive power of capital. He elevated this *pouvoir productif* to the level of another plausible, if not leading, theory of interest. He gained a wide following. After isolating interest from money supply conditions and from the risk premium, Say declared with Turgot that the capitalist advanced a certain sum of value necessary for production. All goods arose from the combined services of nature, labor, and capital. The service of capital could be understood as a form of labor. Capital labored when it "is employed in productive operations."

Say stressed the collaboration of capital and labor. Capital "must, so to speak, work along with human activity, and it is this cooperation that I call the productive service of capital." The value of the goods produced was then parceled out to the three factors of production ("funds" according to Say) and became revenue for their respective owners. Capital worked just as labor did, so that interest, *profit du capital*, was a mirror image of wages. Say made the crucial point that such independent work was over and above the dispensation of the substance (depreciation) of the capital itself. Net profit was necessary.

In detailing how this income of capital came about, Say resorted to both production and marketing processes. First, he remarked that capital had the power to directly create the income value. "The capital employed," he wrote, "pays the services rendered, and the services rendered produce the value which replaces the capital employed." The produced value still meant gross return.

Say next pointed out the necessity for the entrepreneur, typically the borrower, to pay along market lines, since the services of capital created value. The price of capital was conditioned by the product's price. At the same time, the price of the products had to accommodate whatever estimation was deemed right for the remuneration of the productive services. In this sense, Say considered all profit (interest included) as a production cost that had to be paid, for which he brought in the decisive role of the product's buyer: "The more lively the need that the consumers feel for the enjoyment of the product, the more abundant the means of payment they possess; and the higher the compensation that the sellers are able to demand for the productive services, the higher will go the price."

Say thus addressed a critical problem neglected by the English classical economists. He required value exceeding the replacement of capital, that is, net return that included provision for interest. Say, unlike Smith, differentiated between the capitalist and the entrepreneur. He assigned, for example, part of the profit to compensate management labor. Lastly, his Law of Markets, in line with Turgot's view on the determination of interest rates, envisioned the rate of interest declining "the more disposable capitals are abundant" relative to investment opportunities.

About half a dozen other French economists before and after Say discussed interest in their works. Their views revolved around the theories of the major authors, taking the form mostly of restatements, additions, or eclectic combinations. Germain Garnier (1754-1821) was typical. A translator of Smith's book in 1802 and Minister of State under Louis XVIII, he repeated in 1796 Quesnay's identification of advances with capital. He understood profit as the compensation for these advances and mentioned it as "indemnification for a privation and a risk."

Nicolas Francois Canard (d1833), a mathematician, designated interest as rent, *rente mobiliere*, for capital. There were three kinds of rent: rent for land, rent for (the acquisition of) skilled labor, and rent for the products resulting from the previous two rents. Part of these products (capital goods) was invested in commerce: "Commerce . . . like the other two sources of rent presupposes an accumulation of superfluous labour which must, in consequence, bear a rent." Superfluous labor was labor not needed for necessities. It represented profit. Capital therefore was accumulated labor, but Canard did not specify if the rent was for physical capital itself or its service, for the labor embodied in capital, or for the accumulation of capital.

Francois Xavier Droz (1773-1850), a moralist writer, disagreed in 1829 that labor alone was the productive power. Siding with Say, he maintained, that capital was also a primary power. He offered the option of replacing the idea of capital with saving. But Droz did not pursue this topic. He lost the opportunity to contribute to the development of the saving function which was importantly emerging in his time in the theory of interest.

Frederic Bastiat (1801-50) adhered to Senior's abstinence theory. He reinforced the argument. He raised abstinence, *ajournement*, which he sometimes named "delay" and "privation," to being a service, something positive: "Postponement in itself is a special service, since on him who postpones, it imposes a sacrifice, and on him who desires, it confers an advantage." Bastiat continued: "In order to decide to accumulate a capital you must provide for the future and sacrifice the present for it." Furthermore, the efforts to accumulate capital were a service that was not discrete, but spanned time. "To save," Bastiat noted "is deliberately to put an interval between the moment when the services are made for society, and that when the equivalent is received from it."

The service of saving was an exchangeable good. Moreover, it was scarce. Its price was interest. Bastiat based the value of goods on "exchanged services," so that service, this "onerous circumstance," deserved payment, especially in the case of capital which changed hands. The service of the lender was estimated by the postponed value times the length of time of the postponement. From the start, Bastiat was aware that the problem of interest was not to be solved simply by physical and psychological explanations. It had to be tackled to the point of vindicating it, to present it as "natural, just, legitimate, and as useful to him who pays as to him who receives it."

Jean Courcelle-Seneuil (1813-92) tried to improve on Bastiat. In 1858, he propounded the concept of the labor of saving, contrasting it with physical labor. Following Turgot, he included a note of time preference in this saving effort. It consisted of a continuous effort of intelligent foresight assessing present and future needs and of determined willingness that "refrains from enjoyment for a given period of time." This was labor, because it was a painful exertion and "unnatural" to desist from enjoying a present good and instead to work with brawn and brain to secure another article.

Courcelle considered that saving is really industrial labor in another form and therefore a productive force. The labor of saving, like the "labor of the muscles" demanded recompense. Interest of a permanent kind must be paid, because capital conservation and formation necessitated a lasting interest to abstain in light of the equally permanent desire to consume. This perpetual struggle of opposing tendencies was "a necessary condition of industrial life." The amount of interest was determined not so much by the market demand and supply of capital as by the forces behind them, such as the state of business opportunities. Courcelle found support in Josef Garnier (1813-81). A teacher and school administrator, Garnier wrote in 1880 that interest remunerated "the labour of saving."

In 1881, Paul Louis Cauwes (1843-1917), a jurist-economist, also restated Courcelle. He affirmed that "since the conservation of a capital presupposes an exertion of the will, and in many cases even industrial or financial combinations of some difficulty, one might say that it represents a veritable labour . . ." To prove this assertion, Cauwes emphasized the protracted effort required: "In the loan, it may be, there is no labour; but the labor consists in the steadfast will to preserve the capital, and in the protracted abstinence from every act of gratification or consumption of the value represented by it . . ."

Cauwes even went beyond the concept of labor. He made several statements that ascribed to capital its own "active role" in production. From this he drew the "principle . . . that the rate of interest is a direct consequence of the productivity of capital" and that, in addition, "since a certain surplus value is due to capital, interest is one part of that surplus value presumably fixed by contract, which the lender receives for the service rendered by him," regardless of gain or loss on the part of the borrower. Cauwes not only recognized the rigid claim of interest. He also required the existence of a surplus value, although aware that such a surplus may not be directly realized by the borrower in personal consumption loans.

Gustave de Molinari (1819-1912), a homoeopathic physician who wrote on economic subjects from 1846 to 1880, accepted abstinence, in an 1863 book, as reason for interest. He called it "privation" of the satisfaction of urgent needs. He also iterated Say and Cauwes, declaring that "interest is a compensation for the productive service of capital."

Another French economist, who adopted both abstinence and productivity theories and attempted to integrate them, was Pellegrino Rossi (1787-1848), professor, French ambassador to Rome, and papal prime minister. Rossi used the abstinence theory as a general framework that was detailed in productivity terms. In 1865, he wrote that capital ought to be paid "on the same grounds and by the same title as labour." He reasoned that "the capitalist demands the compensation due to the privation which he imposes on himself." The privation was seen as "capitalized saving."

Thence Rossi progressed to the direct productivity approach as he analyzed profit: "Profit is the compensation due to productive power." The rate of profit depended on the degree of productivity, as when efficiency was enhanced by machines. Any displacement of labor meant higher capitalist profit. Additional profit may be realized if the capitalist negotiated lower wages with the remaining labor, but such profit would not be part of the "natural" profit of capital.

Pierre Paul Leroy-Beaulieu (1843-1916), was a member of the Chamber of Deputies, who was appointed in 1879 to a chair in the College de France once held by Say. Author of many economic papers, Leroy-Beaulieu did not even grant Rossi's distinction of "natural" profit. "Capital begets capital; that is beyond question," he stated sweepingly around 1885 and "it is so naturally and materially; in this case laws have only copied nature."

Jacob de Haas, a Dutch economist, introduced a relatively new third dimension to the explanation of the market rates of interest. It would be minutely taken up in the 20th century. The previous dimensions were payment for the principal borrowed (rooted in abstinence or in the hire of capital) and for the risk of default. These two comprised the real rate of interest. The third element added by Haas was the expected rate of change of the value of money. Since the value of money was its purchasing power, this meant price changes, usually understood as upward. The three dimensions combined to form the nominal rate of interest. Thus, Haas saw that nominal rates would trend higher during bouts of inflation and lower during deflationary times. In addition, because of inflation fears, lenders tended to constrict loan supply, while borrowers strove to secure the cheaper credit in real terms.

Summary of the French classical economists. For the French economists, as for the English, assigning interest as the income of capital hardly presented a problem, even if they periodically called that income rent. The French too had graduated from understanding the use of money as its consumption-disappearance to its transformation into goods used in producing more goods and creating value. Money bore fruit, and it was manifestly unjust if the lender was not paid interest.

The more unexplained issue that the French thinkers began to note was, granted that capital had physical productivity, how that productivity directly resulted in profit and how this profit value was to be dissected. It was somewhat naïve to merely state that capital per se had physical productivity. At best, the claim appeared vague. Services undoubtedly had value. But the services of capital seemed to refer to either the operations performed by capital goods or the payment for all services, that is, including those of labor and land. More precision was needed.

The determination of the interest rate was handled more convincingly. The influence of the quantity of money was all but disregarded. Instead, the workings of demand and supply were highlighted. The dominance of the resulting natural "equilibrium" rate was frequently advocated. Rates gravitated to it.

Money was increasingly regarded as funds for lending, while the real goods substratum of capital as the object of credit transactions was emphasized. The important role of saving as related to investment was beginning to attract closer attention. Allusions to land economics and rent still proliferated, but they were employed more to press the right of capital to earn interest than to describe its nature, although the application of rent to fixed durable goods appeared to be sound analogy.

The majority of the French economists agreed that interest was located in the realm of profit. Only one questioned whether this profit was due to capital or to entrepreneurship. But how capital could achieve a return independent of labor still begged definitive proof. Labor's contribution, if not its exclusivity, was strongly and widely advocated.

Nonetheless, momentum was growing for the conclusion that capital could generate not only profit sufficient for its own replacement, which required little economic clarification, since this was in effect repayment of the principal, but also an excess return that included interest. This interest was ascribed to abstinence or risk or time, or to their combination. So far, this net surplus was sourced in product pricing and effective consumer demand, despite the unequivocal declaration of the productive power of capital. The relationship of the surplus to capital itself awaited deeper investigation in the rest of Western Europe, resulting in a few more additions to the list of interest theories.

Chapter 8

BEYOND THE ALPS
AND THE RHINE

The Italians who wrote on interest in the 17th to the early 19th centuries were evocative of scholastic language. Conceptually, however, they largely followed the permissive thinking of Salmasius. The earliest author of note after Salmasius was Scipio Maffei (1675-1755), a count from Verona and a friend of Benedict XIV. Perhaps on account of his position in society and despite his not being a theologian, Maffei boldly published a defense of interest.

Selectivity guided Maffei when interpreting the prohibitions of Scripture and the pronouncements of the Church. He realized that, with the exception of excessive rates, interest was already legally permitted in various credit forms and under external titles that were virtually applicable to all lending. Maffei rejected the natural-law argument of early scholasticism that ownership was transferred in a loan. The lender maintained ownership, because he could still bequeath or donate the value of the loan. He alienated only its physical amount. In addition, ownership could not be passed off absolutely without the lender's consent, which was never given. The free use of money is not tantamount to undisputed ownership.

Maffei also countered the consumptibility argument: "Money does not consume itself in use; on the contrary it multiplies." Money should not be taken as a consumptible or non-consumptible before its actual use. There were indeed cases when "the money is gone," as when lending is for charitable purposes. In other transactions, where less pressing personal needs were met, something of value was left. "Nothing in the world is more fecund," Maffei observed, than money in a business context. Commercial activity needed credit with interest, which the state widely allowed. The loss of profit opportunity legitimized interest. He drew a distinction between consumption and production—a matter overlooked by the classical economists bent on real analysis. A Calvinistic viewpoint was overriding for Maffei. Charity drew the line. He reprehended interest in loans to the poor and those in distress. Like Petty, he did not like interest paid for short-term credit, even in lending of small amounts.

Ferdinando Galiani (1728-87), a Neapolitan abbot, whose writing mainly on the subject of money was a precursor of several key economic ideas, acknowledged Salmasius as the father of the consenting attitude toward usury. Galiani's justification for interest, though, was different. It was strongly based on the temporal values of money. He objected to interest construed as any profit from barren money or from the exertion of another (the borrower). Interest, he proposed, was not profit at all. Its nature merely served to achieve equality in exchange, not in nominal terms, but in terms of value. Equality rested on aligning the near and distant values of money.

In his *Della Moneta* of 1750, Galiani set out the following: "A relation can be established between the certain present and the uncertain future . . . [and] the real value of a good varies with the degree of probability . . . of its use: 100 ducats, obtainable with difficulty in the future, are equal to in value to 90 present ducats. This is their valuation . . . if there is a probability of 90 degrees that they will not be lost, and of 10 degrees that they will be lost. From this arise the rate of exchange and the rate of interest—brother and sister. The former equalizes the present and the spatially distant money . . . with the help of an apparent agio added sometimes to the present, and at other times to the distant money . . . one being reduced because of lesser convenience or greater risk. Interest equalizes present and future money. Here the effect of time is the same as that of spatial distance . . . . The basis of either contract is the equality of the real value . . . . Where there is equality, there is no gain; where the real price is lessened by risk and inconvenience, the offset is no gain."

Galiani's rationale for the varied values of similar amounts of money at different times and places was utility. Utility constituted value. Value "was the relationship of goods to our needs. Goods are equivalent when they provide equal convenience to the person with reference to whom they are considered as equivalent." There was convenience for the borrower and the lender receiving money at hand and later, respectively. In the same way, there was inconvenience for the borrower paying interest at a future date and for the lender parting with available cash. "A loan," defined Galiani, was "the surrender of a good, with the proviso that an equivalent good is to be returned, not more." Persons who would imagine this equality to be objective (nominal) identity, for instance, same weight, "understand little of human activities."

As for risk, which was the other cause of inequality in loans, its premium could vary "because the degree of probability of loss shows extreme variations. This sometimes is very high . . . at other times it is as low as zero . . . and at still other times it is less than zero." Interest also served as compensation for the apprehension caused by the prospect of loss. Galiani phrased this positive risk vividly: "If somebody suffers all the time from palpitations of the heart, this is painful; it is only proper to pay for it. What is known as reward for pain is . . . nothing but the price for palpitations of the heart." The addition of the notion of insecurity likely weakened the time-based cogency of Galiani's theory of interest. By appending the external premium of insurance, it needlessly suggested an insufficiency in the argument that interest created intrinsic equality in loans.

Cesare Bonesana (1738-94), the Marchese di Beccaria, was a Milanese civil administrator, who has been esteemed as the Italian Adam Smith. He commented on the interpretation of the term "use." He distinguished interest, *interesse*, from usury, *usuria*. The first referred to the immediate use of a thing, while the second to the use of a use *l'utilita dell' utilita*, that is, to the use of the goods that money could buy. The latter definition, which recalled Barbon, was thought logical, since money was a measure of the value of goods. Reflecting more past thinking, Bonesana added that as money may embody a plot of land, the rate of usury could be represented by the return on land. Finally, he favored Galiani's comparison of the interest of place in exchange with the interest of time in loans.

The Italian Antonio Scialoja (1817-77), touched on interest in a book he wrote in 1840. He returned to the notion of the productivity of capital without offering much that was new. He declared that the factors of production imparted to and shared with their products their own "virtual" or "potential" value, which was their capacity to produce. Each factor received the value it transferred. Natural interest was the portion of total profit due the capital factor for its active presence during the production period.

Other Italian thinkers espoused capital's productivity at this time. But their contributions were of minor significance. They were more declaratory than explanatory of the objective presence of productivity. William Cesar, the Cardinal of Lucerne, wrote in 1822 that the commercial loan was not a *mutuum*. Business credit did not convey a consumptible, but a "value that will increase by the use one makes of it." In the same vein, Luigi Cossa (1831-1896), a professor at the University of Pavia, restated in 1883 two, by then familiar, aspects of interest, namely, "compensation for the non-use of capital or, as some say, for its formation, and payment for capital's productive service." However, he denied this service as a primary factor of production. Instead, he considered it as a secondary or derivative tool. He may have had the priority of labor in mind.

Marco Mastrofini (1763-1845), a member of the papal court, published a "discussion" on usury in 1828 that was praised by the Vatican. He introduced the term "applicability," which meant the ability to use money and the use itself. Both together harbored a fecund power that was transferred to the goods bought by the proceeds from a loan. The existence of this separate power remained whether the money or goods were used for any purpose or not. Interest had to be paid regardless. However, the presumption of intended use for profit was clear. Regarding the interest rate, Mastrofini was less up-to-date. He thought that the price of money fluctuated with the quantity of money available.

In Germany, the post-Salmasius literature on interest arrived slightly later than in England and France, but its influence grew quickly. In general, the Germans looked favorably on Say's productivity approach, but they frequently tended to still reserve a substantial role to labor in producing value. In 1805, Count Friedrich Soden (1754-1831), writing like a scholastic philosopher, described capital as merely material on which productive power operated. The owner of this material capital initiates its combination with the productive power of others (wage workers) to generate profit. His initiative entitled him a share of the profit with the workers. This was achieved through the negotiation of low wages made possible by the great number of workers compared with the capitalists. While wanting "full value" for wages, Soden counseled against mandated wage hikes lest a point was reached when the capitalist "comes to find that he gets no profit from the power of others" and "will leave dead" all material.

Likewise, Johan Friedrich Lotz (1770-1838) did not acknowledge an independent productive power for capital. "In themselves all capitals are dead," he wrote in 1821. Capital was but a tool for human labor. The capitalist "from the return to labour, and from the . . . goods gained or produced by it, has no claim to anything more than the . . . expense which the furnishing of the capital has caused him; or more plainly, the amount of the labourer's subsistence, the amount of the raw material given out to him, and the amount of the tools . . . that are worn out by the worker during his work. This . . . would be distinctively the rent . . . which the capitalist may claim from the labourer who works for him." Lotz concluded that "there is no place for what is usually called profit, namely, a wage obtained by the capitalist for advancing his capital such as guarantees a surplus over the expenses. Any surplus arising belonged to the worker . . . or to humanity as a whole." Again, business return was gross profit. Net profit for rental-interest was starkly denied.

Lotz's "manifesto" would have heralded another principal theory of interest, namely the exploitation theory, but Lotz retreated back to the common sense of Smith and condescended to discuss net profit. If the capitalist was restricted by labor payments, "he would scarcely decide to advance anything from his stock on behalf of the worker and his work." As a result, the "appropriate extent" of the rent of capital "must be estimated proportionate to the support provided the worker through the use of the capital." Surprisingly, under certain conditions, Lotz would grant nine-tenths of the profit to the capitalist. Still, consistent with his fixation on gross margin, he explained interest as "an arbitrary addition to the necessary costs of production" and as a "tax which the selfishness of the capitalist forces from the consumer." Consequently, net profit, if realized, was partly generated by the purchaser of the final products.

H.F. von Storch (1766-1835), a German with a career spent in Russia, followed Smith's and Say's fundamental idea about the factors of production. Capital, he wrote in 1823, was a source of production, albeit secondary compared with labor and nature. These three factors generated income, because, belonging to different persons, they must be put out on contract, obliging remuneration to one who would bring them together in production.

The natural rate of interest was set more in a monopolistic or oligopolistic manner than competitively. Storch used the theoretical example of a farmer owning and employing all three sources of production. The sale income from his produce should afford him a minimum value equal to the income he would receive if he lent his productive sources. As a creditor, the farmer's rate of income would be bound by the rate set in the market by capitalists and borrowers. As the capitalists were typically rich (and influential) and the latter poor, the market always tended toward higher rates of interest. In reality, however, this higher, market income level was hardly attained by the farmer creditor, since he was the mirror image of the poor borrower. The poor, as the medievalists said, had no choice but to pay a rent for the capital or forego the credit. The poor accepted whatever interest rate was negotiable.

In 1829, Karl Friedrich Nebenius (1784-1857), a follower of Say and a statesman who wrote a treatise on public credit in 1820, was another economist who admitted the productive service of capital, which gave rise to interest. "On the one hand," Nebenius began, "the necessity and usefulness of capital for the business of production in its most multifarious forms, and on the other, the hardship of the privations to which we owe its accumulation; these lie at the root of the exchange value of the services rendered by capital. They get their compensation in a share of the value of the products, to the production of which they have cooperated." Otherwise, people would not bother to accumulate capital. Nebenius placed the objective genesis of value in capital itself, writing that the interest paid to "hire" capital was the fruit of the capital itself, and the amount of the hire was calculated chiefly on the capital's productivity.

Still focused on the idea of productivity, in 1835 an economist surnamed Schon categorized capital as a third source of wealth, although an indirect one. He took rent for capital as proven, since "the produce belongs originally to those who co-operated toward its making," and "it is clear that the national produce must set aside as many distinct rents as there are categories of productive powers and instruments." In procuring the rent for capital, however, he thought this resulted from the restriction of the wages of labor.

Another German economist, surnamed Riedel, was more emphatic than Schon in claiming a unique productive role to capital. He asserted that "it is always incorrect to ascribe the product of capital to the working forces of nature or labour which the capital needs in order that it may be employed. Capital is an independent force, as nature and labour are, and in most cases does not need them more than they need it." He held that the creation of value by capital was evident and could be presumed.

Riedel's analysis, moreover, surpassed those of his immediate contemporaries in Germany. He was cognizant of the shortcoming of gross profit explanations. Riedel required that the resulting value of capital also contain a surplus value besides replacement. Around 1835-38, he wrote: "The productivity which capital when employed universally possesses is manifest on observation of the fact that material values which have been employed, with a view to production, in aiding nature and labour are, as a rule, not only replaced, but assist toward a surplus of material values, which surplus could not be brought into existence without them." Net return was, probably for the first time, explicitly added to gross return. Interest could unquestionably lay claim to part or all of it.

The stricter mathematical calculation of interest next came up for German analysis. Johann Heinrich von Thunen (1783-1850), an agricultural economist who first used the calculus for economics, reintroduced Ricardo's marginal analysis. Ricardo had written that the marginal product, for which rent was paid, was the amount of output lost if a unit of labor or any other factor of production was removed.

Working from this definition, Thunen traced the genesis of interest to the incremental production a worker can achieve by borrowing tools created by another's labor. The added marginal produce was used to pay the rent of capital.

Thunen went on to a second important economic point. He postulated diminishing returns for capital use and consequently declining interest rates. The interest payable was scaled down marginally, that is, by "the use of that portion of capital which is last applied." The sinking efficiency of the final unit of capital resulted in increasing wages. In addition, Thunen thought that the interest rate also paralleled the opportunity cost of money, which was another marginal concept.

The physical productivity of capital was therefore both the origin of interest and the determinant of its rate. Thunen assumed the rent to be gross, covering replenishment of the capital to keep it "in equally good condition" and "equal in value." To this was added a surplus product that was mentioned by Reidel. Why this surplus value was always realized, Thunen left only faintly answered. He often admitted that capital attained its peak rent at a certain level and that producers would (or could) not go beyond this point. This injected some ambiguity to the constant attainment of surplus value, although the action of individual capitalists can hardly coincide to prevent a trend toward zero interest. This vagueness was surprising in an author noted for thoroughness and who had the ability to discern and employ marginal analysis.

In 1832, F.B.W. von Hermann (1795-1868), politician, civil servant, and teacher, published the best treatment of what became known as the use theory of interest. Gleaned from Say's thoughts, the theory claimed two types of usefulness for goods—transitory, such as in cooked food, and durable, such as in tools. The use of these durable goods for as long as they lasted, *Nutzung*, could be taken as a good in itself that could secure an accumulated exchange value, which was precisely interest. Pig iron, for instance, "possesses the exchange value of the three exchange goods employed [ore, coal, and labor], the earlier sum of goods persists, bound up qualitatively in the new usefulness, added together quantitatively in the exchange value."

Transitory goods could also be imbued with durable usefulness through "technical processes" that change "their form qualitatively, while retaining their exchange value." These "lasting or durable goods and perishable goods which retain their value while changing their shape may thus be brought under one and the same conception; they are the durable basis of a use which has exchange value. Such goods we call capital."

Hermann's durability sometimes seemed to mean indestructibility, so that capital was equated with land. The use of this capital or "disposition over quantities of capital-goods during certain spaces of time" (a definition similar to Turgot's), had exchange value, because the use represented a conglomeration of previously distinct economic goods with their own exchangeability. The use formed part of the cost of production. Accordingly, the product price must cover expenses plus remuneration for capital use (interest) and for entrepreneurship.

Capital use was distinct, yet related to capital outlays; both were "sacrificed" or consumed in production. Use embodied a sum of value piled up and held together by technical and commercial processes independent of the substance of capital, so that it was an enhanced finished product that was handed over to the consumer. Hermann inferred that "the uses of capital are therefore a ground of the determination of [product] prices." Price determination was "itself the first to react on the price of the labours and uses." In sum, the additional value embodied in use and realized in price margins explained interest. Moreover, Hermann attributed scarcity to certain uses of capital, thus enhancing the value or price of use in accordance with demand and supply.

Hermann, like many of his contemporary colleagues, did not neglect to bring in labor to his analysis. The underlying principle of his use doctrine distilled all products ultimately to the total of two basic elements: the uses of capital and expended labor. He therefore carefully established the ratio between the contributions of these two factors in terms of their mutual exchange values in calculating the rate of profit. If the supply of labor was held constant and the supply of uses was increased either quantitatively or qualitatively, the exchange value of uses against that of labor would fall and profit relative to total capital would decline. Labor would improve its share in the quantitative gain in production. On the other hand, if the availability or the quality of labor was increased, capital use would gain a premium.

Like the classical economists, Herman tended to identify the rate of interest with the rate of profit. If these rates, however, were considered distinct, then another calculation of proportionalities would have to be suggested. The exchange value of the uses would be compared with the exchange value of the capital goods that provided the uses. If the former value was twenty money units, while the latter was two-hundred units, then the rate of interest would be 10%.

All in all, Hermann clearly disagreed with the pure productivity theory that placed value in capital itself and not in its use. He thought it illusionary "that in the dead mass of capital or land there dwells forces of acquisition." Consequently, for the use of capital, "this hire, this interest, has . . . the nature of land-rent, that like it, it comes to the receiver from the fruit of other people's labour." Hermann never quite forgot labor in his tight reasoning. Use, after all, implied the application of labor.

Writing in 1855 during Hermann's lifetime, Karl August Dietzel (1829-84) briefly tackled the basis of interest. He too invoked capital use, but he combined it with abstinence: "The lender of capital bases his claim on compensation for the using of the capital transferred by him, first, on the fact that he has given up the chance of giving value to his own labour power by embodying it in the object; and second, that he has refrained from consuming it, or its value, at once, in immediate enjoyment. This is the ground on which interest on capital rests . . ."

Initially, Karl Knies (1821-98), a renowned teacher at Heidelberg, was not an advocate of the use theory. In 1859, he likened credit transactions to barter or purchases, in which there was an equal exchange of a thing given in the present and in the future. Knies made little effort to probe the existence of interest. Interest was just an original unspecified part of any loan contract. He changed his uncommitted mind later. He acknowledged that a loan essentially involved a transfer of use. But he hedged on the different values of present and future goods. The difference did not fully explain interest.

Knies further modified the use theory. He sharpened Hermann's designation of use. Use, which "lasts over a period of time and is measured by moments of time," was distinct from the good itself, which was the "bearer of the use." To prove why this use, which was apart from the good, deserved an exchange value, Knies resorted to invoking utility: "The emergence . . . of a price for use, in the shape of interest, is founded on the same relation as that on which the price of material goods is founded." The use, being an object "economically valuable and . . . economically valued," satisfied human needs. Use became simultaneously abstract and concrete.

In 1873, Albert Schaffle (1831-1903), an Austrian cabinet minister, widened Hermann's conception of the use of capital by connecting it to profit. However, in the process he lapsed into some ambiguity with the usual admixture of labor's participation. In his first book, he wrote that profit arose from use. "Profit," he identified, "is to be looked upon as the remuneration that the undertaker may claim . . . inasmuch as . . . he binds together the productive powers economically by means of the speculative use of capital." Loan interest was payment for, or a return from, that use or "functional performance." The rate was set by the supply and demand for the use. Use was one element of cost.

Schaffle differed from Hermann's abstract presentation of use in that he stated the presence of something material and objective in capital, which always had an economic value and "fruitfulness." He defined goods as "stores of useful energies." He called uses as "functions of goods" and as the "releasing of the utility, *Nutzen*, from material goods."

Not wanting to omit labor in his thinking, Schaffle went on to describe goods in complex and difficult expressions as "equivalents of useful materials in living labor" and as "living energies of impersonal social substance." This labor terminology worked its way to Schaffle's later definitions of the use of capital. It was a "working" and "using" of a subject by wealth, a "devoting an employment" of wealth, and a "service" of the entrepreneur.

Eventually, Schaffle, a sympathizer of nascent socialism, attributed all the costs of production to labor. He wrote: "The expenditure of capital . . . can be traced back to labour costs, for the productive expenditure of real goods may be reduced to a sum of labours expended at earlier periods . . ." But he balked at drawing the conclusion of restricting profit uniquely to labor, mindful of existing social structures and perhaps of the impracticality of building new ones. He accepted interest for capital, at least for the time being: "Historically then even capitalism may be fully warranted and profit justified. To remove the latter without having found a better organization of production would be senseless."

Karl Marlo (1810-65), a middle-of-the-road socialist, detailed the capitalist process and ended solidly supporting the right to interest. He saw two sources of wealth, namely, natural power and labor power. Capital was conceived as "perfected natural power," which earned its owners income like labor does. That income was due to a mixture of productivity and use: "If we apply forms of wealth as instruments of work, they contribute to production, and so render us a service. If we apply them to purposes of consumption, we not only consume the wealth itself, but also the service which it might have rendered if productively employed. If we employ wealth belonging to other people, we must compensate the owners for the productive service which it might have rendered. The compensation for this is variously called interest or rent. If we employ our own goods, we ourselves draw the interest which they bear."

Around 1873, Wilhem Roscher (1817-94), a professor at Gottingen and Leipzig, adopted the traditional definition of interest as a first step in his analysis. He defined contractual interest as the price of the use of capital. The amount and rate of interest depended on the number of demanders and suppliers of credit. The rate of contract interest determined the rate of natural interest. But Roscher noted a commonsense market expectation. A low rate of interest was improbable, because it could be prevented by "every extension of the limits of productive land" and by "the numberless persons who would rather consume their capital, or invest it in hazardous speculations than put it out at interest at 1 per cent a year."

Thinking it to be "undoubted," he proceeded to anchor the "legitimateness of interest on two unquestionable grounds: first, on the real productiveness of capital and, second, on the real sacrifice which resides in abstinence from the enjoyment of it by one's self." Either one or both could create exchange and use values. He proved productivity by citing wine that ages. He exemplified abstinence with a fisherman increasing his catch by first taking time to make a net while living off his previous catches. Roscher identified the time spent on fabricating the net as abstinence, although labor was also evidently involved. He therefore took care to remedy this theoretical inadequacy by writing that "the use value of capital to be in most cases synonymous with the skill of the labourer and the richness of the natural powers which are connected with it."

Summary of the Italian and German economists. The first ideas of the Italian economists, who were very cognizant of scholastic interest doctrine, rebutted the long-held inequality view of lending with interest. Interest, they claimed, was not unfair. It actually equalized loan and payment amounts. This was true, because near and distant monies, understood in spatiotemporal terms, had different exchange values. Geographically, distant money had less value, because it could be lost in the future or involve difficulty in being recovered. Present money was worth more than money anticipated in the future. Interest was the value of non-availability of money, risk, and inconvenience. These extrinsic considerations reduced the utility (value) of money to its owner. They provided additional reasons for interest.

As for the productivity of capital, it was acknowledged in a primitive manner. The favored stipulation still was that the use of money referred to the use of the goods purchased. Lent money was not necessarily consumed. That depended on the purpose of its use. Business capital lasted, since it was a factor of production. It transferred the value of its capacity, potential, or active service to its products. Interest was a natural portion of the profit garnered from the finished products, and/or it was payment for the non-use (abstention) of the value of capital. As for the rate of interest, it was thought to be equal to the rent of land or, less proposed, determined by the quantity of circulating money.

The majority in the lineup of German economists chose to mainly discuss the physical productivity of capital as the source of interest, but often with the strong acknowledgment of labor's cooperation. Capital was a factor of production. Thus, the capitalist earned interest for his initiative to offer his "material" to be worked on by labor. This statement meant that the capitalist did not deserve a share in net profit, but only a rental (cost) out of gross return or, as was claimed, out of wages. The rental, however, had to be sizable enough to induce advances of capital.

The view was also presented that the rental amount was due to the incremental output realized by additional capital, subject to diminishing returns. Thus, the rental originated from and was determined by the physical production achieved by capital. The rental or hire was also significantly seen as part of net return, since the emergence of a net return after the production process was always observable. In this case, the rental was not paid for the services of capital, but was the fruit of the capital itself. Its magnitude additionally depended on the market value of this fruit. Rental was evolving toward interest.

An alternative explanation to the unique and independent productivity of capital espoused by the French presently appeared. The use theory of interest was formulated. This forthright doctrine was to become one of the major categories of interest theory. Capital ultimately consisted of durable goods. Their use piled up value, because the use embodied previous economic goods and could last for a prolonged time. But use was distinct from the goods. (In this absolute sense, usefulness could be the more accurate word than use.) Goods were the bearer of use.

Use could be hired. Use was itself a separate value, which passed into the final product sold to the consumer. The purchase price contained the price of this use, which was interest. Use and labor emerged as the ultimate elements of production. They shaped the division of profit, depending on how their quantitative and qualitative substitution changed their exchange values with each other. The rate of profit corresponded with the rate of interest.

The use theory was quickly compounded with other views. As in other material goods, the value of use was ultimately traced to utility and to its functioning over a span of time. The value of use was also ascribed to abstinence. The lender gave up the (business) use itself, bringing up the old idea of foregone profit opportunity.

The presence of labor was definitely not forgotten. In fact, a few of the German economists came close to identifying labor as the only source of value. Use connoted the capital at work in the context of the entrepreneur managing and the laborer applying his skill. This led to the previous extreme claim that capital goods were the sum of past labor and that labor was the total cost of production. Lastly, use was identified with another past specification, namely, that it was productive service. Such service could also be the object of abstinence.

The German economists left the rate of interest relatively untreated. They suggested that it depended on the number of lenders and borrowers and that it tended to fall in the presence of capital's diminishing marginal returns. But they held that a sufficiently positive rate was required to induce capital formation.

Chapter 9

SOCIALIST SURPLUS VALUE

The labor underpinnings that crept into the German analysis of interest assumed prominence with the development of socialist doctrine in Europe. A new approach to interest surfaced aptly called the exploitation theory. A Swiss economist and historian, Simonde de Sismondi (1773-1842), led this progression from the classical labor theory. However, he did not go to the extreme of denouncing interest altogether. In 1819, his book, *New Principles of Political Economy* stated that ascribing rent, profit, and wages to three distinct sources was erroneous. All income came from human labor, and the three types of income were merely ways of participating in the fruits of work. The structure of society ("stage of civilization" in Sismondi's words), where the laborer was unable to possess the means of production, arranged that wealth had the capability to reproduce itself by the labor of others. Since the laborer's need for subsistence was more urgent than the desire for the profit of the landowner or business undertaker, the former's dependence forced him to accept a small share in the output of production.

How did Sismondi, who was not a socialist and was earlier a follower of Adam Smith, justify interest in this oppressive context he described? He appealed to the rights of previous labor and of ownership. The landowner, for instance, by earlier cultivation or even by just occupying virgin land had secured entitlement to rent. Similarly, the capitalist gained a claim to interest on account of the labor originally embodied in the creation of his capital. But time made a difference in this creation of value. The laborer earned only a yearly income by reason of putting in new work. In contrast, the capitalist owned perpetual income from a past input of labor, which was made more valuable by the application of new labor. From this imbalance, Sismondi drew up this rule: "Everyone receives his share in the national income only according to the measure of what he himself or his representative has contributed, or contributes, towards its origin." The representative presumably was the capitalist, as Sismondi insisted that "the rich spend what the labor of others has produced." He was the first to use the term "proletarii" for the class of day-wage earners.

The Frenchman Pierre-Joseph Proudhon (1809-65), a promoter of a sovereign-less state, simply assumed that labor produced all value. The laborer therefore had a natural right to own the total product. The wage that the laborer agreed to really defrauded him. It could not even buy his product. The shortfall was caused by many tolls, *aubaines*, imposed on labor, such as profit, interest, and rent, or by a retention, *retenue*, held back from wages. The rate of interest showed the rate of the tolls. Proudhon conceived a financial system that would abolish interest. Banks would grant free credit against produced goods, or auction them if unsold, and give any excess sums to the producers.

The core of the carefully wrought theory on interest of Johann Karl Rodbertus (1805-75), a conservative monarchist and state socialist, was the proposition, about which "there is no longer any dispute," that all economic goods were the product solely of labor. Specifically, it was that labor which did the material operations of production. This was so ("indelibly imprinted upon the consciousness of the people" were the words of Rodbertus), because labor was the only original power and cost in economic life. Economic goods, as opposed to natural ones, were those that required labor. Economic goods consisted of both immediately produced items and capital goods. In pure justice, the laborer had a natural right to possess the entire product. But since the product could not be shared on account of the division of labor, the claim had to be directed to the whole value of the product, which was exclusively regulated by labor value.

A secondary claim was allotted to "indirect economic labor," that is, labor not materially involved in the production of goods, such as that of professionals and even of the undertakers who "understand how to employ a number of labourers productively by means of capital." These men were like "officers" who were paid a salary. But society did not permit the mode of income distribution visualized by Rodbertus. Laborers received wages corresponding to only part of the value of their product, and the rest went as rent to landowners and capitalists. Rent was obtained not by "personal exertion," but by virtue of ownership. Rent meant profits, interest, and rent of land.

The reason for the prevailing system of income distribution was both legal and economic. The law allowed private property of land and capital. Economically, laborers were compelled by the need for subsistence. Rodbertus vividly portrayed the resulting situation evocative of Sismondi: "For first, the result will be the same as slavery, that the product will not belong to the labourers, but to the masters of land and capital; and secondly, the labourers who possess nothing in face of the masters possessing land and capital will be glad to receive a part only of the product of their own labour with which to support themselves in life; that is to say again, to enable them to continue their labour. Thus, although the contract of labourer and employer has taken the place of slavery, the contract is only formally and not actually free, and Hunger makes a good substitute for the whip. What was formerly called food is now called wage." In further describing this enforced condition, Rodbertus returned to a favorite term of the scholastics for usury. He called it "robbery." As for the rate of profit in manufacturing, he held that competition would drive it toward a uniform rate.

Ferdinand Lasalle (1825-64), another German socialist and an intellectual agitator, remarkably presaged in his Ricardian writing on interest published in 1864 practically the very words to be used by Karl Marx, his famous contemporary. In various passages he wrote: "Labour is source and factor of all values . . . . The labourer does not receive the whole value, but only the market price of labour considered as a commodity, this price being equal to its costs of production, that is, to bare subsistence . . . . All surplus falls to capital . . . . Interest is therefore a deduction from the return of the labourer." He ridiculed the notion that "the profit of capital is the wage of abstinence," mocking the "ascetic millionaires of Europe [standing] like penitents . . . holding a plate towards the people to collect the wages of Abstinence." As for the wages of labor, they were destined to adhere to the level of subsistence according to the "iron law of wages" formulated by Lasalle.

Karl Marx (1815-83), the leading theorist of socialism, drew from his immediate predecessors (notably Rodbertus) in proclaiming the labor doctrine of interest. However, he packed his analysis, largely contained in his massive *Das Kapital* published in 1865-6, with much originality and exhaustive reasoning. Das Kapital was subtitled as a critique of the then current political economy, when "capitalist industry . . . still appeared as an isolated island encircled by a sea of independent farmers and handicraftsmen . . ." Marx, a contemporary of the gentler Mill, vehemently founded his work on the tenet that the value of all goods completely arose from the amount of labor utilized in their production.

How did Marx prove this dogmatic contention? He took labor as abstract human labor, which was "stored" or "objectified or materialized" in goods. "As values," Marx wrote, "commodities are only definite amounts of congealed labour time." Value primarily referred to exchange, not to use. When goods were exchanged, their values were assumed to be equal. The equality was not based on the use value, since their use may be qualitatively different. The equality had to rest on a common component, and this was their being products of labor.

Marx devoted twelve chapters of *Das Kapital* to interest, to both its nature and its rate. Interest, as previous scholarship had gradually shown, was situated in a net profit or surplus value following production. Marx explained surplus value, *Mehrwert*, by denying that the capitalist secured the surplus value by buying commodities below value or selling them above value. Surplus value could not just sprout out of a commodity automatically. It was brought about in the trading of the commodity, namely labor power, which alone, among all commodities, had a use value that also incorporated exchange value. The laborer had to sell his capability, instead of offering the product himself, because he was dispossessed of "all things necessary for the realizing of his labor power."

As derived from Ricardo, Marx wrote that labor power was valued by the labor time required to produce it, that is, to provide the laborer's sustenance. The capitalist paid for this labor time, but actually extracted more labor time, say seven working hours instead of the three required for the laborer's maintenance. This excess value over the wage paid went to the capitalist and was called profit or interest or rent or whatever.

Specifically, the amount of surplus value obtained depended on what Marx called "variable capital," which advanced wages or was the "constituent which is converted into living labour power." The other portion of capital, "constant capital," was advanced for the other means of production. Its amount could "rise, fall, remain unchanged, be little or much, it remains without any influence whatever in producing surplus value." Marx regarded the creation of surplus value by variable capital as entirely occurring at a discrete point of time, not spread over a significant period that would influence commodity values. The rate of surplus value was its fixed ratio to variable capital. "The surplus value," continued Marx, "measured by the total capital is called the rate of profit," which was identical to his rate of interest, which was the ratio between the surplus value and the sum of variable and constant capitals.

Marx assiduously focused his treatment of capital on its monetary aspect. The accumulation of surplus value formed constant capital. "If there were no money at all," he asserted, "there would certainly be no general rate of interest." Money and the credit market played varying roles. Marx divided capitalists into financial and commercial ones. The "circulation" or transactional process of the financier differed from that of the industrialist and the merchant. The latter two moved from money to commodity to money. The financier or creditor moved from money to money (of larger amount). While interest-bearing capital was seen as a commodity, it was "lent instead of being relinquished once and for all." It became a commodity, albeit *sui generis*, because when lent, the "money capitalist . . . alienates a use-value . . ."

Money transformed into credit capital had use value, which was its capacity to create surplus value or profit. Interest was a partial measure of the division of the profit block. "The part of profit," Marx stated, "paid in this way is called interest, which is thus nothing but a particular name, a special title, for a part of the profit which the actually functioning capitalist has to pay to the capital's proprietor, instead of pocketing it himself." Marx called the portion pocketed by the functioning capitalist the "profit of enterprise." A maximum rate of interest of 100% meant that all profit "minus wages of superintendence" went to the lender. The minimum rate was indeterminate, according to Marx, but "countervailing circumstances constantly enter to raise it above the minimum."

Marx sought to clarify the links between the rates of profit and of interest. He believed that "the interest will rise or fall with the total profit, and the latter is determined by the general rate of profit and its fluctuations." The general profit rate, which was partially determined by business competition, but which was not "the specific profit rates that may prevail in particular branches of industry, still less [was it] . . . the extra profit [of] the individual capitalist . . . reappears in the average rate of interest as an empirical given fact, even though the latter is not a pure or reliable expression of the former." Thus, "though it may be impossible to determine, with any precision, the average profits of capital," Marx could say that "some notion may be formed of them from the interest of money." In order to find the average rate of interest, Marx said that "we have to calculate (1) the average interest rate as it varies over the major industrial cycles; (2) the rate of interest in those investments where capital is lent for longer periods."

Since the general rate of profit was decisive in determining the average rate of interest, Marx denied the existence of a natural rate of interest, but at times established the notion unknowingly in his analysis. Over long periods, Marx thought the average rate of interest to be constant, "because the general rate of profit changes only in the long run . . ." In addition, competition would tend to unify the profit rate throughout the economy. On the other hand, the market rate of interest fluctuated permanently, although it was directly determined as a "fixed magnitude at any given moment . . . by the relationship between the supply of loan capital . . . and the demand for it . . ." The concentration of the credit system strengthened this immediate fixing at any given time by the simultaneous presentation of funds "on a mass scale." The consolidation of the interest rate was further induced by "the historical pre-existence of interest-bearing capital and the existence of a general rate of interest handed down by tradition, [and by] the stronger direct influence of the world market . . ."

In contrast, the general rate of profit "only ever exists as a tendency, as a movement of equalization between particular rates of profit." It was determined not only by surplus value, but also by business competition requiring continuous allocation and reallocation of capital. It "simply appears as the minimum limit of profit, not as an empirical and directly visible form of the actual profit rate." Marx held that the profit rate stood "in inverse proportion to the development of capitalist production." In the course of industrial development, the value of constant capital would rise faster than that of variable capital. Assuming that surplus value and the price of capital goods remained unchanged, this formulation allowed Marx to conclude, like economists before him, that the rate of profit would decline in the long run.

Marx realized that "counteracting forces" could "inhibit and annul" his absolute economic law of labor's exploitation. Cyclical phases could raise wages or shorten working hours, for example. But he was confident that his analytical outlook was a barrier that would ultimately halt the operation of capitalism. Marx rejected abstinence as the explanation for interest, considering it as merely exculpatory. Given his derivation of surplus value, he found interest patently unjust. His *Das Kapital* had a lengthy quotation from Aristotle's condemnation of the pursuit of usury and his conception of money as barren, and from Luther's denunciation of usurers that had this last sentence: "And since we break on the wheel, and behead, highwaymen, murderers, and housebreakers, how much more ought we to break on the wheel and kill . . . hunt down, curse, and behead all usurers."

Marx's exploitation doctrine, with its socio-political undertones, understandably invited swift disagreement. An early critic was Karl Strasburger, a member of a group in Jena favoring the productivity theory of interest. His rebuttal, made in 1871, appeared to attempt the riddance of labor productivity altogether. He asserted that capital had distinct powers and that it "produces values inasmuch as it gets natural powers to do work which otherwise would have to be done by man." Capital was scarce too, since "it is not everyone who possesses this means of subordinating natural powers." Hence, this activity of capital was secured ("bought" was the term of Strasburger, not borrowed) by "those who possess no capital . . . by means of their own labor. Or if they worked with the help of another man's capital, they must give over to him a share of the value produced. This share . . . is profit: the drawing of a certain income by the capitalist is founded on the nature of capital." Strasburger's empowerment of capital, although briefly stated, could be taken as representative of reaction to Marxian doctrine at the time. It neatly outlined some of the thought lines of the great controversy to come between the theoreticians of communism and capitalism.

Summary of the socialist economists. In explaining interest, the 19th-century socialists, who could justifiably invoke lineage from the classical economists, did not deny its existence. Instead, they disputed its ownership. In so doing, they improved on previous analysis in one important way. Their notion of surplus value, a term that subsequently proliferated in academic literature, avoided the shortcoming of placing interest in gross profit. Nonetheless, labor wrought all value, including especially surplus value, and value of capital with embedded labor.

Reckoned as a traded commodity, that is, possessing exchange value, capital (always) produced value in excess of its cost, because it worked beyond its price. Surplus value was everything that could be wrung out of a tractable labor force compelled to toil for subsistence wages. Such undervalued costs therefore could easily cause an excess over gross profit. But gross and net profits remained identified as wages. Interest was allocated anywhere outside of gross profit. Social structure and economic status enabled other claimants to this excess value besides the worker. Labor's loss in the surplus value was due to tolls, division of labor, and ownership.

When the capitalist lent capital, he lent its use value, which generated surplus value. The rate of profit depended on the surplus value created and the total (variable and fixed) capital employed. The ratio theoretically approximated, if not equaled, the rate of interest. However, the rate of profit was not immune from market forces that induced changes in capital allocation. The interest rate too was subject to the influence of the credit market. These external factors prodded profit and interest in the long run toward average rates that were constant and roughly mirrored each other. Understandably, the socialists unanimously rejected abstinence as the cause of interest. They did not wish to offer any justification for the conduct of the capitalists.

The affirmation by the socialists of labor's exclusive role in the rendering of value did not bring down the position of the capital productivity school. There were economists of the time who defended the ownership of capital and its contribution in productive activity. They confirmed capital's realization of profit, and they even consented to the validity of calling profit as surplus value, despite its renewed exploitative overtone.

The Marxian critique brought more urgency to explaining surplus value and the source of interest with new approaches. The unfinished task was to buttress the naïve expression of some previous theorists that attributed an inherent power or capability in capital to literally, directly, and immediately create on its own not only gross value, but also additional value. This ability was essentially proved by declaring that excess value was observed to arise regularly after the production process. Explanation of the assertion's logic fell to a subsequent group of economists of varied nationalities. Called "neoclassicals," they enhanced previous reasoning with analytical tools that attained enduring validity not only in interest theory but also in the other fields of economics.

PART FIVE

COMING TO CLOSURE

Chapter 10

THE NEOCLASSICALS

The close of classical economics and its evolution to neoclassicism came about through the introduction of conceptual models whose analytical methods were mainly based on the concepts of utility and the margin. William Stanley Jevons (1835-82) presented the first of such "revolutionary" models. Jevons started as an assayer of a mint in Australia, became a civil servant, and then progressed to a university professorship in Manchester and London. His *Theory of Political Economy* appeared in 1871.

From the start, Jevons rejected the exclusive labor value of Ricardo and the socialists. He put forward a source of value that was mentioned only intermittently and unemphatically in the past in relation to interest: "Repeated reflection and inquiry have led me to the somewhat novel opinion that value depends entirely upon utility. Prevailing opinions make labour rather than utility the origin of value . . . . Labour is found often to determine value, but only in an indirect manner, by varying the degree of utility of the commodity through an increase in supply." Utility as the source of value had been perceived by the scholastics in shaping their "just price" argument. They "lacked nothing but the marginal apparatus" wrote a famed Canadian economist in 1954.

Given the role of utility, Jevons identified the distribution of an economic product as exchange that grew out of market forces. This was unlike in Ricardo and Marx where distribution lay in the production process prior to exchange. Jevons proposed exchange value to be marginal. He referred to it in 1862 as "the final degree of utility," which reflected Bentham's intensity of "pleasure and pain." He defined utility, after Say and Bentham, as "the abstract quality whereby an object serves our purposes, and becomes entitled to rank as a commodity." Utility was not an "inherent quality . . . [but] a circumstance of things arising out of their relation to man's requirements." On the production side, the value of capital itself was measured by the amount of utility (or enjoyment) postponed by its supplier. Jevons introduced the word "disutility," meaning pain as opposed to pleasure, to refer to the burden of labor. He did not state if he intended disutility to mean absence of value, though the context suggested it.

Instead of showing how capital's power directly produced utility, Jevons, like Aristotle defining money, proceeded to follow the functional view of Ricardo and Quesnay. Capital "allows us to expend labor in advance." This disposition of capital was then described in language with a socialist slant. It "consists merely of the aggregate of those commodities which are required for sustaining labourers . . . engaged in work." The time involved in the advance was "the period of production."

Capital was necessary for injecting "whatever improvements in the supply of commodities lengthen the average interval between the moment when labour is exerted and its ultimate result or purpose accomplished." The duration of production, or more exactly of wage-goods, that could be financed determined the mode of production and the resulting product. "The single and all-important function of capital," Jevons repeated, "is to enable the labourer to await the result of any long-lasting work—to put an interval between the beginning and the end of an enterprise." Capital provided the laborer time to use lengthy production methods that resulted in more fruitful work. Each additional capital invested, given the same amount of labor, extended this time.

Jevons saw the relationship between the extension of time and the use of improved technology. The longer the time, the greater was productivity. The profit of capital was the difference between the products that could be produced within the shorter period and the products produced within the extended period made possible by the investment of that capital. The rate of interest was the proportion between this profit and the added capital. This calculation, given an economy endowed with and accumulating much capital, would induce a declining trend in the interest rate as larger incremental capital was invested. In addition, since interest rates on different capitals would tend to come together, they would drift to the lowest level secured by the last increment of capital. Jevons made the important point that interest from the use of capital was based not on the total productivity increase, but on the (diminishing) increase achieved in the last extension of the production process, that is, on the margin.

As a consequence, the prevailing rate of interest set bounds to the feasible period of extended production, subsequently influencing production methods. Thus, Jevons denied the inverse relationship proposed by Ricardo and Lauderdale between the absolute returns to labor and interest, that is, an increase in wages lessens profit. Although "as labour must be supposed to be aided with some capital," Jevons wrote, "the rate of interest is always determined by the ratio which a new increment of produce bears to the increment of capital by which it was produced."

Jevons apparently identified the product increase with value increase, but did not declare that this value increase provided the surplus value required to explain interest. The incremental capital goods could cost more than the old capital, or the additional product could be priced cheaper. If the marginal gain turned out to be insufficient, Jevons inadvertently salvaged the shortfall by his eclectic acceptance of Senior's abstinence theory. He understood abstinence as the "temporary sacrifice of enjoyment that is essential to the existence of capital" or as the "endurance of want."

Jevons looked at an arithmetical calculation for abstinence. He considered it, and interest properly speaking (interest on borrowed capital), as production costs that had to be paid. He counted the payments for abstinence and for risk as the capitalist's income. Jevons strengthened his support of the abstinence theory when he alluded to the valuations men make for present and future enjoyment. "A future feeling," he admitted, "is always less influential than a present one." However, he did not develop this idea despite the frequent citations of it by his predecessors and its relevancy to his extended periods of production.

Carl Menger (1840-1921) was a holder of a chair at the University of Vienna for thirty years and was the founder of the Austrian school of economics whose doctrines constitute major influential lines of thinking in economics. He wrote in 1871 a mature elaboration of the use theory of interest associated with Hermann. In 1888, he enlarged the conception of capital as "productive property [narrowly understood] as a sum of money productively used." He imputed value into the use of capital goods, which incorporates a dimension of waiting time or, from another viewpoint, of "the services of capital." He carefully enlarged the reason why the values of the means of production could equal the higher values of their products for consumption, in other words, create surplus value and account for interest.

First of all, Menger lengthily described his theory of value, divorcing it from the activity of labor and capital goods. He laid down this "universally valid" (no exceptions) principle: "The importance that goods have for us and which we call value is merely imputed. Basically, only satisfactions have importance for us, because the maintenance of our lives and well-being depend on them. But we logically impute this importance to the goods . . . . The magnitudes of importance that different satisfactions of concrete needs . . . have for us are unequal, and their measure lies in the degree of their importance . . ." He concluded: "There is no necessary and direct connection between the value of a good and whether, or in what quantities, labor and other capital goods were applied to its production.

Consequently, the nature and measure of value is subjective, since "goods always have value to economizing individuals and this value is also determined only by these individuals." Menger, however, did not absolutely isolate goods from their factors of production. He merely reversed the direction of causality: "The value of the means of production is determined always and without exception by the value of their products." This interpretation of valuation applied in the same way to both consumption and capital goods. But the latter goods involved more complexity, since they had to be related not only to their final products, but also to other complementary "higher order" goods, such as raw material, machines, inventories, and labor.

In analyzing the role of capital goods, Menger named the means of production "higher order" goods. Final or consumption goods were "lower order." Higher order goods were utilized within a certain time frame. Production, the combination of capital with labor and land, occurred in successive unidirectional stages, where the output of one stage became the input of the next. "One of the conditions of production therefore," Menger said, "is this: the disposal over quantities of real capital during definite periods of time." Thus, a loan was transferred disposal over (the use of) goods. The longer the loan term, the longer was the disposal. Since capital services, which are the "command of quantities of economic goods in an earlier period for a later time, typically are scarce in the face of demand for them ("quantities . . . smaller than the requirements for them)," their use gained a value. Menger, like a few of his predecessors, endorsed scarcity as an element in valuation and interest justification.

Capital services became an economic good in line with Menger's definition of economic goods as "those goods the available quantity of which is less than human need." This scarcity value was augmented by the lengthening of the production process. Value was attained at each sequence of production, with fixed and variable capitals furnishing their own types of addition. Nonetheless, this value "is dependent upon the expected value of the goods of lower order they serve to produce." It could not be "the determining factor in the prospective value of the corresponding goods of lower order." Menger emphasized the word "prospective" to prevent identity with the value of similar present goods. If this prospective value rose, "the value of the goods of higher order whose possession assures us future command of the good of lower order rises also." The reversal of value causation could theoretically mean the erasure of surplus value. But Menger pointed out in turn that the value of the finished goods was determined, as Jevons held, by whatever utility was attributed to them by human wants. Profit for capital services remained possible, if not certain.

It was this process of utility imputation, *zurechnung*, that precisely allowed room for interest. The price of the product, reflecting the magnitude of importance of its power of satisfaction (value) would often exceed the value of its means of production. Menger named two reasons for the expected surplus value, namely, interest and business risk and management. "The aggregate present value of all the . . . quantities of goods of higher order . . . necessary for the production of a good of lower order," he explained, "is equal to the prospective value of the product. But it is necessary to include in the sum . . . also the services of capital and the activity of the entrepreneur. For these are . . . unavoidably necessary in every economic production of goods . . . . Hence the present value of the technical factors of production by themselves is not equal to the full prospective value of the product, but always behaves in such a way that a margin for the value of services of capital and entrepreneurial activity remains." Menger postulated that the effective consumer price would more than fill any value gap.

Given the primacy placed on utilitarian value, Menger, parting company with Jevons, logically rejected the abstinence explanation for interest. He denied the nature of a real exchangeable good to abstinence. In his famous *Principle of Economics* of 1871, he summarized this position: "Some economists represent the payment of interest as a reimbursement for the abstinence of the owner of capital. Against this doctrine, I must point out that the abstinence of a person cannot, by itself, attain goods-character and thus value. Moreover, capital by no means always originates from abstinence, but in many cases as a result of mere seizure (for example, whenever formerly non-economic goods of higher order attain economic character because of society's increasing requirements). The payment of interest must not be regarded as a compensation of the owner of capital for his abstinence (sometimes called "sacrifice" by Menger), but as "the exchange of one economic good (the use of capital) for another (money, for instance) . . ."

Menger also pointed out that interest was an economic phenomenon and that "the question of the legal or moral character of these facts [rent and interest] is beyond the sphere of our science . . . [which] has the task of exploring why and under what conditions the services of land and of capital display economic character, attain value, and can be exchanged for quantities of other economic goods."

Friedrich von Weiser (1851-1926), was probably the best disciple of Menger. He was a professor at the Universities of Prague and Vienna, and later holder of high government positions. Writing in 1891, Weiser, like his teacher, said that "the agents of production, land, capital and labour, derive their value from the value of their products, ultimately, therefore, from the utility of these products."

Since the productive agents "yield a return only by their combined agency," Weiser sought a clue to how this joint return was distributed among them, especially to capital. His answer again evoked Menger: "What is required in economy is not physical division of the product amongst all its creative factors, but the practical imputation of it . . . . It would, for example, be impossible for me to decide whether to purchase a machine and what price to . . . give for it, if I did not know how to calculate the work it would do for me, i.e., what share in the total return to my undertaking should be imputed to it in particular." Ultimately, value devolved to utility afforded by the finished products: "The value of the productive elements is determined on the ground of utility as afforded by the [forthcoming] products, and this holds good of the labour no less than of the coals, the machinery, and all the other means of production."

Linking interest to utility, Weiser specified in a new way the Roman title of profit foregone and the scholastic lost opportunity. They were the deprivation of utility. "By our investing a certain amount of capital," he wrote, "during a certain time in a certain product, we deprive ourselves of the interest which some other investment of our capital would fetch. The sacrifice of utility which we make in production consists therefore not only in the consumption of capital, but also in the sacrifice of interest, which is larger in proportion as the capital is larger and the period of investment longer. Accordingly, the current interest . . . is to be reckoned in the cost of production, and determines, together with the other elements of cost, the value of the products." At this point, Weiser clearly held the opposite to Menger's value-determination path from product price to factor price. Weiser's view, however, was shared by other economists.

Weiser was laying an a priori claim on the creation of value on behalf of interest. Sufficient value had to be, and was, realized without help from the products. Weiser rebutted the anticipated rejoinder from other theorists "that interest is a surplus of profit over expenditure, that it is conditioned by the value of the products and cannot, therefore, itself determine the value of the products." He distinguished absolute and relative values: "But is not the value of the productive commodities also conditioned by the value of the produce? And yet we say that it, as cost value, itself jointly determines the same. Equally are we entitled to say the same of interest. The [absolute] value of iron depends on the value of iron products, but the relative value of the iron products is determined by the mass of iron required. The rate of interest depends upon the value of the goods, but the relative value of the goods is determined by the quantity of capital required and by the length of time during which it is invested."

Weiser next confronted what was "essential to the complete solution of the problem of the value of capital" and of how interest was deducted from the value of the produce. He followed Menger in establishing net interest. "I start," he said, "from the notion of imputation. A portion of the product must be assigned to capital. But of this share we must first replace as much of the capital as was consumed. Now experience shows that this being done, the reward of capital as a rule is not exhausted, a surplus of clear profit remaining over. That capital is in this sense productive is just as truly a fact of experience as that the soil always brings forth fresh produce . . . . [The] field cleared of its harvest must be less than the value of field plus crop. The difference between the value of capital and the value of gross profits can only disappear if capital ceases to be productive and yield profit."

Since capital goods had value independently, so money as a capital fund similarly had its own value without depending on product pricing. Accordingly, Weiser drew the following mathematical instructions: "1—The value of circulating capital is found by discounting, i.e., by deduction of interest from gross income. 2—If a capital of 100 can after a year be converted into 105, then is the sum of 100, which can only be claimed after a year, of less value than 100. Future goods have, therefore, less value than present goods. 3—The value of fixed capital is reckoned . . . either through [continuous] discounting or capitalizing, attention being given to the principle of amortization or sinking fund." With these rules, Weiser astutely translated the stream of income from a slave observed by the Roman jurists pondering interest into modern accounting. But he did not fully realize that these calculations could themselves lead to a sufficient explanation of the nature of interest and that their development would render his and Jevon's imputed-utility argument for interest superfluous.

Leon Walras (1834-1910), a Frenchman who lived in Laussane, besides being an early marginalist, has been credited as the author of the modern theory of money. He was equally esteemed for his general equilibrium work—that condition when all aspects of an economy are in balance or at rest or stable indefinitely or, if disturbed, tends to right itself. Within the general equilibrium model, Walras developed his interest theory from his theory of capital. Writing in 1874-77, he considered, as undeniable, that surplus or net revenue arose from capital goods. Capital was narrowly defined for the first time as fixed stock, that is, "all durable goods . . . which are not used up at all or are used up only after a lapse of time." Variable or circulating capital (wage goods and raw materials) was excluded. Producer capital essentially provided productive services.

The price of this flow of services was directly determined in the market and therefore was influenced by the prices of all products. It had to be proportional to the net (after depreciation and insurance) return of the services. The rate of net return was the ratio of the net rental (price) of each unit of service to the value of the capital good. The value of the capital good was consequently equal to the net price of the unit service divided by its net return. This value also equaled the cost of the production of the capital good. The net return was the same for all capital goods in competition-induced equilibrium.

Walras pre-positioned his capital-interest discussion on the basis of net return. The total capital goods demanded equaled the total of saving. Saving depended on the maximum utility choices of individuals for a theoretical commodity of "perpetual net revenues" and for all other commodities. An individual's choice between present income and streams of perpetual income determined his total saving. Hence, the resulting single price facing both household demand for a perpetual net income and industry demand for capital goods in terms of a unit of net product value per unit of time resolved into the reciprocal of the perpetual net revenue. This price was identifiable with the real rate of interest. In this particular equilibrium, the behavior of the interest rate would be induced by changes in the values of capital goods relative to their costs to firms. The interest rate was a passive element here. But Walras injected money into his real analysis and money became an active segment.

Given the imperatives of his general model, Walras departed from the classical practice of dealing with production and exchange separately, so that prices assumed a central importance, including the money rate of interest. Walras inserted another market in his system called the capital market, *marche du capital*, which was equivalent to the market for capital goods, *marche des capitaux*. In this financial market, what capitalists saved and borrowed was money. The commodity traded in this market was the service rendered by money, *service d'approvisionnement*, which was a perpetual flow of income. Its price was the reciprocal of the rate of interest. Its equilibrium price was where people's demand for money for transaction purposes, *encaisse desiree*, equaled the existing stock of money. Taking money as a common denominator, the rate of interest should be such as to effect this equalization. Saving then would run on the same line as the supply of loanable funds. At the extreme high and low levels of interest rates, savings would tend toward zero. Borrowing and lending would cease.

In equilibrium, saving would equal the value of newly produced capital goods. From the general simultaneous equilibrium viewpoint, however, the interest rate would affect the values of capital goods and stock and, through them, all other prices in the system. It also would influence the amount of transactions in the economy and therefore on desired money holdings, but Walras characterized this latter result as "indirect and feeble" and disregarded it. On the other hand, Walras recognized the variations of bank credit, especially its "abusive" prerogative to lend to businessmen without equal borrowing from capitalists (savers). This could destabilize the economic process.

Overall, the introduction of money made it difficult for the Walrasian system to maintain its professed static nature. The system also neglected the investment process and production time. Walras did underline the consequential distinction between the entrepreneur borrower and the capitalist. Interest was a cost (expenditure) for the former and income (revenue) for the latter.

Eugen von Bohm-Bawerk (1851-1914), another brilliant student of Menger, was a dedicated public servant and a professor at the universities in Innsbruck and Vienna. He published his major work entitled *Kapital und Kapitalzins* in 1884 and 1889. Early on Bohm-Bawerk was keenly aware of the twin problems facing the theorist—the problem of the existence of interest and the problem of the determinants of its rate.

He rejected the supposition, dating back to the scholastic doctrine of fungibles, that the sum paid should be equal to the sum lent. The value of goods, he said, did not "depend simply on their physical qualities, but to a very great extent, on the circumstances under which they become available for the satisfaction of human needs." These other circumstances were principally time and place. Coal, for instance, did not have the same value at the pit, the rail stockyard, or the fireplace at home.

As for time, Bohm-Bawerk insisted that "it is impossible . . . to assume it as a self-evident principle that there is a complete equivalence between the present goods given in loan and the goods of like number and kind returned at some distant period. Such an equivalence . . . can only be a very rare and accidental exception." He repeated the same idea in various ways, for instance, that "the actual presence of the immediate object of desire" afforded a higher value than the same object anticipated in the future, even with certitude, or that a premium (agio) was due people with wealth who did not immediately seek their claims from the economy.

The "only" mistake of the scholastics, according to Bohm-Bawerk, was to assume the "independent use of the loaned goods as a fiction." A loan was "a real exchange of present goods against future goods," and "present goods invariably possess a greater value than future goods of the same number and kind, and . . . a definite sum of present goods can, as a rule, only be purchased by a larger sum of future goods . . . . Present goods must have an agio as legitimate consequence of the constant fact that present goods are more useful and more desired than future goods, and that they are never present and offered in unlimited abundance. This agio is thus organically necessary . . . . This agio is interest. It is not a separate equivalent for a separate and durable use of the loaned goods, for that is inconceivable; it is a part equivalent of the loaned sum, kept separate for practical reasons. The replacement of the capital plus the interest constitutes the full equivalent."

Bohm-Bawerk footnoted his insistent argument for the disparity between present and future values with an acknowledgment of Galiani, Turgot, and Knies for "the germs of this view." But he overlooked Lessius who was the first to teach it at some length and the other earlier thinkers who merely hinted the same idea. And he ignored the use theory of interest which was then gaining momentum.

Bohm-Bawerk showed why a man may be ready to pay more than lent from the principle of a "subjective undervaluation of future goods compared with present goods." He gave three specific reasons, which harked back to previous economists like Menger and Thunen. "The first great cause of difference in valuation," he wrote "consists in the different circumstances of want and provision in present and future." This meant that people could anticipate to be better situated income-wise in the future (declining marginal utility of present income), or have urgent needs in the present, or possess a durable asset that can be either currently or later used.

Secondly, he said that "to goods which are destined to meet the wants of the future we ascribe a value which is really less than the true intensity of their future marginal utility . . ." This underestimation of the future happened because of lack of imagination to foresee future needs and the inability to overcome the desire to enjoy present goods or satisfy present needs knowing the uncertainty of life. Lastly, in a reason that was related to the first two reasons, he cited the "technical superiority of present over future goods" since the former was utilized for production whose value was greater than the produce of future goods. The current investment of capital had a greater present value than the same investment carried out the following year.

These reasons coalesced to form Bohm-Bawerk's theory of interest. He defined capital as "a complex of goods that originate in a previous process of production, and are destined, not for immediate consumption, but to serve as means of acquiring further goods." In this realm of capital goods, "the technical facts of production, which I describe as the greater productivity of time-consuming methods of production, provide a partial ground for the higher valuation of present goods, the possession of which permits the use of those more productive time-consuming methods. From this point of view, the technical and psychological facts are coordinated from the start." He concluded that "the [higher] subjective use-value of present goods" was manifested in "a higher objective exchange value and market price for present goods."

The objective value sourcing interest was Bohm-Bawerk's postulate that longer or "more roundabout" production processes increased productivity on the average. Roundabout production, as opposed to direct methods, meant the employment of "an aggregate of intermediate products" of varied types. He illustrated this with the example of a fisherman progressing from fishing with his hand to using a hook and, finally to casting a net. Another example was getting a drink of water. One could cup his hands at a spring, put water in a bucket and store it, or construct a pipeline to his house. The additional productivity attained by these technical upgrades that took time to implement gave rise to interest that was not a market rate paid to creditors, but an internal rate of return, although in an equilibrium condition, both would coincide.

Bohm-Bawerk's proof for the increased output from roundabout production was everyday knowledge. He wrote: "It must be emphatically stated that the only basis of this proposition is the experience of practical life. Economic theory does not and cannot show *a priori* that it must be so; but the unanimous experience of all the technique of production says that it is so. And this is sufficient; all the more that the facts of experience which tell us this is commonplace and familiar to everybody."

Eventually, due to the competitive pressure of producers seeking additional capital, the market rate of interest, as Jevons held, would tend to equal the ratio of the incremental product gained by extending time to the added capital needed. Expressed as a mathematical model, with the supply of labor and capital seeking investment as givens, the wage level, the production period, and the rate of interest would be determined simultaneously. The interest rate would be equal to the marginal product of capital. In the long run, the output increase gained on the margin of lengthening time would fall, everything else held constant. How did the producer determine the optimum extension of the production time? The optimum period occurred when the average rate of return on capital per time unit was maximized, and this point was attained when this average rate equaled the marginal rate of return on the additional amount of capital placed to prolong the production period (usually graphically represented as the intersection of two lines).

The supply of capital for investment was in turn determined by the subjective present-versus-future elements of Bohm-Bawerk's theory. The agio must meet the desired rate of return. In other words, new capital goods had to realize a positive return in order to be produced or retained. Without this yield, saving would hardly materialize. Bohm-Bawerk made the valuable point that interest was the realization of a discounted value of a flow of expected returns. Like Weiser, but in contrast to Menger whose production analysis lacked a time dimension, Bohm-Bawerk took value, capital, and interest as intertemporal phenomena. Moreover, his time discount of future satisfactions was general. It referred to the returns of all types of productive services besides physical capital goods.

As for the abstinence theory, which partially related to his first two grounds for interest, Bohm-Bawerk qualified the implication of permanent deprivation. "The man who saves," he wrote "curtails his demand for present consumption goods, but by no means his desire . . . . The abstinence connected with saving is no true abstinence, but a mere 'waiting.' The person who saves is not willing to hand over his savings without return . . . . For the principal motive of those who save is precisely to provide for their own futures . . . . [and] to increase proportionately their demand for consumption goods in the future."

Bohm-Bawerk discerned a double-counting in abstinence, as some considered it also as a cost together with labor in producing a capital good. Such a finding likely arose from the ambiguity surrounding the demarcation between gross and net returns. Bohm-Bawerk, however, sided with Lasalle, who disagreed with Senior. For Bohm-Bawerk "the existence and the height of interest . . . inevitably correspond with the existence and height of a sacrifice of abstinence." This accorded with the view that the positive interest rate was not an absolute price for something, but was sourced in intertemporal pricing. It was based on the intertemporal behavior (valuation and allocation) of both consumer and producer.

In summary, Bohm-Bawerk attacked the previous simple productivity theory, calling it naïve, and the use theory as explanations of interest. The mere physical productivity of capital was inadequate to prove the production of surplus value. The utilization of a tool, for instance, to increase the quantity of output or the rent from the use of a house did not by itself necessarily result in a permanent net return over cost and depreciation. Instead, in what became known as the roundabout-production theory of interest, which was developed partly in answer to Marx's surplus value (labor, according to Bohm-Bawerk, was entitled to the entire product only if production was instantaneous), Bohm-Bawerk asserted that the productivity of a definite quantity of capital was increased by the extension of the production period.

Expositions before Bohm-Bawerk superficially discerned that capital permitted this lengthening. Jevons believed that the sole purpose of capital was to enable this necessary interval between the beginning and end of the production period. Even earlier, Ricardo had observed "the time distance between investment and the emergence of the corresponding consumers' goods." And a contemporary of Senior, Mountfort Longfield, remarkably foreshadowed Bohm-Bawerk. In 1834, Longfield wrote that production took time, because the division of labor necessitated different capital goods whose use lengthened the production process. Profits resulted from the added productivity endowed labor when capital was invested in machines. With the entrepreneur conceived as performing both funding and managerial functions, Bohm-Bawerk viewed interest as an element of profit like the classical economists. Ownership strengthened the entrepreneur's right to interest.

Alfred Marshall (1842-1924), son of a cashier in the Bank of England and professor at Cambridge University, was the dominant pioneering figure of the marginalist school of economics. As a marginalist, he was understandably concerned with the rate of interest. Marshall, whose *Principle of Economics* was published in 1890, held that a rise in the money rate reduced the use of capital goods, since their net surplus would have to exceed that rate, and vice versa. Marshall termed this inverse relationship the "marginal utility of capital" or its "marginal net utility."

He explained the marginal utility of capital this way: "Suppose that the rate of interest is 3 per cent per annum . . . and that the hat-making trade can turn [the absorption of one] million pounds' worth of capital to so good account that they would pay 3 per cent net for the use of it rather than go without any of it. There may be machinery which the trade would have refused to dispense with if the rate of interest had been 20 per cent . . . . If the rate had been 10 per cent more would have been used . . . and finally the rate being 3 per cent, they use more still. When they have this [maximum] amount, the marginal utility of the machinery, i.e. the utility of that machinery which it is only just worth their while to employ, is measured by 3 per cent." Hence, the money rate of interest determined how far investment would be undertaken, given the schedule of capital's marginal utility.

The market interest rate in turn was influenced by supply and demand: "Interest, being the price paid for the use of capital in any market, tends toward an equilibrium level such that the aggregate demand for capital in that market, at that rate of interest, is equal to the aggregate stock forthcoming there at that rate . . . . An extensive increase in the demand for capital in general . . . will be met for a time not so much by an increase in supply, as by a rise in the rate of interest; which will cause capital to withdraw itself partially from those uses in which its marginal utility is lowest. It is only slowly and gradually that the rise in the rate of interest will increase the total stock of capital." Marshall's use here of "capital" and "stock" indicated his intent on real analysis. The price of capital goods was what equated the supply and demand for such goods. Operating behind the demand for capital goods was the diminishing productivity of each marginal addition to them.

Marshall had difficulty in making a clear-cut distinction between real and monetary rates of interest, even though his *Principles of Economics* of 1890 ostensibly dealt with the real economy. Loan funds, for which Marshall sometimes used the term capital, implied saving. Marshall disliked the term abstinence as rather misleading and preferred Bohm-Bawerk's "waiting," which more clearly signified a positive time preference, that is, "the sacrifice of present pleasure for the sake of the future" and "the postponement of enjoyment." Like Senior, Marshall found the primary motivation for saving in human nature's readiness to postpone consumption to reap more in the future. "We are justified," he explained, "in speaking of the interest on capital as the reward of the sacrifice involved in the waiting for the enjoyment of material resources, because few people would save much without reward; just as we speak of wages as the reward of labour, because few people would work hard without reward." The creation of additional capital goods by saving would stop at the point where their net yield would drop to zero, that is, where earnings would merely repay their cost. Abstinence should mean not only a desire, but also an ability, to secure a reward.

Marshall recognized other conditions for saving. The saver's level of income, for instance, could be so high that accumulation would occur even if the interest rate dipped to zero or below. He therefore clarified abstinence: "This term has been misunderstood: for the greatest accumulators of wealth are very rich persons . . . some of whom . . . certainly do not practice abstinence in that sense . . . which is convertible with abstemiousness. What economists meant was that, when a person abstained from consuming . . . , his abstinence from that particular act of consumption increased the accumulation of wealth."

Marshall used abstinence or "waiting" in his rebuttal of the doctrine of surplus value of Rodbertus and Marx which denied the legitimacy of interest. He wrote: "It is not true that the spinning of yarn in a factory, after allowance . . . for the wear and tear of the machinery, is the product of the labour of the operatives. It is the product of their labour, together with that of the employer and subordinate managers, and of the capital employed; and that capital itself is the product of labour and waiting: and therefore the spinning is the product of labour of many kinds, and of waiting. If we admit that it is the product of labour alone . . . we can . . . be compelled by inexorable logic to admit that there is no justification for Interest, the reward of waiting; for the conclusion is implied in the premises."

Marshall's real analysis avoided construing profit as entered in business balance sheets. He distinguished between real economic costs of production and expenses of production. The first was constituted by the disutility of labor and the sacrifice of providing necessary capital. Both were subjective in that they implied personal toil and trouble. Real costs were not equivalent to money costs, except in terms of exchange. In the long run, the real earnings of factors of production would equal marginal real cost, so that real interest would align with the marginal sacrifice involved in saving, just as wages would be identical with the marginal disutility of work. Marshall had a term, "normal rate of profit," which he apparently identified with the long-run real interest rate, which in another context seemed to be the reward for waiting. The normal profit rate would be realized in long-run competitive conditions from all investments in all lines of production.

As for nominal interest, Marshall disassociated the quantity of money from the interest rate: "The supply of gold exercises no permanent influence over the rate of discount . . . . All that the influx of gold does is to make a sort of ripple on the surface of the water. The average rate of discount is determined by the average level of interest . . . and that is determined exclusively by the profitableness of business, gold and silver merely acting as counters with regard to it." Marshall deemed any interest rate effect of an increase in the supply of money as temporary at best.

Marshall was the first to use both nominal and real terms for interest rates. Like Thornton and Haas, he perceived another element impacting the rate of interest, namely, inflation. Inflation eroded the purchasing power values of a loan's interest and principal. A nominal rate of 5%, for instance, meant a minus 5.5% real rate, assuming a 10% rate of inflation. Inflation forecasts extrapolated from past inflation were slow to adjust to actual inflation, and such forecasts differed among market participants affecting credit supply and demand. Insofar as business accounted for the bulk of credit transactions, the slow and different adjustments contributed to economic cycles.

Marshall's merger of classical supply-demand analysis and utility marginalism led to his designation as introducing a neoclassical stage in economics. The classical trait was shown by his developing the analogy of man-made capital goods to land, as previous English economists did. The two were similar in the short run, because their supplies were both fixed. The yield to previous capital investment was like rent, or "quasi-rent" in Marshall's terminology. Quasi-rent disappeared in the long run. "It cannot be repeated too often," Marshall cautioned," that the phrase 'the rate of interest' is applicable to old investments of capital only in a very limited sense." It was the (marginal) earnings of "floating" (variable) and of current investments that shaped the rate of interest.

Vilfredo Pareto (1848-1923), an Italian engineer, taught at Laussane where he created a school of economic thought carrying his name. Pareto had a pair of brief opinions on interest. According to him, that physical capital earned interest was "not more a problem than is the fact that the cherry tree bears cherries." In addition, to look for the precise cause of interest was an error. The interest rate was not determined by any specific element, but was simultaneously established by all the factors in a Walrasian general equilibrium system. The complex computation involved in such a universal determination would have been a far cry from the simple money quantity theory of the first mercantilists.

Summary of the neoclassicals. The neoclassicals endowed "utility" with unique prominence in the vocabulary of interest theory. A few went to the extent to claim that utility alone, not labor alone, imparted value to goods and capital. Consumers evaluated goods on the basis of the utility they saw for themselves. The higher the subjective utility assessed, the higher the price (objective exchange value) readily paid. Producers also calculated the utility that the service of capital goods afforded. The saver gave up utility by holding off on consumption. In this sense, utility could be taken as an extension of abstinence, which was central to another theory of interest.

Interest was recompense for lost or delayed utility, whose measure was the amount and the term of the capital invested. Capital provided needed advances (its use or services) in order that labor could engage in productive activity over a period of time. There would be diminishing returns on capital inputs, so that the market rate of interest would at a certain point force production adjustments. The marginal utility of capital had to meet the market rate of interest.

The market demand of the consumer was one solution to the problem of profit exceeding gross return, that is, of creating surplus value to cover interest and the risk and industry of the businessman. This approach departed from the focus on capital itself and the production process, both of which concerned the neoclassicals, given their real analyses. Hence, utility was also assigned capital. Capital goods possessed utility in their use or services. This utility was sometimes seen as consumer utility imputed to them. Their degree of utility was in direct proportion to the degree of consumer utility. Capital goods utility commanded a price that was a proportion of the net return. Since capital was required over an extended production period as advances, it progressively became scarce, and the use of a scarce commodity was valuable. It provided heightened utility.

The lengthened or roundaboutness of the production process resulting from intensified capital inputs was a key proposition for understanding the productivity of capital. Roundabout production, which employed a sizable amount of intermediate goods over an extended period of time, resulted in increased output on the average. The gain obviously occurred regularly and needed no theoretical proof. The increased capital productivity was augmented by the addition of the value found in the higher estimation of present goods (the intermediate goods made available or advanced for manufacturing use) over future goods. Thus, profit could be understood as the difference between immediate and delayed output. This variance relative to the added capital employed gave the rate of interest. The prolonged time of the production process led to the re-terming of abstinence to waiting. Waiting implied an assured expectation of the interest premium.

Critical significance was also attached by the neoclassicals to the term "marginal." Utility and value were calculated on the last unit of satisfaction and production. These incremental dimensions determined interest rates. Households looked to satisfy their goal of a perpetual income from the last unit of saving. Industry demanded net revenue on the basis of the marginal utility of capital, that is, the final unit of product per unit of additional time. The price that met both sides of the market was the real rate of interest, toward which the market rate would drift. Households and firms were expected to maximize this equilibrium price.

Chapter 11

MONEY REVISITED

The development of general equilibrium systems was not confined to real interest rate analysis. Since interest was constantly associated with money and loans, a completely realistic study needed to incorporate its monetary aspect as Walras attempted to do. John Gustav Knut Wicksell (1851-1926), a Swedish mathematician, social reformer, and professor at the University of Lund, thoroughly addressed this issue. His model of long-run equilibrium contained both aspects—physical capital and money interest. Wicksell laid the foundations for much of modern monetary economics.

Wicksell began with "the purely imaginary assumption" of the absence of money and credit, and then proceeded to show the interactions resulting from their presence. He pointedly stated that lending money was not "a lending of real capital goods in the form of money . . . . For in actual fact it is money which is lent, not the goods purchased by means of money. The rate of interest is a matter for negotiation with the owners of money and not with the owners of goods." Wicksell, however, admitted that "money is only one form of capital . . ."

Wicksell followed Bohm-Bawerk's insight that capital made a longer period of production possible. He admitted that the longer the period (the more capital used), "the greater will be the annual production of finished consumption goods, provided the same number of workers and the same [land] area . . . are involved." But he parted from Bohm-Bawerk

197

by thinking of capital (production goods), as the labor value theorists did, as consisting of dated "saved-up labour and saved-up land." Capital was differentiated from the investment of current labor and land directly used for making consumption goods. The wages and rent paid for the original or saved-up capital stayed invested from start to finish in the production of consumption goods. But the marginal productivity of the saved-up capital was greater than that of current labor and land employed because of its use over a longer span of time. Real interest originated from this difference (surplus value). Wicksell differed from the view of previous economists, like Jevons, that confined interest (at least its rate) to either variable or current capital investment. He recognized the contribution of fixed capital.

Bohm-Bawerk conceptualized an average production period and calculated with simple interest. Wicksell, computing from the marginal productivities of the quantities of his dated capital, had to use compound interest to arrive at a uniform rate of interest for all kinds of labor and land investment for a given period. The final real rate of interest that equilibrated the supply of and demand for capital eventually represented the scarcity of saved-up capital, since its "marginal productivity . . . was greater, simply because current labour and land exist in relative abundance for which they can be employed, whilst saved-up labour and land are not adequate in the same degree for the many purposes in which they have an advantage."

This inadequacy of saved-up capital was "explained by the circumstances which limit the accumulation of capital." Physical conditions limit the supply of capital goods. Also, if available capital was increased due to decreased consumption (augmented saving), the equilibrium real rate of capital would drop, discouraging saving and investment. Wicksell's real capital rate, which he also called natural or normal, was a net return to physical capital. It was "the rate consistent with the then existing marginal productivity of capital." It would be the rate set if all lending were done in real capital goods. It was described by the English economist, John Hicks, in 1965 as "a rate of exchange between wine now and wine a year hence . . . or any good now and the same good a year hence," while the money rate was "a rate of exchange between money now and money a year hence."

The real rate derived from the marginal productivity of physical capital, while the money rate was related to the marginal yield of investment. The money rate should correspond to the movements of the real rate like a shadow image, ensuring price stability. It was possible that the money rate could diverge from the real rate, resulting in the two rates losing their identity. The expansion of bank credit, for example, could prevent the money rate from gravitating towards the real rate. Wicksell saw the money rate as "essentially variable."

A relatively low loan money rate would inflate prices as increasing demand for cheapened loans raised the economy's liquidity. The consequent diminishing of the supply of loans would restore the money rate to its normal level. The banks, however, could maintain the low rate for some time "in an elastic monetary system." They could also adopt an opposite loan rate policy, so that the money rate, where "the demand for loan capital and the supply of savings exactly agree, and which more or less corresponds to the expected yield on the newly created capital, will then be the normal or natural real rate." The loan rate would fully reflect its determination by the supply of and demand for still non-invested real capital. Fundamentally, the convergence of the two rates meant stability in the general level of prices.

Wicksell, however, knew that in reality rising prices usually did not come with falling money rates, so he reversed his analysis and maintained that the dissimilarity between the two rates arose because the real rate was "not fixed or unalterable in magnitude," while the money rate remained relatively unchanged or lagged behind. Wicksell wrote: "An exact coincidence of the two rates . . . is unlikely. For changes in the (average) natural rate may be presumed . . . to be continuous, while the money rate . . . is usually raised or lowered only in discontinuous jumps of one half or one per cent . . . ." The real rate depended on a host of factors: "the efficiency of production, available amount of fixed and liquid capital, supply of labour and land, in short on all the thousand and one things which determine the current economic position of a community." He also perceived that rising prices could depress the real rate: "There is no doubt that when a sudden violent rise in prices has set in, people . . . are compelled to curtail consumption, and to that extent should lower the real rate."

The divergence of the interest rates was unlikely to prevail in the case of individual lending, but not for bank loans. Because of the banks' power to create credit and unsettle equilibrium, Wicksell in 1898, perhaps the first economist to do so, called for government policies to control interest rates as a means of stabilizing the economy. Since the natural rate could not be known precisely, Wicksell proposed the following rule: "So long as prices remain unaltered, the banks' rate of interest is to remain unaltered. If prices rise, the rate of interest is to be raised; and if prices fall, the rate of interest is to be lowered; and the rate of interest is henceforth to be maintained until a further movement of prices . . ." To the objection that these actions would mitigate bank profits, Wicksell, a social reformist, replied that "their obligations to society are enormously more important than their private obligations . . ." If banks were unable to meet these obligations, Wicksell wryly urged their nationalization.

Given his regard for studying money interest, Wicksell moderately differed from classical economics and declared that "interest on money and profit on capital are not the same thing, nor are they immediately connected with each other; if they were, they could not differ at all, or could only differ a certain amount at every time. [But] there is no doubt some connecting link [exists] between them . . . . If we look only at credit transactions between individuals . . . the connection . . . indeed seems obvious. If by investing your capital in some industrial enterprise, you can get, after due allowance for risk, a profit of, say, 10 per cent., then . . . you will not lend it at a much cheaper rate; and if the borrower has no recourse but to individuals in the same situation as you, he will not be able to get the money much cheaper than that." Capitalists invariably estimated their lending rate in conjunction with the industrialist's expected rate of return and vice versa.

John Maynard Keynes (1883-1946), famed English economist and statesman, founder of a major school of economic thought, gave primacy to the treatment of money interest. Commenting on Locke, he asserted that the mercantilist view that interest meant interest on money was "the view, which is, it now seems to me, indubitably correct." While often alluding to analysis done in the past, Keynes' monetary approach to interest published in his *General Theory of Employment,*

Interest, and Money in 1936 and in other publications either rejected or reworked some long-held theories of the classical economists. Keynes discussed interest itself and the dynamics of its rate, giving interest more independence as an individual analytical variable capable of being linked to aggregate quantities like national income, consumption, saving, and investment.

At the head of his departure from the non-monetary tradition was the proposition, "that interest is not derived from, or expressive of, anything that has, in whatever form, to do with the net return from capital goods." Interest, as "the percentage excess of a sum of money contracted for future delivery," was a price, and Keynes proceeded to show how this single entity played a vital macroeconomic role, both as determined and as a determinant. He criticized the old saying that interest was "the reward of not-spending" or saving or waiting. He declared instead, reminiscent of Lessius, that "whereas in fact it is the reward for not-hoarding . . . for parting with liquidity." The key to the tendency to hoard money was precisely its need "to determine the rate of interest at which the aggregate desire to hoard becomes equal to the available cash." Keynes said that hoarding had its "own interest," which was an idea used by Malachy Postlethwayt, an English economic writer in 1757, to define interest as payment to "overcome reluctance to part with cash."

In 1937, Keynes formally defined interest: "Interest on money means precisely what the books on arithmetic say that it means; that . . . it is simply the premium obtainable on current cash over deferred cash, so that it measures the marginal preference (for the community as a whole) for holding cash in hand over cash for deferred delivery. No one would pay this premium unless the possession of cash served some purpose, i.e., had some efficiency. Thus we can . . . say that interest on money measures the marginal efficiency of money measured in terms of itself as a unit." Thus, "the marginal efficiency of money in terms of itself is . . . a function of its quantity (though not of its quantity alone), just as in the case of other assets." Keynes went on to say: "The rate of interest is not the price which brings into equilibrium the demand for resources to invest with the readiness to abstain from present consumption. It is the price which equilibrates the desire to hold wealth in the form of cash with the available quantity of cash."

This basic point of Keynes strikingly recalled Lessius (without the marginal and equilibrium concepts) and Walras. Keynes, in what is now a classic enumeration, laid down three motives behind people's behavior in holding money. People kept money to use in transactions, to serve as a precautionary measure, and to engage in speculation. The first motive signified circulating money. The second and third motives referred to inactive funds. People maintained liquidity to meet unforeseen contingencies ("the desire for security as to the future cash equivalent of a certain proportion of total resources") or to take advantage of an investment opportunity ("the object of securing profit from knowing better than the market what the future will bring forth"). The second motive involved avoiding a loss by liquidating financial assets, while the last concerned making a profit by investing.

The amounts of cash to be held under the first and second motives were determined by the cost incurred in holding them. This cost was the interest earnings foregone. If the interest rate was low or moderate, there would be less hesitancy to retain the convenience offered by a liquid position. Normally, only relatively high interest rates would change this disposition, since the volume of transactions and contingencies were relatively stable. In other words, transaction and precautionary balances were not very responsive (inelastic) to the interest rate in contrast to speculative balances.

Elasticity was pivotal in the Keynesian system. It determined the steepness of the slope of the downward curve of the demand for money at various rates of interest. The intersection of this downward curve with the vertical line representing the existing stock of money determined "what the [equilibrium] interest rate is," assuming no change in aggregate income levels. If such a change occurs, which would primarily affect transaction demand, the demand for money curve would shift up or down. This scenario clearly provided leeway for policy-making by the monetary authority. It could change the supply of money or the interest (discount) rate or both.

Keynes formulated the demand for money in the so-called "liquidity preference function." His equation had the actual quantity or supply of money on the left side. This was equaled on the right side by the people's demand for money as dependent partly on their income, which influenced the volume of their transactions and of precautionary activity, and partly on the rate of interest or, more accurately, on its near-future movements relative to the current rate required for speculative decisions. The rate was the long-term rate as representative of all rates and yields, so that the buy and sell actions of holders of government bonds were Keynes' chief illustration of such interest expectations. In brief, money demand would rise as the interest rate declined, money supply held constant.

How did Keynes handle saving and investment? The classical theory considered saving as dependent on the interest rate. The higher the rate, the greater was the saving. The rate also influenced investment. The lower the rate, the more investment was induced. The intersection of these tendencies indicated the equilibrium interest rate (and also an economy at full employment). The interest rate therefore brought saving and investment together. Keynes did admit that the classical economists were right in thinking that saving depended positively on the interest rate. But he took saving as primarily positively dependent on (disposable) income, while investment was controlled by profit expectations that had to be evaluated against the interest rate. Lower rates induced more investment, since larger profits were likely with lesser interest rates.

Keynes further digressed from the classical school in an important point. The classical economists believed that savings always equaled investment. Keynes said that not all saving was automatically invested. Saving could mean saving in the form of money. Instead of leading to the formation of capital, it could cause unemployment and the loss of capital.

Keynes' analysis of interest progressed to an economy-wide system. He arrived at an equilibrium interest rate for the entire economy by joining the money and goods markets. In terms of a graph, with the interest rates on the vertical axis and national income on the horizontal axis, he laid the downward sloping curve of the demand-for-money schedule across the upward sloping curve of the saving-investment schedule. Their intersection showed the equilibrium interest rate for the economy at a given price level. At this point, the amount of money desired would be equal to the actual money supplied, and the actual saving and investment would equal desired saving. In this way, Keynes achieved a determinate and integrated theory of interest.

Keynes also treated capital from a monetary viewpoint. He attributed value to capital (physical goods) not on account of its productivity. He found it "much preferable to speak of capital as having a yield over the course of its life in excess of its original cost, than as being productive. The only reason why an asset offers a prospect of yielding during its life services an amount having an aggregate value greater than its initial supply price is because it is scarce. It is kept scarce because of the competition of the rate of interest on money. If capital becomes less scarce, the excess yield will diminish . . ." Capital was scarce, as the neoclassicals pointed out, since it was utilized in a lengthy or roundabout production method that could result in its expected return (marginal efficiency of capital) to exceed the costs of direct labor use and depreciation. If there was no excess return, the supply of capital would be halted. Capital "has to be kept scarce enough in the long run," Keynes wrote, "to have a marginal efficiency which is at least equal to the rate of interest for a period equal to the life of the capital . . ."

Keynes based the calculation of the value of capital on a series of annual returns foreseen for the life of the capital good and on the rate of interest discounting this income series. Investment would be induced as long as this value exceeded the replacement cost. Expressed differently, investment would come as long as a spread existed between the marginal efficiency of capital and the market rate of interest. Keynes rigorously defined the marginal efficiency of capital, a pure number like the interest rate, as "that rate of discount which would make the present value of the series of annuities given by the returns expected from the capital asset during its life just equal to its supply price."

Capital's marginal efficiency related an investment's future returns to the present income to be sacrificed for that investment. This method for investment decisions developed in the wake of legacies from the past. The present money versus future money principle was discernable. So were Marshall's normal profit and one meaning that Wicksell gave his natural rate of interest, namely, that it would equal the "expected yield on the newly created capital." Wicksell's marginal productivity of physical capital, which was also identified with natural interest, touched the same line of thought.

The rate of interest therefore was an overriding element in the demand for capital and as a criterion for investment, so that Keynes favored government policy intervention in either the money supply or the interest rate or both. He advised that "the justification for a moderately high rate of interest has been found hitherto in the necessity of providing a sufficient inducement to save. But . . . the extent of effective saving is necessarily determined by the scale of investment and that the scale of investment is promoted by a low rate of interest . . . . Thus it is to our best advantage to reduce the rate of interest to that point relatively to the schedule of the marginal efficiency of capital at which there is full employment."

Keynes essentially followed the mercantilist view that more money meant low interest rates that fed investment that increased output. Yet he recognized that blockages could occur in this pattern. He also replicated the interest rate theory of Irving Fisher, his contemporary in America. Keynes observed that "in a period of rapidly rising prices, the money rate of interest seldom adjusts itself adequately or fast enough to prevent the real rate from becoming abnormal. Thus . . . the businessman who borrows money is able to repay . . . with what, in terms of real value, not only represents no interest, but is even less than the capital originally advanced; that is, the real rate of interest falls to a negative value, and the borrower reaps a corresponding benefit."

Keynes further elaborated on investment with these interrelationships: "The equilibrium rate of aggregate investment . . . depends on the readiness of the public to save. But this in turn depends on the rate of interest. Thus for each level of the rate of interest we have a given quantity of saving. This quantity of saving determines the scale of investment. The scale of investment settles the marginal efficiency of capital, to which the rate of interest must be equal." This general analysis was also worded in individual terms by Keynes: "The owner of wealth, who has been induced not to hold his wealth in the shape of hoarded money, still has two alternatives . . . . He can lend his money at the current rate of money-interest or he can purchase some kind of capital-asset. Clearly in equilibrium these two alternatives must offer an equal advantage to the marginal investor in each of them. This is brought about by shifts in the money-prices of capital assets relative to the prices of money-loans."

Writing the *General Theory*, Keynes had occasion to review interest rate theories of the past. He paid tribute to the work of the scholastics:

"I was brought up to believe that the attitude of the Medieval Church to the rate of interest was inherently absurd, and that the subtle discussions aimed at distinguishing the return on money-loans from the return to active investments were merely jesuitical attempts to find a practical escape from a foolish theory. But I now read these discussions as an honest intellectual effort to keep separate what the classical theory has inextricably confused together, namely, the rate of interest and the marginal efficiency of capital. For it now seems clear that the disquisitions of the schoolmen were directed towards the elucidation of a formula which should allow the schedule of the marginal efficiency of capital to be high, whilst using rule and custom and the moral law to keep down the rate of interest."

Keynes saw a rationale for and benefit from the ancient and medieval usury (maximum ceilings) rates. During those periods, "the destruction of the inducement to invest by an excessive liquidity-preference was the outstanding evil . . . . since certain of the risks and hazards of economic life diminish the marginal efficiency of capital whilst others serve to increase the preference for liquidity. In a world . . . no one reckoned to be safe, it was almost inevitable that the rate of interest, unless it was curbed by every instrument at the disposal of society, would rise too high to permit of an adequate inducement to invest."

Keynes consequently defended Smith "as extremely moderate in his attitude to the usury laws. For he was well aware that individual savings may be absorbed either by investments or by debts, and that there is no security that they will find an outlet in the former." To promote investment, Smith "favoured a low rate of interest." Bentham, Keynes pointed out, severely took Smith to task unfairly, when Bentham complained that capping rates discouraged entrepreneurs (called "projectors" by Bentham) from "striking into any channel of invention." Keynes doubted that Smith intended this meaning.

Keynes additionally noted that the mercantilists "were emphatic that an unduly high rate of interest was the main obstacle to the growth of wealth; and they were even aware that the rate of interest depended on liquidity-preference and the quantity of money." He repeated a mercantilist quotation of 1621 that Locke had used: "High Interest decays Trade. The advantage from Interest is greater than the Profit from

Trade, which makes the rich Merchants give over, and put out their Stock to Interest, and the lesser Merchants Break." All in all, Keynes presented a formal and comprehensive monetary theory of interest and an alternate examination of the capitalist process.

Ludwig von Mises (1881-1973), an Austrian classmate of Bohm-Bawerk, "professor extraordinary" at the University of Vienna, and professor at New York University after his immigration to the United States, had a meager and scattered treatment of interest. Nevertheless, some of his views managed to be controversial. They either opposed or upheld long-held beliefs. He disagreed that interest was an income secured from capital goods or that it was "the price paid for the services of capital."

For Mises, interest was the common and unavoidable fact of time preference, which was "operative in every instance of action." Time preference was the higher estimation given the present than the future. As such it would arise even in an exchange economy without production, and it would do so even more in a production economy, since production took time. Thus, Mises underscored a definition of interest valid for all types of lending.

Mises maintained that capital should not be construed as capital goods or their totality, but be defined as the money value of an owner's assets in a business. In this he resembled Menger who tried "to rehabilitate the abstract concept of capital as the money value of the property devoted to acquisitive purposes against Smith's real concept of the produced means of production." Mises, deplored the (physical) aggregation of capital, since "the totality of the produced factors of production is merely an enumeration of physical quantities of thousands and thousands of various goods. Such an inventory is of no use . . . a description of technology and topography . . ." This heterogeneous collection was meaningless.

The measurement of capital was to serve economic calculation, and "the capital concept is operative as far as men . . . let themselves to be guided by capital accounting." Capital was assets minus liabilities. Mises, unlike his mentor, Bohm-Bawerk who followed Smith's notion of capital, dismissed any role for the physical aspects of production.

Capital in relation to the historical start of physical capital was irrelevant. Mises was firmly planted on monetary ground, and he argued wholly on subjective time preference and emphasized prospective business decision-making.

Mises similarly dismissed the idea of his fellow economists, the Americans John Bates Clark and Frank Knight, that capital was a self-perpetuating fund. It was "nonsense that capital reproduces itself and thus provides for its own maintenance." The market value of such a fund, taken in isolation, was subject to flux caused by changed and changing business expectations. Accordingly, Mises spurned as a blunder the explanation of "interest as an income derived from the inherent productivity of capital." He considered capital goods as unfinished consumer goods. They were not productive like labor, land, and time. Capital accounting merely drew "a boundary line between the consumer's goods which [an individual] plans to employ for the immediate satisfaction of his wants and the goods . . . which he plans to employ for providing . . . for the satisfaction of future wants."

Mises detailed how this time preference generated interest, that is, how an excess value of the produced goods emerged. Without (positive) time preference, the price of a capital good would equal the non-discounted total of the marginal values of that good's future services. The market prices of the produced consumer goods would approximate the prices of the factors of production. But with time preference, the prices of the factors would be only the discounted values of their multi-period services. "As production goes on," Mises pointed out, "the factors of production are transformed or ripen into present goods of a higher value."

Besides the interest from time-increased value, Mises added a second item to interest earned in a loan. He observed that capitalists were necessarily entrepreneurs as well, speculating and running risks, so that "interest stipulated and paid in loans includes not only ordinary interest but also entrepreneurial profit." The economic approach of Mises was the individual ("actor") making decisions. In the case of the entrepreneur, the decisions were planning future activity based on accounting data.

Friedrich Von Hayek (1899-1992), was a student of Mises, Nobel Prize winner in economics in 1974, and professor at the University of Freiburg, of Chicago, and the London School of Economics. A free-market classical liberal influenced by Menger, he was, unfortunately, somewhat lost in the shadow of Keynes, some of whose views he opposed. He adhered to the tradition of Bohm-Bawerk's Austrian school and of Wicksell that interest and capital were rooted in the temporal nature of production.

Nonetheless, Hayek's *Pure Theory of Capital* published in 1941 raised questions about the views of his predecessors. Hayek moved away from their static equilibrium analysis. The problem he saw was that "we [cannot] assume from the beginning that the same stock of instruments will be constantly reproduced . . . . since saving and (new) investment are activities which imply by definition that the persons undertaking them want to alter their future position, and consequently will do in the future something different from what they are doing in the present." Hayek therefore objected to capital as an enduring subsistence fund of value and to an average period of production used as givens by previous economists. He wrote that "the quantity of capital as a value magnitude, no less than the different investment periods, are not data, but are among the unknowns which have to be determined."

His solution to this problem of variability was to take as the point of departure the stock of real capital goods existing at the moment and the investment periods of each productive input and subject them to the dictates of a single will that fully knew all the income streams they can produce. This "dictator" would construct an income stream that was constant and maximized and that was effective immediately. This income stream consisted of consumption goods required by the community, and its composition could internally undergo successive modifications by substitution. Hayek gave the following reason for the continuous changeability: "We start out with an assortment of non-permanent resources (capital goods), which is the result of a particular historical development, and which will consist in large part of items which it is either impossible or else unprofitable to reproduce."

The direct relevance of interest in this presentation lay in the effort of maintaining a fixed income stream. Hayek's principle was that "whenever the rate of increase of the product which can be obtained by lengthening the investment periods of some units of input is greater than the rate of decrease of the product caused by shortening the investment periods of other units of input by the same interval of time, it will be advantageous to make the corresponding changes . . . . Hence the condition for maximizing the total income stream . . . is that this rate of increase of the product due to an extension of the investment period by a given interval shall be the same for all investments." This rule implied that the internal rate of return of all inputs would have to be the same and be equal to the prevailing rate of interest. If not, then input-output adjustments had to be made. Hence, the given stock of real capital, the output relative to the investment periods, and income maximization determined the interest rate.

Hayek continued to explain that "the condition that all input must be invested in such a way that the ratio between the marginal rate of increase of the product and the size of the whole product is the same for all units of input, also determined the period for which each of the units of input has to be invested." Hayek qualified this statement, which partially revised Jevons' interest rate formulation ("rate of increase of the produce divided by the whole produce"), as true only "for all processes maturing at the same time . . . . This does not mean that these ratios must also be equal for processes terminating at different moments. That is true only under stationary conditions." The implication was that the interest rate could undergo changes in time, while the income stream remained the same, bringing to mind the analogous issue of the term structure of interest rates.

Concretely, the interest rate was determined in the market for new capital, that is, in the interplay of the productivity of new investments and the readiness to save against the background of present versus future income choices. All of Hayek's generalizations that required choosing a given structure of capital goods and visualizing successive unit periods of time integrated three themes in connection with interest theory: time, real capital, and monetary accounting.

Bertil Ohlin (1899-1979) was a Swedish winner of the 1977 Nobel Prize for Economics, a university professor in Stockholm and Copenhagen, and a member of Parliament. He was part of the so-called Swedish school rooted in the teaching of Wicksell that emerged in the early 20th century.

In 1937, Ohlin contrasted Keynes' liquidity preference theory with the loanable funds theory of interest, which had been intimated by the classical and neoclassical economists, such as Cantillon, Turgot, and Mill. Mill had written that "the rate of interest . . . depends essentially and permanently on the comparative amount of real capital offered and demanded in the way of a loan," so that "fluctuations in the rate of interest arise from the variations either in the demand for loans or in the supply." The loanable funds theory maintained that the rate of interest was finalized in the market for credit (a flow), while the liquidity preference theory held that the determination occurred in the market for money (a stock).

The ensuing esoteric debate ended inconclusively. The two theories were seen either to be equivalent, or resulted in the same interest rate movements, or were really different. Ohlin's opening position faulted the classical position: "Obviously, the rate of interest cannot . . . be determined by the condition that it equalizes the supply of and the demand for savings, or, in other words, equalizes savings and investment. For savings and investment are equal *ex definitione*, whatever interest level exists on the market . . . . How, then, is the height of the interest level determined? The answer is that the rate of interest is simply the price of credit, and that therefore it is governed by the supply and demand for credit." Nonetheless, since Ohlin observed that "the banking system—through its ability to create credit—can influence . . . the interest level," he asked the question: "Does this mean that [the interest level] has no connection with the disposition of individuals and firms to save and with other elements in the price system?" His realistic reply was "of course not."

Ohlin prescribed two types for credit that recalled the distinction between new and old capital. There were net or new credit and gross credit that included outstanding old credits. He showed how rates of interest were actually determined for these credits: "The willingness of certain individuals during a given period to increase their holdings of various claims and other kinds of assets minus the willingness of others to reduce their corresponding holdings gives the supply curves for the different kinds of new credit during the period. Naturally, the quantities each individual is willing to supply depend on the interest rates. In other words, the decisions are in the nature of alternative purchases and sales plans." Similarly, the "total supply of new claims minus the reduction in the outstanding volume of old ones gives the demand—also a function of the rates of interest—for the different kinds of credit during the period. The prices fixed on the credit market for these different claims—and thereby the rates of interest—are governed by this supply and demand in the usual way."

Supply and demand were rendered equal by the prices in the bond, stock, and bank deposit markets. Excess loan demand would cause the interest rate to rise and excess loan supply the opposite. At the end of the given period (*ex post*), "one finds equality between the total quantity of new credit during the period, and the sum total of positive individual savings." Since the loanable funds theory covered all types of credit instruments, especially claims or interest-bearing securities, it did not require a single interest rate. Each supply and demand, with its attendant risks and terms, determined its own yield. Moreover, the theory was valid either for stock or flow approaches, although it favored the latter for a given time period. Demanders were listed as new investors, consumers, and those desiring to build up balances. Suppliers were newly created money, those who dishoard, and savers.

Ohlin emphasized that the willingness to make financial investments depended on changes in production, incomes, and planned savings. Changes in all markets or price systems, including the commodity market, were relevant for determining the combination of interest rates. Interest was equally a real and a monetary phenomenon as was indicated in Wicksell's treatment of the natural and money rates of interest. The loanable funds theory presented only a partial equilibrium system, as prices and income were given. As such, it did not invalidate Keynes' liquidity-preference formulation in determining the rate of interest.

Frank Ramsey (1903-30), an English wunderkind, wrote brilliant studies in philosophy, mathematics, and economics. His two papers on economics were edited by his friend Keynes who rated one of them, *A Mathematical Theory of Saving*, "one of the most remarkable contributions to mathematical economics ever made, both in respect of the intrinsic importance and difficulty of its subject [and] the power and elegance of the technical methods employed . . ." Ramsey's model followed Frank Knight, an American economist, in that the determination of the rate of interest at a given time was unrelated to time preference or the rate of investment. It was completely determined by the existing stock of capital goods referenced to the marginal product of capital.

Ramsey's approach differed from Keynes and the loanable funds theory. Keynes directly related the investment rate of return to the rate of occurring investment. Investors then would attempt to align the rate of return to the market interest rate, which was determined elsewhere, by modifying their investment efforts. The loanable funds construct simultaneously determined the interest and investment (saving) rates, and this interest rate uniquely indicated the equality of the marginal rate of return of investment and the marginal rate of time preference. Despite the differences, all three models implied that the rate of interest would align with the marginal rate of investment in equilibrium. Ramsey's analysis also concluded that saving did not depend on the interest rate, unless this actually was zero. It was demand for consumption in the future that motivated saving, but this intention could be seen as partaking of time preference.

Summary of the monetary-oriented economists. The return to money interest analysis did not mean abruptly abandoning the treatment of real interest. The achievement of greater productivity by the prolonged utilization of capital goods was extensively acknowledged. Interest, however, was largely disassociated from profit. Also, a distinction was made between old capital and ongoing or new capital. The former, being scarcer and in use longer, produced more value than the latter. Real interest came from this difference. Its rate derived from the marginal productivities and equilibrated the demand and supply for newly created physical capital. The money rate, which equilibrated loan demand and savings supply, followed the real rate like a shadow, but this trend could be disrupted by bank credit operations or by variations in the real rate based on expectations of real profit.

The break from interest as secured from capital goods or their services was strengthened. Interest increasingly became a matter of purely subjective time preference. Capital was interpreted as the money value of net business assets. It was not an aggregation of various goods. Neither was it a self-perpetuating fund, since the market value of such a fund was subject to fluctuations. It was the result of accounting that separated goods for immediate and future satisfaction. Time preference produced surplus value, because the original prices of capital goods would not equal their future marginal values, but would approximate their discounted values. The prices of the finished consumer goods would surpass the prices of the factors of production.

Additionally, the idea of time in relation to capital was repeated, but in a different vein. Time brought changes. The capital stock was affected by new investment and altered allocations. The remedy to this instability was to posit a fixed income stream from existing capital and prospective investments. This income stream was maximized by assuring that any rate of product increase of some input units by each extension of the production period was greater than the rate of decrease of other units due to any shortening of the production period. With the marginal output increase rendered the same for all inputs relative to the total product, the internal rate of return of these inputs should then equal the prevailing interest rate. Given the invariable income stream, changes in the interest rate would require input-output adjustments.

The logic that interest was primarily a monetary phenomenon was boosted by the appearance of the liquidity preference theory of money. Interest was not a net return from capital goods. It was the reward for parting with cash. Current liquidity possessed a premium over deferred liquidity. The marginal efficiency of (cash) money depended largely on the supply of money. People had three motives for holding cash—for transactions, contingencies, and investment. The lower the interest rate, the lower was the cost of keeping money for the first two motives, although this relationship was not too responsive to the rate. The third motive was more elastic to the level of the interest rate.

The crossing of these three demand motives as consolidated into one statistical curve, given the stock of money, marked the equilibrium interest rate of the money market. The demand for money and the joint magnitudes of saving and investment comprised another set of relationships affecting the interest rate. The intersection between the demand for money and the scale of saving-investment, when set against national income, showed an equilibrium interest rate for the total economy (money and goods markets).

Business investment proceeded from the premise that value was not attributed directly to capital goods, but to the series of yields over their lifetime that exceeded their supply or replacement price. The prospective annual returns of the investment were capitalized at the market rate of interest to find the value of the capital goods. As long as this value surpassed their cost, it would pay to invest. In effect, the rate of return over cost, designated as the marginal efficiency of capital, matched the rate of discount. The sum of the yearly returns had to yield a return above cost, that is, the sum involved a discount, depreciation, and risk insurance. This relationship of investment and the interest rate was the investment demand schedule. Investment would grow to the point where the marginal efficiency of capital equaled the market interest rate.

Previous statements of the classical and neoclassical economists about the credit market, as opposed to the money market or to saving, were also formalized in a new major interest theory. The theory essentially based the determination of the interest rate on the demand for and supply of loanable funds. Credit was a flow concept, while money was a stock concept. The interest rate was the price of credit. The supply of new credit was defined as increased asset claims minus reduced asset holdings of individuals. The demand for this credit was the total of new claims minus the reduction in old claims. Since there were multiple types of credit instruments, various rates equilibrated their respective demand and supply. Movement in these rates was also affected by developments in the real sector, such as production, income, spending, and prices in the various markets.

Chapter 12

ACROSS THE ATLANTIC

In the independent United States, early ideas about interest were fragmentary. Benjamin Franklin (1706-90), acknowledged polymath and one of the Founding Fathers of the country, in a pamphlet on currency in 1729, echoed the English views of his time. He affirmed that a too little quantity of money raised interest rates and cheapens land. Franklin displayed a strong affinity with the capitalist ethic and the value of missed gainful opportunities. Money deserved esteem. It gave rise to profit. "Remember," he enjoined, "that time is money . . . . Remember, that credit is money. If a man lets his money lie in my hands after it is due, he gives me the interest, or so much of as I can make of it during that time."

More fundamentally, Franklin reverted to Aristotelian vocabulary, writing that money was not sterile: "Remember, that money is of the prolific, generating nature. Money can beget money, and its offspring can beget more, and so on. Five shillings turned is six, turned again it is seven and three pence, and so on, till it becomes a hundred pounds." Admittedly, this statement was not a direct reference to money lending or the interest rate, despite its apparent indication of a goodly earnings percentage. Its context alluded to man's industry as opposed to idleness and being a spendthrift. But it contained some theory by denying the barrenness of money.

William Douglas (c1691-1752), a Scotsman who settled in Boston, was a physician of versatile talent and a pamphleteer. His study of

British plantation currencies together with his belief that expansion of money did not reduce interest rates, but raised them instead, led him to distinguish two rates of interest in connection with purchasing power. He was perhaps the first formally to do so. He foreshadowed the expansive analysis of interest rates done by Irving Fisher, a fellow American, particularly in connection with inflation.

Douglas identified a nominal rate, which was a measure based on paper money, and a real rate denominated in silver coin. If paper currency were to easily increase, it would depreciate against coin money, since it was not convertible to coin. The value of paper-currency loans would accordingly decline relative to loans based on coin. Lenders of the former loans would ask for a premium to fully offset the difference. As Douglas wrote: "The quantity of paper credit sinks the value of the principal, and the lender to save himself, is obliged to lay the growing loss of the principal, upon the interest." In short, the nominal rate equaled the real rate plus the foreseen inflation rate. The nominal rate fully adjusted for inflation resulting from the overmuch issue of paper currency. Thus it neutralized the real income effects on both sides of the credit market.

Another Scottish-born settler in Boston from 1821 was John Rae (1796-1872), a respectable classical scholar and mathematician. Although not trained in economics, he published a book in 1834 that was frequently quoted by Mill and known by Senior. The book contained what has been considered an insightful and forward-looking theory of capital, with ideas resembling time preference, abstinence, and roundabout production.

Rae held that in the estimation of men "the actual presence of the immediate object of desire" endowed it with greater benefit than the same object to be surely realized in the future. The desire of society to save was measured "by the length of the period, to which the inclination of its members to yield up a present good, for the purpose of producing the double of it at the expiration of that period, will extend." Rae suggested that the rate of interest determined the total amount of waiting supplied. He also said that "lengthening" the production process would typically increase the physical quantity of the final products.

Henry Charles Carey (1793-1879) was a wealthy publisher and later in life an economist-sociologist of some repute. In his *Principles of*

Social Science published in 1858, he presented an analysis of interest not through abstractions, but through pictorial vignettes. Because of their simplistic nature, they portrayed, more clearly than anywhere else, the common confusion with gross and net returns, whose distinction was essential to a deeper perception of the nature of interest.

Carey used the characters in *Robinson Crusoe* as his example. Robinson offered to lend his canoe to Friday, saying "Working without the help of my canoe, you will scarcely . . . obtain the food required for the preservation of life; whereas with it, you will, with half your time, take as many fish as will supply us both. Give me three-fourths of all you take and you shall have the remainder for your services." The capital good here obviously caused a productive surplus or profit for which Robinson quoted a price. Carey identified this price, which was for a gross use (or hire) of capital, with interest.

Carey positively connected the amount of interest with the high or low value of real capital. Robinson would have demanded a bigger share if he was lending a motorboat. Value was determined by the cost of producing a good. Since capital goods progressively cost less to make (required labor input decreases) as an economy developed, their prices would drop and the rate of profit or interest would decline even as the absolute amount of profit increased. In other words, the proportion of the product that went to the capitalist diminished, while that to the laborer grew. This scenario governing capital and interest became the "great law" of Carey. It was illustrated by the loan of an ax. The man who lent the first ax in a primitive society could demand more wood in recompense than one who lent an ax in much later times when reproducing axes cost less. A point would be reached when the laborer's proportional share would exceed that of the capitalist.

To prove his proposition of capital's declining share, Carey then made the facile shift from discussing interest to explaining the rate of interest. He cited the steady historical decline of interest rates—from Brutus in Rome lending at 50%, to Henry VIII's cap of 10%, and to the 4% in contemporary England. The confusing (and questionable) transition arose from Carey's first referring the term "proportion" to the price of capital (the hire) as related to the total return obtained by labor with the use of capital and, subsequently, as the relation to the value of the capital. The former percentage would be much higher than the latter. It was not clear which ratio Carey was identifying as the rate of interest. The latter would be the correct calculation of the interest rate, but, rising too rapidly as the capital value fell, would have been an unrealistic choice. Moreover, the ratio would be contrary to Carey's initial depiction.

Henry George (1839-97), a journalist turned economist, was cognizant of the classical triad of factors of production. Total product was equal to total income, which consisted of rent plus wages plus interest. However, George did not consider that wages and interest depended on the produce of labor and capital, but upon what was left after rent was removed. This residual concept held true even in cases of rent-free land or the poorest land. Rent was imputed if actually absent. The behavior of rent constrained wages and interest. A century later than Quesnay, George's context for economic activity was still primarily agricultural.

Francis Amasa Walker (1840-97), was a Civil War veteran, supervisor of the censuses of 1870 and 1880, Yale University professor, and president of the Massachusetts Institute of Technology. He was apparently well acquainted with the views of the English economists, especially their concern with the relation of the interest rate to land, the quantity of money, and national prosperity. Walker held that rents tended to rise and interest to fall as wealth increased. But he admonished that rent and interest must not be treated together. Rent was analogous to profit (of capital). Profit did enter into the price of a product or reduced wages. The price of a good was determined by its (highest) cost. Walker believed that all capital bore the same rate of interest, except for differences in risk.

John Bates Clark (1847-1938) was known as the dean of American economists, a graduate student of Knies in Heidelberg, professor at several prestigious American universities, and the last to discover marginal analysis independently. He reformulated the concept of capital in 1885 along with "certain leading principles of economic science."

Clark found ambiguous the conventional understanding that mixed two ideas—capital in terms of money or value and of concrete goods. He acknowledged that capital was real individual goods, even including land and natural agents, but he extracted from this collection of productive power a second notion of capital, that is, a permanent fund of value or "pure capital" or "social capital" as he called it. Clark did not formally give this abstraction of productive power (Knies regarded capital as "fundamentally nothing but a mere abstraction") a monetary or value definition, but conceived it as still composed of physical entities. He likened it to a waterfall, which, although consisting of vanishing drops of water, maintained its static existence. Similarly, capital goods could wear out (and be replaced), but the same pure capital remained, a "single entity" embodying everything common in all real capital.

This concept was analogous to capital as contained in business financial statements. In this way, Clark sought to establish capital as a lasting factor of production deserving of a permanent net yield. Concrete goods earned rent. Pure capital earned interest. This analysis, applied in tandem to labor working land and capital, led Clark to often use the word rent for interest. He virtually generalized the income from all capital goods as a rental sum in place of a percentage. Capitalization of this income stream would show the size of the pure capital fund.

"One law," Clark averred, "governs wages and interest—the law of final productivity." Clark detailed this law of final productivity in various marginal ways. It was "the rate that the market puts on the final unit of the supply of [labor or capital] . . . and . . . on the entire supply." Or: "No increment of capital can get for its owner more than the last increment produces . . ." or, "no form of capital can claim and get for its owners in a year a larger fraction of its cost than the least productive form produces." If this law was otherwise, an entrepreneur would refuse to borrow. "Final" did not necessarily mean the last, but either the average or the least productive.

Clark represented "the law of interest by the process of building up, increment by increment, the fund of social capital and of measuring the product produced by each unit of it . . . [so that] the addition to the product caused by the last unit of capital fixes the rate of interest." Clark separated "the rent of the fund of social capital" from the wages component of production. Interest could be fixed by the law of final productivity, resulting in wages being a surplus. The reverse could also be said, so that "all interest is thus a surplus, entirely akin to the rent of land . . . . [and] it is a concrete product, attributable to the agent that claims it as an income." In this alternative approach, the surplus could be loosely considered a residual "left in the hands of the entrepreneur." But the entrepreneur would be forced to pay the capitalist (and the laborer as well) what the law of the final productivity of capital (and labor) has directly determined. After his interest and wage payments, the entrepreneur, in subsequent marketing, may or may not be left with "pure profit," which would be true "residual income." Such profit also could be realized by the undervaluation of labor or capital or both.

Clark hung his theory of wealth (income) distribution on the productivity peg. Capital was productive; thus interest existed. "Paying interest," Clark explained, "is buying the product of capital, as paying wages is buying the product of labor." Wages, interest, and profit were equitable. They were a law that society had to follow, because "the law itself is universal and hence natural." Productivity theory postulated that "the different classes of men who combine their forces in industry have no grievances against each other." In addition to the yield on capital, Clark was the first to formally assign a return for technical, commercial, and managerial factors. This was profit conceived as a surplus over interest, rent, and wages. Clark also perceived the stock of capital growing faster than the supply of labor. As a result, the interest rate would tend to decline.

There was, lastly, a psychological element in the theory of interest. Like previous economists, Clark said that interest provided a motive for abstinence, which not only led to new capital goods, but also maintained the existence of past goods. The valuation of pure capital rested on this present generative abstinence or sacrifice, rather than on the anticipation of future use. As for interest rates, Clark presented a two-rate analysis similar to that of Douglas. He considered the real loan rate as constant.

Frank William Taussig (1859-1940) had a long economics professorship at Harvard University interrupted by a brief stint as the Tariff Commission Administrator. He has been characterized as the American Alfred Marshall for the classical and neoclassical traits of his teaching. He began his explanation of capital in his *Principle of Economics* book first appearing in 1911 with a lucid recapitulation of previous teaching: "Some writers have distinguished between 'capital' and 'capital goods.' By the latter term they mean the concrete apparatus of production . . . . But by the word 'capital' alone these writers mean the value of the concrete apparatus; and they sometimes speak as if there were a sort of distillation or essence of capital, distinct from the tangible capital goods in which it is embodied."

Taussig validated "capital" interpreted alone, by asserting that "the only measurable element common to all forms (of capital) is that they have value and price, and the only way of reaching a quantitative statement as to the whole is in terms of value and price. But it is not to be supposed that there is any such thing as capital distinct from the capital goods. The only . . . existent thing is the concrete apparatus of production. Its value and price is merely a relation to other things, a mode of measuring it."

Taussig then referred the cause of this value to the productivity of capital, guardedly expressed in the language of Ricardo: "This consequence has . . . been stated by saying that capital is productive; a phrase which must be used with care. The strictly accurate statement is that labor applied in some ways is more productive than labor applied in other ways. Tools and machinery . . . are themselves made by labor, and represent an intermediate stage in the application of labor. Capital as such is not an independent factor in production, and there is no separate productiveness of capital." Taussig cautioned that the productivity of capital must be "taken as expressing concisely the result of the capitalistic application of labor." This "production with capital" evoked Bohm-Bawerk's "indirect or roundabout method of production." In addition, Taussig appeared to suggest that capital was in a sense the wage fund of the classical economists, that is, advances for command over labor.

After clarifying "these questions of terminology," Taussig proceeded to ask why interest, "expressed in terms of a percentage paid each year," was demanded and willingly paid. He made it clear that "what the borrower wants is not the money itself, but that command over commodities and services which money buys . . . . for his own immediate use or for use in operations of production." The explanation of interest therefore was "not to be found in the use of money, but in the nature of the operation which it facilitates . . . . Interest, then, appears as the result of an act of exchange by which a quantity of money (or commodities) now in hand, is given for a greater quantity of money (or commodities) to be returned in the future." While not completely forgetting the importance of the time element, Taussig thus found the reason for the borrower's readiness to pay in excess of the principal debt by analyzing the "conditions of his demand" as a producer.

The conditions were, first, production was "spread over time," which increased the productivity of labor in accordance with Bohm-Bawerk's thesis. Second, capitalists were a separate class: "The persons who do the saving and possess the surplus are commonly . . . a different set from those who do the labor." These double conditions—"labor applied in roundabout ways and [the process of] surpluses saved"—created interest and capital, respectively. "The long-maintained application of labor in successive steps," Taussig explained, "is possible only if at the outset there has been a surplus—if there has been saving and accumulation." He pointed out, as Quesnay did, that "all the operations of capitalists resolve themselves into a succession of advances to laborers." As a result, "the laborers as a whole produce more than they receive. Those who borrow and then hire the laborers can afford to pay back more than they borrowed."

On the supply side of the credit transaction, savers, looking at the rate of interest, also faced certain conditions. First, long-run "competition will bring the return in all channels of investment to the same level." Second, this uniform level depended on the degree of labor productiveness caused by the capital stock. This meant that "the gain, or premium, or interest, which the owners of capital will secure, will be determined by the least productive use of capital; or, to be quite accurate in language, by the addition to the ultimate product of labor which results from the least effective phase of the roundabout or capital-using process . . . . It is the effectiveness of the last installment of capital (last in the order of productiveness) that determines the rate of gain for all capital. Or . . . in other words, the return to capital depends on the marginal productivity."

Taussig faithfully reiterated the statements of Clark and the marginalists. The least productive constituent of capital was what would be first relinquished in production if compelled by, say, management rationalization. Thus, the "bank rate of interest oscillates above and below what may be called the true rate of interest—the return on steady investments." The rate of interest did not "depend on the quantity of money. More money makes higher prices, not lower interest." With this statement, Taussig literally anticipated the soon-to-emerge monetarist school.

Like previous theorists, Taussig admitted that changes in the level of the interest rate affected the amount of saving, particularly marginal saving. But he doubted the universal necessity of interest for saving to occur, but he did not mention the functional role of income. Taussig also added an afterthought determinant of the interest rate arising from the division of gain and from basic supply and demand: "The larger the number of first-rate managers, and the smaller the supply of present means, the more likely is it that the savers will get the lion's share, and rates of interest tend to be high; with the opposite results if savers are many and managers scarce."

Irving Fisher (1867-1947) was granted Yale University's first doctorate degree in economics in 1891 where he later became a professor. A mathematician turned economist, he invented the rolling card index that made him a millionaire. He ran up a fortune of approximately $9 million in the stock market and lost it all in the 1929 crash. (Keynes also suffered financial losses at this time and received support from his father.) Fisher stated that the return on capital goods was not interest, but more like quasi-rent, since such goods were fixed in the short run. He thus reflected the thinking of Thornton and Marshall. His major books on interest were *The Rate of Interest* and *The Theory of Interest*, published in 1907 and 1930, respectively. In the dedication to the latter work, he paid tribute to John Rae and Bohm-Bawerk "who laid the foundations upon which I have endeavored to build."

Fisher's theory of interest rested on two main ideas, namely, time preference and investment opportunities, which were subjective and objective elements, respectively. Fisher considered time preference "the central fact in the theory of interest." He also called it "impatience," which he thought was "a fundamental attribute of human nature." He therefore labeled his doctrine "the impatience and opportunity" theory. However, Fisher correctly realized that time preference had been recognized in one form or another as far back as the scholastic period, so that he claimed originality largely on his investment concept.

Like Bohm-Bawerk, Fisher alluded to the brevity and uncertainty of life as reason for time preference. His exposition of time preference began with the assumption of an individual's flow of income from his work or property within a time frame of one year, The income, however, was conceived as realized at a point of time. The current income flow was related to income expected exactly a year later. The individual thus confronted various combinations of present and future incomes, ranging from an equal mix to combinations favoring more or less of one of either incomes. If the individual chose 110 units of future income and 100 units of present income, then his time preference was 10%. The degree to which the individual selected to exchange present for future income and vice versa was his marginal time preference.

This intertemporal allocation of income, however, was only one side of time preference. The individual could lend or borrow to modify claims to present and future income. Assumed rates of interest would result in specific income combinations for him. To lend or to borrow would depend on his marginal time preference and the given rate of interest. The rule was that both should be equal. The aggregation of these individual choices (credit demand and supply) gave society's time preference, which in turn influenced the market rate of interest. At equilibrium, the marginal time preference of every individual equaled the market interest rate. The rate of time preference therefore was determined mainly by an individual's income "as to its size, time-shape, and probability."

Other factors also influenced this determination: tastes, investment possibilities, credit terms, and even shortsightedness. But positive time preference would always tend to be the outcome. Fisher treated time preference as the purchase and sale of future incomes and the price being the interest rate. "Thus, the rate of interest," he concluded, "is the common market rate of preference for present over future income. Those who, having a high rate of preference, strive to acquire more present income at the cost of future income, tend to raise the rate of interest. These are the borrowers, the spenders, the sellers of property yielding remote income, such as bonds and stocks. On the other hand, those who, having a low rate of preference, strive to acquire more future income at the cost of present income, tend to lower the rate of interest. These are the lenders, the savers, the investors."

Fisher did not formally incorporate risk or uncertainty in his time preference model. The income stream and the one-period interest rates were anticipated with perfect foresight. The capital market was presumed to be efficient. However, he recognized the effect of future price changes. He sought to identify the real interest rate by bringing in expected inflation: "We have found evidence . . . that price changes do, generally and perceptibly, affect the interest rate in the direction indicated by a priori theory." Later research showed that this positive association, known as the Fisherian effect, was about one-to-one. The nominal interest rate would go up 1% for every 1% rise in prices. The inflation-adjusted nominal rate was crucial for the decisions of lenders and borrowers.

Like other economists, Fisher suspected the real rate to be more or less constant. To control prices, he relied on the management of the money supply, whereas Wicksell saw the interest rate as the adjustment mechanism for monetary conditions. Fisher's exposition of the nominal-real interest rate relationship was considered at the time as culminating analysis on the subject. He held that expected inflation would push the market or nominal interest rate upward. Past and current inflation bred expectations of higher prices. To compensate for the loss of future purchasing power, financial investors would demand an interest premium, while borrowers would accommodate this premium anticipating repayment in cheaper money.

Fisher visualized the nominal interest rate, plus an adjustment for the inflation rate, as the real rate. He thought this adjustment to be full and instantaneous on the premise of complete foresight of price trends. But later evidence indicated the adjustment to be insufficient and lagged due to imperfect estimation of the actual inflation rate. The result was a modified real rate. The real rate inversely moved with the nominal rate and could be negative in periods of spiking inflation. Lastly, price expectations were not only imperfect, but unequal. Business borrowers were better forecasters than lenders, so that demand for (cheap) loans would rise in the early stage until the "sticky" nominal rates were brought in line with actual inflation. This interlude of expected windfall profits was part of Fisher's explanation of trade cycles.

For the second leg of his interest theory, Fisher linked time preference to the process of investment. Investment meant favoring future over present income. The larger the present income sacrificed, the greater was next year's income. Investment would be carried out until what Fisher called the "marginal rate of return over cost" (Keynes' marginal efficiency of capital) was equal to the market rate of interest (and the marginal rate of time preference). Figuring the marginal rate of return over cost (in producing capital goods) essentially involved a rate for discounting a series of expected yields. Fisher said "that rate, which employed in computing the present worth of all the costs and the present worth of all the returns, will make these two equal." Arithmetically, this equilibrium was future value minus present value divided by present value.

To foster new investment, "the rate of return over cost must exceed the rate of interest" and the marginal rate of time preference. Otherwise, the growth of investment would cease. Fisher was not clear if he included equities in his treatment of investment. However, their inclusion as equivalents to real investment would not be inappropriate in terms of the individual. Fisher construed investment as business capital in money terms and, like Keynes, interest earning as a percentage of a principal sum. "The rate of interest," Fisher wrote, "is a ratio and the two things which it connects are both sums of money." This standard idea of interest meant a strict reference to liquid capital or readily disposable purchasing power, since "the resources of an individual are in the form of general purchasing power."

Fisher knew that "in a world of chance and sudden changes," other factors could affect the desired investment interest rate. He mentioned risk and the importance of liquidity of investments. "Salability," he cautioned, "is a safeguard against contingencies which make selling advisable . . . . For this reason, the rate of interest on individual mortgages will be higher than the rate of interest on more marketable securities . . . . The most salable of all properties is, of course, money . . . . The convenience of surely being able . . . to dispose of it for any exchange . . . is itself a sufficient return upon the capital which a man seems to keep idle in money form. This liquidity of our cash balance takes the place of any rate of interest in the ordinary sense of the word." Time preference, after all, could be understood as individuals allocating their consumption over time in the best manner, given their patterns of income and cash positions. Thus, Fisher distinguished between interest and rent. The owner of capital "earns an income," while the entrepreneur "pays a cost [rent]." Interest as percentages of a principal sum could be applied only to liquid assets, that is, to purchasing power readily available. Physical capital was not purchasing power.

In summary, if a person preferred to exchange a unit of consumption in the future for one in the present, that person exhibited a positive time preference. If time preference existed, then it was essential for the emergence of a positive interest rate. From another perspective, interest was the occurrence of an excess value in final consumer goods over the value paid to the factors of production. Bohm-Bawerk and Fisher were in agreement in the proposition that prospective wants and needs were usually valued less than they were in the present. Fisher, however, had a broader, if not all-encompassing, understanding of interest.

Fisher believed that "distribution has been erroneously defined as the division of the income of society into interest, rent, wages, and profits." Interest was not an income share, but a certain conception of every kind of income. Every agent of production received a stream of income that can be capitalized. When the agent related his prospective income to the capitalized value as a percentage, he could think of interest, so that "interest is not a part, but the whole of income." This universal nature of interest was a meaningful leap from Smith's interest is profit and profit is interest. But it was a quantum jump from the pure labor theory of value. It virtually supplanted the assertion that all income was to be thought of as wages in one form or another.

Joseph Schumpeter (1883-1950) was an Austrian-American economist and a long-time professor at Harvard University. He characterized his theory of interest as monetary. He asserted that "it is impossible to pierce the money veil . . . . If one penetrates through it one penetrates into a void." The money form "is not shell but kernel."

Schumpeter saw no problems in the emergence of interest even in a static economy. In consumption loans, for example, interest was evident as long as there was an individual caught in unforeseen difficulties or an individual seeking increased income in the future who valued money on hand to money in the future. Government loans also fitted this category where interest payments were taken for granted.

Schumpeter considered commercial loans—"the payment made by the entrepreneur to the capitalist for the use of purchasing power"—to be more challenging to analyze. The entrepreneur borrowed and wanted to pay interest, because he aimed to make profits from the acquisition of capital goods. But how could interest, which was a permanent income flow, come from profits, which were variable and temporary? Schumpeter's answer was that, while profits were earned from specific goods, interest was earned from "liquid purchasing power." The use of this power could flow from one source of profit to another in a growing economy. Interest therefore was not identical with profits or "adhered to concrete goods." Interest was a tax. It was a transfer from profits to the capitalist.

For the supply of loanable funds, Schumpeter introduced saving in the form of reinvestment of profits. In his interest theory, economic development was a vital element. It provided the dynamic solution to the dilemma posed by perfect competition theories that the full value of consumer products should be ascribed back to the original factors of production, namely, land and labor, leaving no allocation for interest. Perfect competition was a static equilibrium system that hardly prevailed in the real world. Instead "the number of innovations is practically unlimited . . . . Every step forward opens new prospects . . . . Consequently the demand for productive loan funds with interest at zero would always be greater than the supply, which is always limited." Excess demand would push the interest rate above zero. But the prices of factors would not go up to blunt the process of excess value, because previous utilization determined those prices and not prospective uses. The inadequacy of this dynamic solution, understood as theoretical and not empirical, was that continuous qualitative innovation or disequilibrium, not just growth or extension of the existing capital structure, was required for the existence of interest. Schumpeter's theory needed some integration with other theories, especially time preference.

Frank Knight (1885-1972) was a professor at the University of Chicago. He founded monetarism, the school of thought which was commonly positioned opposite Keynesianism. But like Keynes, he demarcated the monetary and real aspects of interest. He wrote: "Even in an entrepreneurial economy using money, the relation between capital and its yield, or between rent and interest, has no essential connection with the borrowing and lending of money . . . . If the role of capital in a situation without exchange or lending is understood, the explanation of the market value of sources, and of the yield as an annual rate per cent of their value, will present no difficulty."

Knight understood capital in an extremely broad and aggregated sense—any source of productive power, that is, land and labor besides capital goods. Every capital good yields a return, which was its rental. A capital good has value solely by its being a source of a flow of services and hence of a perpetual stream of income. The individual owning any productive power would want to maximize the return from its use. Savers had this revenue or income stream in mind. Knight wrote that "all that any individual or any society can do is to save and invest, or disinvest, as the case may be, up to that point at which his preference of present over future goods is measured by the rate of return." This yield rate was the ratio between the yearly income from the perpetuity and the sum or cost invested in the source.

Faced with numerous investment opportunities, an individual attempted to equalize the present value of future returns with the cost of investment for each of these opportunities. He then chose the most profitable investment, which is the one that offered the highest rate of internal return. This best return represented the productivity of capital at the margin. It was the rate that would eventually pervade throughout a perfectly competitive and maximizing economy. Fundamentally, this would "make the marginal productivity of capital the causal determinant of the interest rate" to which savers would tend to align their marginal time preference. In the real world, however, the rate of saving would also be an important determinant, particularly if the demand for capital is quite inelastic in relation to the interest rate.

Knight explained this optimum return at length in 1941: "The rate of return on 'capital' is the maximum perpetual income obtainable under the given conditions, through the creation of a new source of income, or the maintenance of old sources, measured as a rate per unit of time, divided by the aggregate present consumption sacrificed in making any such investment. An 'investment' is . . . to be understood as an increment of investment, made or maintained at the margin for the total productive plant of an economy." The value of the marginal product depended on its price, which was determined by demand ("tastes and purchasing power of the buying public"). As in Wicksell, the rate of interest, however, had to be based on the stock of capital existing at a single point of time, not on the smaller flow or rate of current investment as in Keynes, since interest at a given time originated from the productivity of the existing stock of capital and not from time preference.

Over a longer period, diminishing returns on capital would cause the interest rate to very slowly fall. But Knight observed in 1944 that "if all productive agents can be freely augmented by the use of all those which already exist, there will not be diminishing returns, for, if the growth of investment leads to progressive satiation of wants, it will affect in the same way the cost and the yield and consequently will not affect the rate." Capital formation would be infinite. Wants would constantly change. The economy would never be stationary. Knight had a metaphor for capital. It was the "Crusonia" plant—a type of vegetation that required no attention and met all human wants, but ceaselessly grew at a geometric pace "except as new tissue is cut away for consumption."

Knight provided a second version of his interest theory, because he believed that his first presentation of equality between the present value of the stream of future income and the cost of the best investment was inadequate. He reasoned: "Equality does not prove causality, still less show the direction of causality. To deal with this problem, it is necessary to consider the rate of return, or the valuation of income sources, in the usual terms of value or price theory, in the terms of demand and supply." Knight developed the solution in two ways by regarding either the rate of interest (perpetual income stated as a percentage of the capital) as the price of the capital or the capital as the price of the perpetual income. The first method showed the customary view of a demand curve for capital sloping downward to the right as larger quantities of capital supplied progressively lowered the intersection or equilibrium points with interest rates, indicating diminishing returns of increasing investments. Knight attributed the diminishing returns not to capital, but to "the diminishing utility [on the margin] of total economic income to the individual." He added, however, that technology could positively alter the productivity of capital.

The second method—capital as the price of the perpetual income—considered future income as the commodity demanded. Its price was the present value of such income or, alternatively, of the market value of the income's sources (capital goods). The supply of perpetual income depended on the cost of producing it or, identically, of producing the capital goods. Knight figured the cost as moderately decreasing, so that the supply curve represented in a graph tended slightly downward. The volume of available saving stood for the demand side represented by a vertical line, since saving was assumed as constant in the short run. As saving grew, advancing the vertical line rightward, the intersection of demand and supply would occur at progressively lower interest-rate points. If ever capital goods became free goods, Knight theorized that the interest rate would drop to zero.

According to Knight, the constant enlargement of the capital stock, which is characteristic of a capitalist economy, presumed abstinence, not waiting, because new capital was supposed to last. In fact, the decision to save evaluated "large, short segments of income flow with thinner streams reaching out to the indefinite future." Investors usually did not think of disinvesting. Abstinence would have to be "continuously incurred" for old and new investment. Interest was long-term normal profit.

Frank Fetter (1863-1949) was a moderately known exponent of the Austrian school of economics in the United States and a professor at Cornell, Indiana, Stanford, and Princeton universities. From 1900 to 1927, he attempted to inject unity and consistency he found wanting in the theorems of income distribution. He objected to certain prevailing explanations of capital, interest, and rent. Given that the prices of the factors of production are determined by their marginal productivity in producing consumer goods, that is, every capital good earns a rent, Fetter asked, reprising Schumpeter's problem, "why the market price of the machine . . . is not bid high enough to equal the sum of expected future rents . . . . why there [is] a net return to the investor."

To identify the source of extra income for interest, Fetter replaced the usual answer given in terms of the capital good's productivity (the reason for its rent) with the basis for discounting. "Rents are discounted to get the present capitalized value of the factor" due to the principle of time preference. In this sense, interest was a future rental or, more specifically, a rate or ratio "between future earnings and present price or payment." Accordingly, Fetter disagreed with Clark that capital was a permanent fund of value, in which production (output and input) was synchronized, thus removing the time dimension.

Fetter upheld a difference between rent and interest. Rent was the marginal productivity of scarce factors of production. Interest was the present valuation of future services. Fetter declared that interest theory "must set in their true relation the theory of rent as the income from the use of goods in any given period, and interest as the agio or discount on goods of whatever sort [wheat was one analog of Keynes], when compared throughout successive periods." Thus, all factors of production could be treated in a standardized manner as "yielding uses and "bearers of rent" or as "salable at their present worth . . . as discounted sum of rents (wealth or capital)." Interest from capital goods came from the latter method.

Fetter declared that the market rate of interest for loans revealed the economy's general rate of time preference. Conceptually, however, capitalization preceded the existence of the loan money rate. The capitalization rate reflects the long-run normal or natural profit rate for businesses. If the supply of present goods were to increase, their marginal utility would decrease relative to future goods. Time preference would tend to fall and the interest rate would drop. Fetter's insistence on pure time preference to explain interest had the merit of being applicable not only to production loans, but to consumer loans as well.

Milton Friedman (1912-2006), was a professor at the University of Chicago, Nobel Prize winner in 1976, laissez-faire believer, and the foremost advocate of the monetarist school of thought. He owed much to the work of Fisher. He reversed the simple inverse association of interest rates with the supply of money. Instead, he cited empirical evidence indicating that a rapidly increasing quantity of money, while hiking prices as usual, also raised interest rates. To explain this "paradox," Friedman offered three sets of effects: the liquidity effect, the income effect, and the price anticipations effect. The liquidity effect followed the conventional view of the larger the quantity of money, the lower the interest rate. This happened because monetary authorities typically expand money supply by increasing bank reserves, which lead to heightened loan capabilities. In addition, if the higher prices induced by the monetary expansion were not anticipated or slow in occurring, people would adjust their portfolios, that is, unload excess cash holdings and bid up the price of securities, thus depressing interest rates.

The income effect worked in the opposite direction. Rapid money growth would raise nominal income, tending to increase spending. Rising business demand for loanable funds would force interest rates up. In addition, the higher income would require bigger liquid balances which required higher interest rates to induce people to hold money. In fact, the upward trend of interest rates could overshoot the equilibrium level in the short run. The third effect also dictated interest rates to rise. Anticipation of continued high prices would increase the cost of keeping cash. Real balances kept would tend to be lower and the circulation (velocity) of money would increase. Inflation would exert an additional upward pressure on nominal interest rates. Friedman's analysis of the response of interest rates to accelerated money growth concluded thus: "an initial decline, a subsequent rise and an ultimate attainment of a level higher than the initial one." The initial decline lasted about six months and the return to the initial level about eighteen months. Full adjustment took longer for long rates than for short rates.

Summary of the American economists. Early American thought on interest was cursory. But it contained kernels of received theory, namely, the fecundity of capital, mercantilist rate determination by the quantity of money and by the risk factor, likeness to rent, and profit as a residual. Lengthier explanations did not take long to appear. There were descriptions of time preference, roundabout production, and the productive function of capital. Interest was identified with gross gain, much as European analysis did at the same time. As an economy developed, capital goods became cheaper to manufacture. The cost of their hire was reduced, and the share of labor relative to capital in the total return increased as a result.

The turn of the century saw American analysis attempting to refine and amalgamate the nearly completed body of interest theory achieved so far and to develop a few relatively new ideas. The critical dichotomy of capital as money and as physical goods was reexamined. This led to the abstraction of capital into a fund of value generating income. The lasting quality (durability) of capital's pure (inherent) productive power was what earned a yield or interest. In contrast, rent was due concrete goods, but since this rule equally applied to all capital goods, interest was also taken as a rental sum (not a percentage) capable of being capitalized. The size of the return followed the principle of marginal productivity, which fixed the rate of interest. Interest was separated from wages, so that interest was part of the residual profit. A descriptive definition of interest was as a purchase of the product of capital.

Additional conclusions were reached, some of which were paraphrases. A return for entrepreneurial work was named as added surplus value. Increased availability of capital, which came from continued abstinence, would lower the rate of interest. The quantification of capital could only be done by a common measure, that is, by its value and price. The productivity of capital, qualified with the application of labor, was repeated as the source of value. Interest was paid not for the use of money, but for the profitable operations from what the money could buy.

A definition to push analysis forward also emerged. Interest resulted from an exchange of commodities (or money) in hand to more commodities (or money) in the future. There were two reasons behind the future outcome of more commodities (or money). First, the businessman and the saver were distinct classes. The former engaged in spreading production over time resulting in larger output due to the extended application of labor. The latter undertook the task of creating advances resulting in increased capital and making possible the successive hiring of labor. Labor produced more than it received. Second, the resulting profit depended on the marginal labor-capital productivity, meaning the least productive utilization of capital. The true rate of interest, around which bank rates oscillated, reflected this least productive constituent of capital. But productivity, dependent on the acuity of entrepreneurs, typically surpassed this minimum level. With the new definition of interest, rate determination by the quantity of money was disregarded, and marginal savings influenced by the interest rate was acknowledged.

Most important in the development of American interest theory was the definitive presentation of the positive time preference theorem. The return on capital goods was interpreted as quasi-rent instead of interest. Interest was primarily placed on subjective time preference or impatience and secondarily on objective investment opportunities. Time preference was described as an individual's choice relative to present and future income in a year's time frame. The individual could mix present and future income in combinations that suited his desires. This would give the rate of his marginal time preference. In addition, the individual could lend or borrow to modify his income, in order to equalize his marginal time preference and the prevailing rate of interest. The aggregation of the individual time preferences into society's as a whole determined the market rate of interest. Those who weighted present income more than future income tended to raise this rate. The opposite group, the frugal, lowered it. The time preference theory was essentially psychological and individual. It ultimately came down to a person's allocation of consumption.

As for investment, interpreted as favoring future over present income, business capital was estimated in money terms. Interest was similarly reckoned. Investment occurred as long as the market interest rate equaled the marginal rate of return over cost. The equalization of costs and returns involved the discounting of a series of expected yields showing the income stream with the highest present value. This desired investment rate, which should pervade in a competitive economy, was also influenced by conditions of risk and the degree of liquidity of investments.

The determination of the interest rate in the time preference theory was shown in two ways using supply and demand statistical curves. In the first method, the curve of the demand for capital sloped downward to the right as larger quantities of capital supplied progressively lowered the intersection or equilibrium point with interest rates. This indicated the diminishing marginal utility of total economic income to the individual. In the second method, the maximum future income was the commodity demanded. Demand was represented by the volume of available saving. The supply curve of perpetual income depended on the cost of producing it or, identically, of producing capital goods. As saving grew, the intersection of demand and supply would occur at progressively lower interest rates. Abstinence would have to be continuously practiced to sustain old, and to grow, new investment.

Interest was finally explained solely on the basis of time preference. Productivity as the source of return on capital was discarded. Capital goods did earn a rent from their marginal production of consumer goods. But this rental sum (the price of the capital good) was not high enough to account for a net return to the investor. The needed extra income was generated by discounting the rent to its present capitalized value, which was time preference in effect. Interest was future rental in a broad sense or, specifically, a rate or ratio between future earnings and present price or payment. Rent was income for use in a given period. Interest was comparative income over successive periods.

The insistence on pure time preference to explain interest via discounting made the theorem applicable not only to production loans, but to consumer loans as well. A constant influence on the interest rate was also brought to the fore. This was the behavior of prices. The real value of money or purchasing power should be kept equal at both term ends of a loan. The nominal rate had to appropriately incorporate expected inflation (or deflation). It should become equal to the real rate plus the rate of inflation. Inflation was typically unanticipated, and the pace of adjustment of the interest rate to the actual price level was usually lagged. The delay opened a window of advantage to borrowers in real terms. In the case of commercial loans, it induced borrowing in light of brighter profit expectations. Such demand contributed to trade cycles. Ultimately, the interest rate would adjust fully to the inflation rate.

PART SIX

ANALYTICAL OVERVIEW: TWO THEORIES

Chapter 13

THE NATURE OF INTEREST

What is interest? Can economic analysis stop at merely declaring that it is a payment (universally agreed to) without describing what it pays for and what forms it takes? Whence and how does it originate? Is it restricted to borrowing and lending? After centuries of progressive inquiry, conclusive responses to these questions are possible, but they are complex. It must be realized at the outset that the analysis of interest, which is fundamentally a search for value, is done at two levels—real and monetary. There is real (imbedded and proceeding from real things) interest and money (nominal) interest. The difficulty is evident in how early economic studies went back and forth between the two. Today, the distinction still is often misunderstood, if not unknown.

At the start of this book, interest was defined as the payment for the use of money. This conventional definition is inadequate. To say that the nature of interest is a payment and to stop there is true, but it also begs the question. What kind of payment and for what remain unanswered. Moreover, further explanations cannot be generalities. They need to be clarified and detailed, perforce in an eclectic and integrative manner, given the voluminous and varied theories of interest constructed through the centuries.

The "use of money" specification of the payment's purpose indicates that interest may originate from use. Use can be variously interpreted. Is it use absolutely, pure use, an abstraction (use-ness residing in a piece of paper)? One hardly pays for an abstraction. It is difficult to regard an abstraction as intrinsically having material value. Hence, at best, a real power or function must be assigned to the word "use," so that it evolves into "usefulness." Use then becomes the embodiment of some kind of service or utility.

Money has been called the "merchant's tool." What is the service of money, assuming money loans? The economic definition of money is itself functional as Aristotle wrote. Money serves as a medium of exchange. Still, interest cannot be identified with money as such. Interest directly is not, or is paid for, the service of exchange. Interest still hangs in the air.

However, money does exchange for commodities—goods and labor. It possesses purchasing power that endows it with value. It enables the transition from the monetary to the real economy. This capability provided an early path to tentatively establish the nature of interest. Classical economics shifted from scholasticism's chief focus on money contracts, particularly high-interest (usurious) consumption loans. The business sector offered a fertile field for unearthing the source of interest. Commercial loans are principally incurred to purchase capital goods and real estate property. Goods are "borrowed," not currency. Many economists call capital "business advances."

Capital is variously categorized. There is capital in a physical sense. From an individual's viewpoint in the 17th century, it is one's "store of economic objects" or "one's substance." It is "anything valuable," "article of wealth," "saved goods," and "movable wealth" of "accumulated values." It is defined in a substratum sense as "gifts of land" or stored-up labor, since all capital is sometimes seen as having its ultimate origin either in land's fertility or the work of labor. It is also designated as that "part of a [person's] stock from which he expects to derive income."

With the development of industry, physical capital increasingly becomes a stock limited to directly productive items, such as machinery and tools, but may include structures, inventories of semi-finished goods and raw material, and sometimes even consumption goods for the upkeep of labor or land. Capital ranges from the primitive fishing canoe to multi-tasking computers. But it may even be restricted to goods that exclusively manufacture other producer goods. However construed and aggregated, capital goods become "the complex of intermediate products" with varying durability appearing in the stages of production. (The intermediate products are sometimes seen as unfinished consumption goods, since consumer goods are the final object of production.)

This "mass" conception of capital is enabled as corporations increasingly assume ownership of capital as tangible assets. Since their use produces both durable and consumption goods, their productivity is patent. Material output is the fact-of-life outcome of their operations. The physical productivity of capital goods with its positive return emerges as an obvious reason for interest, whether in cases where the capitalist and the entrepreneur are identical and earn all the income or the businessman is financed by borrowed funds. Thus, the analysis of interest advances from exchange to the use of the productive goods secured.

The use of capital goods results in production. Economists adopted a number of approaches to define interest from this truism. The residual interpretation, introduced by classical economics, follows the expected business process. Sales exceed costs. Gain is realized after the sum of costs is deducted from total revenue. To consider interest as coming from this residual is reasonable. Interest is lodged in the profit, either all or part of it. Thus, the nature of interest may be expressed in this way: interest is profit and vice versa. Both are the results of capital productivity.

Is the profit referred to gross or net? The question is not trivial. Important theorists in the past overlooked the issue. If the costs are comprised solely of labor expenses (wages), then interest is easily found in gross profit. However, capital disbursements (acquisition, depreciation, replacement) can absorb the rest of gross profit, leaving no proper room for interest. The situation amounts, as it were, to paying back only the principal. To simply claim, therefore, that interest is intrinsically business profit is deficient. The value of produced goods by a given outlay of capital must be greater than the total costs. If they are equal, gross profit is the outcome. The difference between the value of the capital goods and the value of the goods they produce must have a larger margin. There must be net profit. Common experience shows that increased value typically arises from the production process over and above gross margin.

The desired profit outcome is reflected in the observable difference between the rate of profit and the rate of interest. The latter, set in the money market, is typically lower than the former, even if the profit is considered "normal." If the profit is generated from wholly owned funds of the entrepreneur, it can be broadly construed as interest (sometimes called "originary" interest, more conventionally "implicit" interest). This interest may be found in gross profit.

If all or a portion of the capital is borrowed, that is, when the capitalist does not participate in the production process, but gives his money for a fixed compensation for temporary use, the compensation is called "contract" or "explicit" interest. This type of interest is sourced in net profit. However, accounting reckons interest paid for borrowed financing as a cost for deduction (like taxes) to arrive at net profit. Hence, loan interest does not have to be ascribed to accounting "net profit." In fact, from the lender's viewpoint, interest is not an economic cost, but income originating from the net profit (value created) of the business.

The use or operation of capital goods in relation to describing the productivity theory of interest resurrected the tendency to abstract usefulness. Usefulness is concretized as itself a raw entity existing in capital goods. It is durable and harbors exchange value compressed from past inputs of valuable labor and capital. It finds expression in the German noun *Nutzung*, which conveys the notions of utilization and revenue. It commands the payment of interest. This so-called use theory of interest attempts to give the conventional definition of interest a real specification. But the enhancement may be unsatisfactory. Interest becomes payment for use (in goods).

Productivity theorists were tempted likewise to grant abstract existence to productivity. The extent of their abstraction ranges from assigning a productivity substantially apart from capital goods to one resident in capital goods. The latter reference to capital goods consists as conveyance of their capacity or potential, that is, of their value. However, the validity of this type of productivity approach provides vague support to stating that interest is payment for or buys productivity. The definition is awkward, as if productivity is picked off a shelf. The deeper issue confronting the economists is to sensibly explain why and how production expands not just value, but value to pay for interest. Interest cannot have an incomplete rationale.

The postulated enlarged output of production is traced to a characteristic of capital-intensive operations. Physical capital, which by their nature lasts for a long time, makes a lengthier period of production possible. The employment of a sizable and variegated amount of intermediate goods, typically in successive stages, stretches the duration of production or, equivalently, the utilization of time-consuming methods. Drinking water, for example, can be secured by a cupped hand or from a faucet following the extended construction of a modern waterworks system. This roundabout technical process results in increased output on the average, allowing ample leeway for excess value. The more capital goods used, the greater the output. The longer the period, the scarcer, and hence more valuable, capital becomes. Besides scarcity, capital goods are said to embody the conglomerated use of previous economic goods, including land use. This is stored up value that compounds current product value.

Two distinct, but related, meanings can be given capital productivity. A stock of capital assets is productive, because only a portion of its services is needed to maintain and replace that stock. With such costs met, an excess of services remains. Part of the income generated sources interest. The other meaning says that part of the excess is not consumed, but reinvested to build more capital assets, which would further increase the excess potential. Unsatisfied with the "it undeniably happens" evidence for excess productivity, some economists add the ultimate reason for it in the growth of knowledge, invention, and technology. But these explain interest only indirectly.

The centrality of excess or surplus value brings up a supplementary economic theory, which antedates the formal scrutiny of interest. It is the endeavor to define value and to discover its origin. It concludes that labor creates all value in goods. The assertion of labor's contribution to production resonates throughout the development of interest theory and is never denied. For example, the application of human industry to borrowed money is often used to prove that money is not barren, but bears fruit. The fecundity helps prove that interest is deserved and moral. The issue comes down to the degree of labor's participation. Is it behind all or part of gross and net returns?

The answer rests on the interpretation of original source. There is current and past labor in the making of all economic goods. Labor is embedded in capital goods. A conclusion of socialism is that profit and interest are ultimately wage values channeled away from labor. Labor always produces a net return or surplus value, because it works more than its due. In effect, labor sells itself below cost. Their price is merely the cost of its subsistence.

The exclusive assignment of value to labor activity is disputed by examining the resources and results of the production process. Financial capital is advanced for maintaining labor in the interval between the start and end of production. Such advances enable a longer production period, resulting in more output. Moreover, the output of labor working alone is different from output generated with the use of capital goods. Production with their aid typically results in either larger quantities or better quality or both. Fishing by hand is less efficient than fishing with a trawler.

No less important, the quantitative and qualitative gains include the realization of new goods that labor by itself could not manufacture—"beyond the reach of the personal exertion of man to accomplish." Capital goods substitute for labor, operate longer hours, and utilize improved technology. They uniquely harness the natural powers of land and man. Pure labor is unable to account for the resulting total product. There is a distinct value proceeding from capital goods that passes on to final goods. As has been stated: "It is nonsense that labor created capital. Capital was produced by capital and labor working together. Capital is as old as labor."

The distribution of income develops another old supplementary tenet employed to define the nature of interest. If the use of capital goods is productive, is this not similar to the cultivation of land? It appears to be so, and the use of capital goods, which are fixed in the short run, may be construed as rent. The return on capital is "rentals of particular machines, derived from the demand price for commodities which they could help to produce."

The rent of capital goods is qualified as quasi-rent. This designation maintains the distinction between capital and land, thus preserving them as independent factors of production with their respective earnings. The economics goes beyond nomenclature if interest is identified with rent. Objections arise. For one, interest is a percentage of a certain amount, while rent, like wages, is commonly an absolute sum. Interest has essential relative aspects of wealth and capital. Also, excess value could be seen as amounting only to gross return if interest is a rental (hire for use), with the capitalist merely lending his "material" to be worked on by labor and receiving replacement payments. As for personal consumption loans, rental has limited relevance. The interest for money borrowed to buy food is hardly a rental payment. Defining interest as rent is easily controverted.

The realization of excess value is lastly attributed to external elements. The alternative theory, which reverts back to humans, is persuasive, namely, that additional increased value arises from final product pricing. The selling price of goods, calculated by managers with marketing expertise, achieves comfortable margins. Ultimately, buyers, with their subjective estimations of utility, pay the interest bill. This market-oriented view, however does not deny, the independent productivity of capital goods. Capital goods cause with their own contribution the existence of final products. Product prices handed down to buyers are partly determined in relation to the prices of utilized capital.

The recourse to marketing activity is further amplified. It can be interpreted as either reinforcing or replacing the capital productivity argument for interest. Entire value is again assigned to a single concept, namely, utility. The satisfaction of wants and needs is imputed to goods by consumers and businessmen. Utility is a highly individual and subjective estimation. It is conditioned by different times and places. This variability allows product prices to be flexible and to realize excess value (net profit) that arguably is not necessarily a deduction from wages.

The presence of utility in commodities causes individuals to want to buy them, rationally seeking the maximum utility as measured in the last unit. Utility theory acts like scissors in forming value in goods. Individuals act on the demand side, and capital goods constitute the supply side. Nevertheless, like the rigid notions of use, usefulness, and service, utility has the image of a universal idea. The sense of appearing semi-abstract is a theoretical, but not fatal, weakness. The definition "interest is payment for utility" cedes only priority in time to "interest is payment for purchasing goods."

Nonetheless, utility reasonably fulfills the payment-for-value requirement of interest. In fact, the external entitlements to interest validated in ancient Rome and medieval Europe on the basis of damage incurred or profit lost were transformed to designate loss of utility. Utility is also ascribed to, even substituted for, the use of capital goods. Capital goods are defined as "every durable foundation of utility which has exchange value." Thus, utility favorably compares with previous explanations of interest. Interest was first linked to the goods acquired, then to capital goods secured, then to their use, followed by their service, then to their productivity, next to profit realized, and finally to net profit. All of these prescriptions mainly involve commercial credit. Utility offers a more comprehensive rationale. It is applicable to consumer loans as well.

Utility with its individual characteristic leads to another major description of interest that is based also on personal psychology. Introduced prior to the utility doctrine and thereafter long propagated by many economists, the abstinence theory of interest transfers attention to the role of savers (lenders) of money. The theory endows abstinence with value and deserving of compensation. Abstinence is defined in several ways. One is that it means postponement or delay of the satisfaction of utility. It goes to the extent of foregone consumption spending by the capitalist. The act of abstaining is even seen as the simultaneous creation of utility in the capital goods resulting from the investment of savings. The time lag of utility is erased.

The economic argument for the direct value of abstinence lies in the worth of a human endeavor. Abstinence involves an effort of the will to endure prolonged privation, to forbear immediate enjoyment, to be frugal, in a word to sacrifice. It is therefore extended labor whose psychic cost has been called disutility. As labor, abstinence qualifies to be a vital factor of production. It works to fabricate new capital goods and maintain old ones and thus to make profit. Like the treatment of labor's production cost, "wages" are due abstinence. Abstinence is the labor of saving. This special service transforms money into *rentier* wealth. "Waiting" has been the word intermittently preferred for abstinence, because the deprivation is not permanent, though considered perennial in the context of the habit of saving. Increased prosperity is expected sometime in the future. In any case, interest is payment for abstinence. Interest is a reward, recompense, or restitution for hardship undertaken.

The formation of capital, psychological aspects, and temporal parameters connected with abstinence constitute an appropriate transition to the relatively recent, and probably final, analysis of the nature of interest. Known as the time preference theory, its formal model has substantial roots in the legacies of previous thinking and was technically elaborated only in the 20th century. It is analysis essentially on the monetary level. Interest is viewed as having to do with money, not goods or profit from production. Money is borrowed and not goods. Money is paid. The switch from physical to money capital is held to be the proper way for analyzing interest.

Moving from the real to the monetary aspect of interest, the concept of capital undergoes a change. Capital is now understood as a fund of wealth, a financial sum, an estimate, or a (market) value. Capital is "economic wealth whose quantity is expressed in a general value unit" at an instant of time. It is a stock as opposed to a flow of income. As wealth, capital can be conceived broadly. It shades into so-called social capital, which in turn can mean national wealth. However, with regard to interest, capital is delimited. It must be bounded by features of productive employment and income generation.

Capital is any economic good "held for the purpose of gaining wealth." Capital is acquisitive; it is investable wealth. It is an investment fund denominated in currency. It is defined by some theorists as self-perpetuating, a permanent fund yielding perpetual fruit. It is a passive abstraction if named as "effective social utility" nor a "fund of wages." Rather it conforms to the usage of the business world. Capital is the total amount of money tied up in the firm, a monetary value that can include intangibles like patents and goodwill. A refined definition would be net business assets.

Nevertheless, it should be acknowledged that for one school of economic thought, the changeover to financial capital does not vitiate the argument regarding interest originating from the productive use of real capital and the resulting enlargement of value. The money measurement of capital merely veils the underlying composite of capital goods, which alone can be deemed to have material existence. Interest remains as a payment, albeit monetary, for the acquisition and use of, or command over, the means of production.

A look at business credit transactions makes this connection obvious. One lends money to an enterprise expecting a profit at a fixed interest rate which is presumably drawn from the firm's consequent return. Even to invoke the realization of surplus value through the selling price fails to avoid reverting to the goods produced. At the very least, physical productivity can be accepted as one of the factors explaining the origin of money interest and justifying its payment.

The group of monetary-oriented economists that considers the connection of capital goods with interest to be superfluous resembles the medieval thinkers intent on the money loan contract. They firmly regard interest to be unlike rent, which is due from concrete goods. Interest "is not derived from . . . anything that has . . . to do with the net return from capital goods." Interest is "the percentage excess of a sum of money contracted for future delivery." Lending's closest link to the physical world consists only in the loss of purchasing power or of command over resources. Lending with interest is likened to barter. It is simply an exchange—money for money of an agreeable higher sum. Specifically, interest is a reward for not hoarding money. Interest is the inducement for parting with liquidity.

Behind the reluctance to relinquish cash are accepted economic dicta. Money has efficiency. It is demanded for day-to-day transactions, meeting contingencies, and investment speculation. Amounts remaining for the last motivation will be invested in securities (loaned) as long as the price (interest) is right. If capital goods are to be brought into the discussion, they are interpreted in terms of having a yield over the course of their life in excess of their original (replacement) cost. Evaluating this income stream requires an interest rate calculated against a fixed magnitude.

The demand for liquidity is germane to the positive time preference theory. Like the need for liquidity, the existence of time preference is undoubted. It is considered "a fundamental attribute of human nature." People are impatient. If given a choice, they would select to be given a dollar today than tomorrow. They prefer the present to the future, a bird in hand than one in the bush. In other words, they place more value on the present use of goods than on their future use, on present than on future consumption, and on present than on future utility. (Analogically, capital goods are current goods temporarily given up for the satisfaction of future goods.)

People choose present income to expected income. Waiting is disliked, but it is precisely part of the essence of lending. Talmudic law describes interest as the "wages of waiting." Money today is exchanged for money tomorrow, for instance, a year later. But time preference does not merely involve tenses. It has a quantitative element—the expectation of more income and consumption in the future. Interest is therefore equivalent to the difference between what is paid for to obtain or consume goods today (current value) as opposed to their cheaper price tomorrow (future value).

The doctrine of time preference is structured on the individual with given wealth endowments, faced with choosing between present and future incomes within a definite time frame. The individual decides on a certain mix out of a whole range of combinations of the two types of income. In addition, he can modify his endowment position by lending or borrowing money to arrive at a desired trade-off point that represents maximum satisfaction. A lender decides to forego some consumption now if this will allow him to increase his consumption bundle later (greater endowment). The lender augments future income by interest earned, while lessening present resources. On the other hand, the borrower undertakes the opposite substitution pattern. He pays interest for increasing money on hand by acquiring cheaper future money. Firms follow similar intertemporal procedures (saving-investment choice) in terms of output.

The interest rate is clearly a decisive element in the exercise of time preference that involves lending and borrowing. It is the price at a certain future date of a dollar secured now. Rates must meet endowment and budget conditions. The magnitude of time preference is the ratio of the amount lent to the larger amount to be received in the future.

The aggregation of the time preferences of individuals is society's time preference. Social time preference is known as the consumption rate of interest, which is a community's weighting of consumption on the margin.

The arithmetic of the comparison of present and future values is present value discounting. The method brings a future sum in line with a present sum by discounting the former, that is, by finding the current value of the sum due after the lapse of a designated period. The actual loan amount will be smaller than the total future payment. The difference is the interest premium. The size of the difference is dependent on the rate of interest. Interest must be a recognition of the higher worth of present money, assuming the absence of price inflation.

Since the yield or return of business capital is a percentage per unit of time (not a rental sum) applied to the total money value of all capital assets of an enterprise, the intertemporal logic of the time preference theory is basically valid for business investment. However, the net present value computation, which corresponds to determining the internal rate of return, instead of discounting a single amount available in the future, discounts expected net return in the form of an income stream or a series of free cash receipts. The business cost incurred today is compared with the present value of this future inflow of revenue. An interest rate, whether the market rate or an arbitrary one, is essential to this computation.

Hence, this capitalization of business assets hinges on a suitable interest rate reflecting the opportunity cost of the capital (the minimum rate of return or the rate of an alternative riskless investment plus a risk premium). The level of the rate will decide whether to go ahead or not with an investment project or to select one from several ventures. The assumption, in relation to interest theory, is always the realization of a net gain. The net gain allows a place for interest, properly speaking, for any credit secured.

The feasibility of a venture (the highest present value chosen) is associated with, but not dependent on, individual time preferences. The level of the capitalization rate influences the willingness of individuals to part with liquidity and to invest. In addition, a business net return revealed by discounting reestablishes the net productivity of real capital as a rational origin of interest.

The studies on the nature of interest are replete with different theorems. The degree of their divergence and convergence, of their filiation and cross-pollination, relies on the latitude of interpretation. A number of theories can be discarded, such as interest is a tax deduction on the earnings of laborers. Others require lengthy amplification. For example, the old external titles for interest are twice removed unless elaborated to connect with productivity and profit. A few have been weakened by modern practices. Although likely default, delay, and variability risk influence the fixing of (higher) interest rates, they and other forms of loss and damage are nowadays also recompensed by separate or subsequent penalties.

Missed business opportunities are too vague and impractical criteria for interest. Not only must the creditor be a bona fide merchant, but the prospective success of the business has to be guaranteed. At most, the title to profit foregone only makes the general statement that money is potentially fecund. The risk of incurring damage still merits coverage, but it becomes academic when loans are withheld on account of doubtful creditworthiness. Risks for questionable borrowers also may be covered by collateral. In the last analysis, any provision of added interest for risk does not explain the intrinsic nature of interest. A lender still charges other interest on the loan. Interest is charged even on a riskless loan. As a rule, interest theorists seek to probe pure interest, that is, without extraneous factors such as risk.

Several theories meld into an accepted principal doctrine that explains real or natural (as contrasted with monetary) interest. The core tenet of the synthesized doctrine is the net productivity of capital goods. Abstinence is an appendage here, because it contributes to the formation of capital. The use and services theories are likewise adjuncts as long as they incorporate the productive operations of capital goods and are not taken in abstract isolation. The roundabout theory is very pertinent. It details the production process, and it relates its extended periods of production to abstinence and the time preference theories. The residual profit theory recognizes the enlarged output of capital goods. Finally, the relevance of the utility theory may be accepted by its imputation of value to capital and consumer goods.

All the preceding theories can serve as partial definitions of interest to varying degrees. They are, however, subsumed in the conclusive identification of the nature of interest as the productivity of capital that generates a surplus value. The exclusive labor theory of interest is excluded, except perhaps in an ideological, moral, or ontological sense. Capital and labor both contribute to the manufacture of intermediate and final goods. Besides, the overriding consensus is that interest, whether as a cost or income, is peculiar to real or monetary capital. Interest is not unqualified payment for labor.

The other principal doctrine is the positive time preference theorem. It competes with the productivity theory in explaining the nature of interest. Most economists regard it as a superior, if not the conclusive, answer to the interest inquiry. The definition derived from the productivity of capital goods and the profit outcome is arguably more of a finding in the search for the origin of interest than for its nature. To predicate interest as payment for a share of business profit can be truthfully restated as interest is business profit.

Some of the other theories can be associated with time preference. Abstinence as waiting involves withholding on the present and anticipating the future. Roundabout production stretches the period between the use of present goods and the later realization of final products. The utility theory offers an ultimate criterion for those engaging in intertemporal choice.

The second fundamental definition of the nature of interest thus rests on the proposition that a difference exists between present money and future money. The former has more value than the latter. One would opt to be given one thousand dollars now than two after a year. The foregoing of present income creates the differential that must be paid for later. Time is of the essence. Interest then can be defined formally as payment for time. This economic definition is highly acceptable, because it has universal applicability. Unlike the capital productivity theory, time preference is not confined to commercial credit. It provides the reason for interest on consumption loans, indeed for any type of lending. It is present whether grain is lent or currency.

The two leading definitions of interest separately account for real and money (nominal or market) interest. Typically, interest means the latter, a monetary claim. As a result, the metamorphosis or monetization of the real concepts generated by meticulous theoretical research is not convoluted. The net productivity of capital-profit theory are initially expressed as surplus value, but later discussed in money terms in reference to the price of capital goods, the rate of return, and the belief that surplus value is realized in the market prices of the final products. The imputed valuation of utility is reflected in sale prices. More significant, capital is redefined as a fund of financial value and the yield of invested capital is understood as a series of cash receipts. Discounting such sums to their present value is monetary evaluation.

The liquidity preference theory is straight-forward demand for money. Its precise concern is retention and disposal of cash holdings that represent a store of value. In a similar vein, the time preference theory presents the framework of individual income endowments for either lending or borrowing, which entails a trade-off between present and future money units. These monetary expressions indicate the nature of (nominal) interest. It is an excess sum of money, that is, it is a percentage of a separate principal amount, regardless of the nature of the loan. The money is either a share of business net revenue or remuneration for the loss in selecting distant income for near money.

The centuries-long continuum of scholarly examination of interest fluctuated between non-monetary and monetary approaches. Some dealt with the short run, for example, medieval consumption loans, and others looked at the long run, investment credit for instance. Cognizance of the analytical reasoning invites a review of the common definition of interest as payment for the use of money. The definition can be accepted as true. But it leaves much unsaid. A summary explanation can fill the void.

A creditor earns and a borrower pays interest, because what is lent and borrowed embodies value. Firstly, it produces goods worth more than they cost so the profit margin provides for and justifies the interest payment. Secondly, interest is earned, because the creditor gives up current (immediate satisfaction of wants) income for increased income later. Thus, a single definition for interest suffices. Interest is payment for either created value or exchanged time or both. For now, the latter has the favor of economists. Interest is payment for time.

A quasi-epilogue is an insight proferred by the author of the time preference theory. Commenting on the allocation of income into wages, rent, profit, and interest, he thought interest should not be considered as a share of divisible total income. Interest instead is a manner of conceiving all types of income. The argument may or may not be persuasive. Every income stream received by economic agents can be capitalized. When expected income is related to the capitalized value as a percentage, the idea of interest is evoked. The whole income and not part of it can be understood as interest. Thus, interest is all income and all income is interest. This sweeping identification of the nature of interest is rock-bottom definition.

Chapter 14

THE RATE OF INTEREST

Mathematically, an interest rate is a pure number. It is a ratio in which the numerator and the denominator are specified in identical units, in this case, currency units. The rate of interest (percent per year) is the price of money. This is clearly brought out in the liquidity preference theory. The rate of interest dissuades or persuades the owner of money to dishoard cash assets. In other words, the price must be right.

In terms of positive time preference, the interest rate is a measurement of the rate at which individuals wish to exchange present wealth endowments (income or goods and services) for those in the future. The underlying premise is that the present has more worth than the future. Assuming zero inflation and a yearly market interest rate of 5%, a loaf of bread eaten today is prized 1.2 times more than a loaf of bread eaten tomorrow. A premium needs to be paid to overcome the higher cost of the earlier consumption. An increase in the interest rate means that the cost of present consumption further rises relative to future consumption. Thus, the interest rate (either actual or anticipated), being options over time and a positive magnitude, partly determines the saving (refraining from consumption) and investment decisions of people.

Translated to the financial markets, the interest rate is the price of credit or of the exchange for a currency unit today for another tomorrow. But there is nothing in the financial market like "the" interest rate. Participants in the capital, credit, and money markets are heterogeneous.

There is a whole spectrum of credit products and of interest rates, just as there are different prices for even similar goods. For instance, the rates are different for a fifteen-year and a thirty-year mortgage.

Two conditions essentially cause the differentiated structure of rates. One is the term to maturity, and the second is risk of all types, such as the likelihood of default. Other features are influential too, such as taxation, calls, rights, and coupon size in the case of securities. However, interest rates are basically classified into two types. There is the nominal rate and the real rate.

The nominal rate hardly requires explanation. It is in everyday usage. It is the market or money rate, that is, yield measured in prevailing currency. It is the published rates of financial institutions. It is written into credit contracts. It "refers to the premium on a unit of a monetary claim compared to a unit of monetary claim in the future." It is "the number of dollars per dollar after maintaining the dollar amount of capital intact."

There is a multiplicity of nominal rates, since they are subject to market forces. Competition, size and term, debtor creditworthiness, regulation, and other factors shape the final level. Also, banks follow the principal rate settings of the central banking authority. The rates are a major tool of monetary policy. The Bank of England wielded tremendous power with its Bank Rate. An American study in 2010 in the wake of the recent financial crisis showed that variations in the rates across a range of credit markets followed a change in the federal funds rate. However, most rates in the market tend to congregate over time at a certain level, depending on the type of credit. Mortgage rates, for instance, are more or less uniform in the banking industry. An equilibrium force is always present reacting to demand-supply conditions.

The nominal rate cannot be negative, since the cost of holding money or the permanent stream of income that money wealth represents is basically zero. Zero lies above any negative rate. However, in certain rare instances of securities trading, negative nominal interest rates may briefly emerge.

The real rate, sometimes called the natural rate because value is based on material entities in nature (more specifically, on the marginal physical productivity of capital), is the return on funds measured in terms of goods and services. Formally defined, it is "the premium on a unit of a commodity or real consumption income today compared to a unit of the commodity or real consumption income in the future." It is "the number of dollars per dollar after maintaining the *real* amount of capital intact." The perspective is that real things are being lent, not paper money, and real things of equal value are expected in return for the goods foregone.

As a footnote, in academic macroeconomics, the terms market and natural rates of interest were formally introduced in 1898. The market rate "denotes the actual value of the real rate of interest," and the natural rate is the equilibrium rate of this market rate. Equilibrium refers to the coordinated balance between household saving and business investment and between supply and demand in the credit market.

The behavior of commodity prices, therefore, is pivotal. The onset of inflation may (and almost always does) jeopardize the prescribed quantitative equivalence, since the purchasing power of future money is lessened. Adjustment must be made for higher prices. Hence, the real rate is the nominal rate corrected for expected inflation. It is the nominal rate minus the rate of inflation. In an economy with constant prices, the nominal and real rates are the same. Basic economic theory often assumes an inflation-less context to simplify analysis. Nominal rates are usually sticky in responding to rising prices, so that it is a not a neutral measure of real value.

The underlying idea of the real rate is partially illustrated by the so-called own rate of interest used in economics. For every commodity, a rate of interest can be assigned in terms of itself. For example, if a quantity of wheat amounting to 110 bushels is to be delivered a year later, and this amount has the same exchange value for 100 bushels for spot delivery today, then the wheat rate of interest is 10%. Borrowing wheat, like borrowing money, is really buying a spot claim and selling a future claim on wheat. The own rate of wheat and other own rates can be transformed into a common standard of measure, for example, into the money rate by the use of an adjustment factor. All rates are fundamentally equal in equilibrium when estimated in the same units or single standard, whether that standard be money, food, or clothing. Money as the standard happens to be customary and convenient.

At times a distinction is made in the real rate—*ex ante* and *ex post*. The *ex ante* rate is the expected rate of real return to be earned or paid. It weighs heavily in saving-investment decisions. It is always positive, because lending will not willingly be made for a negative yield, and credit market competition would remove such an outcome. The *ex post* rate is the actual return realized. Thus, it can be zero or above or below zero. A negative real rate means an unexpected transfer of wealth from lenders to borrowers.

A most important theoretical point about the interest rate is that it plays a triple role. It can be the determinant or the determined or both discretely or at the same time. The interest rate in the liquidity preference theory partially guides money holders in choosing to dispose of current liquidity or not, especially in relation to their speculative motivation. In turn, the resulting demand for money in tandem with movements in the supply of money determines the equilibrium interest rate.

In the case of time preference, the income choices of an individual, calculated either in goods or money, exerts some influence, as a supplier or demander of money, on the interest rate, which is the price next year of, for example, a bushel of wheat or of a dollar that is lent this year. At the same time, changes in the interest rate not only shape the decision to maximize income by lending or borrowing, but also how much to lend or borrow. The higher the rate, the more is generally lent and the less borrowed by savers. Matching the lending against the borrowing of all individuals gives us the equilibrium interest rate. Up and down variations of this rate result in the usual demand and supply adjustments of the time patterns of consumption.

In commercial credit, the interest rate is equally potent. It affects both sides of business activity. It is a criterion for saving and investment. The higher the rate, the more inducement there is to save. Saving (sacrificing current consumption) supplies funds for investment (increased future consumption). The resulting stock of capital faces demand for it from productive enterprises that compare their expected rate of return with the cost of borrowing. If the rate of return is higher than the market rate of interest, the investment is undertaken. Otherwise, the investment is postponed or abandoned.

As firms carry out the competitive process of allocating investment, the rate of return and the market rate eventually gravitate to an equilibrium level. The two rates become equal. They are real rates, as inflation is considered absent. Thus, given the current capital stock, the interest rate determines investment, rationing funds to lucrative projects. In the long run, the equilibrium rate drifts downward, as capital is accumulated and diminishing returns reduce the rate of return. In addition, the interplay between the net productivity of capital and household thrift behavior also determines the long-run equilibrium interest rate.

The interest rate figures in the discounting equation for undertaking investments. The commercial agent projects transforming present resources into a future income stream with a view of maximizing a present value. Maximization is calculated at an external appropriate rate of return, which is the going market rate of interest. Similarly, the general market rate of interest is also indispensable in the time preference rationale for interest. It should equal the intertemporal rate of exchange. In fact, the latter is said to give rise to the general market rate.

Another area where the interest rate is a vital element is the credit market. This market handles the supply of and demand for loanable funds. The interest rate is the price of credit. The relationship of the interest rate is no longer focused on the quantity of money as in conventional economics, but on lending and borrowing. Here the interest rate both determines and is determined. Suppliers and demanders of credit refer to existing interest rates when deciding to lend or borrow. The amount of the resulting loanable funds that they plan to bring to market and the need for them will fix the equilibrium interest rate. This reciprocity provides a format for forecasting rates. Such a function is useful, since securities or financial assets can be substituted for loanable funds. To borrow, for example, is to issue bonds, and to lend is to buy them. The relationship between bond prices and interest rates is inverse.

As there are several basic interest rates in the formal financial market, much study and empirical research has been devoted to the behavior of the structure of rates. It is a difficult area to analyze due to its complexity and dynamic nature. The last word about it has yet to be stated, particularly with regard to trading movements. The received doctrine so far indicates a core of elementary principles, greatly abstracted from real world conditions. The simplifying assumptions are lack of uncertainty on the part of investors, absence of risk and institutional rules, and unhindered arbitrage.

Investors are expected to maximize their returns. Their efforts induce an adjustment in security prices, so that the effective net yields for any given term become equal, regardless of term. Demand and supply will force the removal of any differentials among security net returns. The implication is that the yield to maturity of long-term securities will equal the average of the current and anticipated short-term rates over the rest of the life of the securities. If the holding of a string of short-term securities yields more than the holding of a long-term instrument, then arbitrage will operate to approximately remove the difference in the rates. This generalization is consistent with the logic of modern theories of interest rate determination.

This term rate-structure analysis suggests that long and medium rates often move together in the same direction. Occasionally, long rates themselves can move in opposite directions. Short rates also could intermittently move in different directions from each other or from long rates. Most of these movements are the result of dispensing with the simplifications of theory. Factors such as sudden changes in expected future rates (uncertainty), the supply of securities, and liquidity preferences are allowed into the analysis.

Leads and lags also occur in all these trends, typically influenced by business cycles. Long rates usually lead short rates. The yield curve (the relation between bond yields and maturity lengths) is known to be a good statistical predictor of economic activity in general and of recessions in particular. The slope of the curve (upward or flattening) and the spread between the yield curves of long-term and short-term interest rates are the key indicators. The inversion of the yield curve (short-term rates rising above long-term rates) has an especially good record of preceding economic downturns.

In the early 1990s, a modification of the real interest rate was introduced by monetary authorities in the United States. Identified as the neutral real rate of interest, it refers to the condition when the real rate is at a level that "if maintained, would keep the economy at its production potential over time." If the real rate of central bank funds is below the neutral real rate, then policy would have to be expansive, and, if above, policy would be restrictive. However, it is difficult to exactly estimate the neutral real rate, since it is not directly observable, and it also can change.

Somewhat similar to the neutral real rate is the definition of the natural rate expanded in 1898. The natural rate also became that loan rate "which is neutral in respect to commodity prices, and tends neither to raise nor to lower them." The new natural rate is an equilibrium rate too, but it specifically refers to the rate of central bank funds that is consistent with real Gross Domestic Product expanding along its potential in the long run with price stability. Again this rate can change in the wake of changes in macroeconomic supply and demand. It should rise, for example, if budget deficits grow or potential gross product rises.

Clearly, the interest rate is a dynamic economic variable. It is a powerful ally of fiscal policy as well to stimulate an economy or slow it down. It affects choices of temporal patterns, types of assets, and organization of production. Fisher in 1907 summarized the role of the rate of interest this way. It is "not a narrow phenomenon applying only to a few business contracts, but permeates all economic relations . . . . It is the link which binds man to the future and by which he makes all his far-reaching decisions. It enters into the price of securities, land, and capital goods generally, as well as into rent, wages, and the value of all 'interactions.' It affects profoundly the distribution of wealth. In short, upon its accurate adjustment depend the equitable terms of all exchange and distribution."

BIBLIOGRAPHY

Books

Abrahams, Israel. *Jewish Life in the Middle Ages.* New York: Atheneum, 1981.

Ackley, Gardner. *Macroeconomic Theory.* New York: The Macmillan Company, 1961.

Ackley, Gardner. *Macroeconomic Theory and Policy.* New York: Macmillan Publishing Company, 1978.

Angell, Norman. *The Story of Money.* Garden City, New York: Garden City Publishing Company, 1929.

Aristotle and Louise Ropes Loomis (editor). *On Man in the Universe.* Roslyn, New York: Classics Club. 1943.

Arkin, Marcus. *Aspects of Jewish Economic History.* Philadelphia: Jewish Publication Society of America, 1975.

Bacon, Francis. *The Essays.* New York: The Heritage Press, 1944.

Barber, William J. *A History of Economic Thought.* New York: Frederick A. Praeger, 1967.

Barker, Ernest. *The Political Thought of Plato and Aristotle.* New York: Dover Publications Inc., 1959.

Barker, Ernest. *The Politics of Aristotle.* London: Oxford University Press, (reprint) 1946, 1981.

Baron, Salo Wittmeyer. *A Social and Religious History of the Jews, Volume 14.* New York: Columbia University Press, 1969.

Barrow, R.H. *The Romans.* Middlesex, England: Penguin Books, 1984.

Baumol, William. *Economic Theory and Operations Analysis, (4th edition).* Englewood Cliffs, New Jersey: Prentice-Hall Inc., 1977.

Ben-Sasson, H.H. (editor). *A History of the Jewish People*. Cambridge, Massachusetts: Harvard University Press, 1976.

Bieler, Andre. *La Pensee Economique Sociale de Calvin*. Geneva: 1959.

Bohm-Bawerk, Eugen V. *The Positive Theory of Capital*. London: Macmillan and Company, 1891.

Bohm-Bawerk, Eugen V.and William Smart (translator). *Capital and Interest*. New York: Augustus M. Kelley Publishers, (reprint) 1970.

Boker, Ben Zion, (translator). *The Talmud, Selected Writings*. New York: Paulist Press, 1989.

Bonder, Nilton Rabbi. *The Kabbalah of Money*. Boston: Shambhala, 1996.

Boorman, John T. and Thomas M. Havrilesky. *Money Supply, Money Demand, and Macroeconomic Models*. Boston: Allyn and Bacon Inc., 1972.

Bouwsma, William J. *John Calvin: A Sixteenth Century Portrait*. New York: Oxford University Press, 1988.

Brems, Hans. *Inflation, Interest, and Growth*. Lexington, Massachusetts, 1980.

Brunhoff, Suzanne de. *Marx on Money*. New York: Urizen Books, 1973.

Cassel, Gustav. *The Nature and Necessity of Interest*. New York: Kelley and Millman, Inc.,(reprint) 1903, 1957.

Cathcart, Charles D. *Money, Credit, and Economic Activity*. Georgetown, Ontario: Richard D. Irwin Inc., 1982.

Chamberlin, E.R. *The Bad Popes*. New York: Barnes and Noble, 1969.

Chazan, Robert. *Medieval Jewry in Northern France*. Baltimore: John Hopkins University Press, 1973.

Choudhury, Masudul Alam. *Contributions to Islamic Economic Theory*. New York: St. Martin's Press, 1986.

Coats, A.W. *The Classical Economists and Economic Policy*. London: Methuen & Company, 1971.

Cochrane, James L. *Macroeconomics Before Keynes*. Glenview, Illinois: Scott, Foreman and Company, 1970.

Conard, Joseph W. *Introduction to the Theory of Interest*. Berkeley: University of California Press, 1966.

Cole, Charles L. *The Economic Fabric of Society*. New York: Harcourt, Brace & World Inc., 1969.

Copeland, Thomas E. and J. Fred Weston. *Financial Theory and Corporate Policy*. Reading, Massachusetts: Addison-Wesley Publishing Company, 1980.

Davidson, Paul. *Theories of Aggregate Income Distribution*. New Brunswick, New Jersey: Rutgers University Press, 1960.

Dewey, Donald. *Modern Capital Theory*. New York: Columbia University Press, 1965.

Dobb, Maurice. *Theories of Value and Distribution since Adam Smith*. Cambridge: University Press, 1973.

Dodds, J.C. and J.L. Ford. *Expectations, Uncertainty and the Term Structure of Interest Rates*. New York: Barnes and Noble, 1974.

Dougherty, Christopher. *Interest and Profit*. New York: Columbia University Press, 1980.

Duby, Georges. *Rural Economy and Country Life in the Medieval West*. London: Edward Arnold (Publishers) Ltd., 1968.

Eagly, Robert V. *The Structure of Classical Economic Theory*. New York: Oxford University Press, 1974.

Eatwell, John, Murray Milgate, Peter Newman (editors). *Money*. New York: W.W. Norton & Company, 1987, 1989.

Eatwell, John, Murray Milgate, Peter Newman (editors). *Capital Theory*. New York: W.W. Norton & Company, 1990.

Einzig, Paul. *The History of Foreign Exchange*. New York: Saint Martin's Press Inc., 1962.

Engels Frederick. *Engels on Marx's Capital*. Moscow: Cooperative Publishing Society of Foreign Workers in the U.S.S.R., 1936.

Epstein, Isidore. *Judaism*. Middlesex, England: Penguin Books, 1980.

Fairweather, Eugene R. *A Scholastic Miscellany: Anselm to Ockham*. Philadelphia: Westminster Press, 1956.

Feavearyear, Albert. *The Pound Sterling, A History of English Money, (2nd edition)*. Oxford: Calrendon Press, 1963.

Fetter, Frank A. *Capital, Interest, and Rent: Essays in the Theory of Distribution*. Kansas City: Sheed Andrews and McMeel, Inc., 1977.

Finley, M.I. *The Ancient Economy*. London: Chatto and Windus, 1973.

Fischer, Stanley and Rudiger Dornbusch. *Economics*. New York: McGraw-Hill Book Company, 1983.

Fisher, Irving. *The Theory of Interest (reprint)*. New York: Macmillan Co., 1930; New York: Augustus M. Kelley Publishers, (reprint), 1965.

Friedenthal, Richard. *Luther: His Life and Times*. New York: Harcourt Brace Jovanovich Inc., 1967.

Friedman, Milton. *Price Theory*. Chicago: Aldine Publishing Company, 1976.

Feuerwerker, Albert. *State and Society in 18th Century China, The Ch'ing Empire in its Glory*.

Galbraith, John Kenneth. *Economics in Perspectives, A Critical History*. Boston: Houghton Mifflin Company, 1987.

Galbraith, John Kenneth, *Money*. Boston: Houghton Mifflin Company, 1975.

Gies, Joseph and Francis Gies. *Merchants and Moneymen*. New York: Thomas Y. Crowell Company, 1972.

Gordon, Barry. *Economic Analysis before Adam Smith*. New York: Harper and Row Publishers, 1975.

Groseclose, Elgin. *Money and Man*. New York: Frederick Ungar Publishing, 1967.

Gurley, John G. and Edward S. Shaw. *Money in a Theory of Finance*. Washington D.C.: The Brookings Institute, 1960.

Guttentag, Jack M. and Phillip Cagan. *Essays on Interest Rates 2 vols*. New York: NBER, Columbia University Press, 1969.

Hahn, Frank. Money, Growth and Stability. Cambridge, Massachusetts: the MIT Press, 1985.

Haney, Lewis H. *History of Economic Thought. (4th enlarged edition)*. New York: The Macmillan Company, 1949.

Hansen, Alvin H. *A Guide to Keynes*. New York: McGraw-Hill Book Company, 1953.

Harrington, Wilfred J. *Key to the Bible, 2 vols*. Garden City, New York: Image Books, 1974.

Harrod, Roy. *Economic Dynamics*. London: Macmillan, St. Martin's Press, 1973.

Harrod, Roy. *Money*. London: Macmillan, 1969.

Havrilesky, Thomas M. and John T. Boorman. *Monetary Macro-Economics*. Arlington Heights, Illinois: Harian Davidson Inc., 1978.

Hayek, Friedrick A. *The Pure Theory of Capital*. London: Macmillan and Company, 1941.

Hayek, Friedrick A and Roy McCloughry (editor). *Money, Capital, and Fluctuations: Early Essays*. Chicago: The University of Chicago Press, 1984.

Hazlitt, Henry. *The Failure of the New Economics*. New Rochelle, New York: Arlington House, 1978.

Heer, Friedrich. *The Medieval World*. New York: New American Library, 1962.

Homer, Sidney. *A History of Interest Rates*. (*2nd edition*). New Brunswick, New Jersey: Rutgers University Press, 1977.

Hughes, Philip. *The Church in Crisis: A History of the General Councils, 325-1870*. New York: Hanover House, 1961.

Hume, David and Eugene Rotwein (editor). *Writings on Economics*. Freeport, New York: Books for Libraries Press, 1972.

Jacobs, Donald and Richard Pratt (editors). *Conference Proceedings, Savings and Residential Financing Conference*. Chicago: Savings and Loan League, 1968.

J. Gardner, Wilkinson. *A Popular Account of the Ancient Egyptians*. New York: Bonanza Books, 1988.

Jalee, Pierre. *How Capitalism Works*. New York: Monthly Review Press, 1977.

Jardine, Lisa. *Worldly Goods: A New History of the Renaissance*. New York: Doubleday, 1996.

Kahn, Mohsin S. and Abbas Mirakhor, (editors). *Theoretical Studies in Islamic Banking and Finance*. Houston, Texas: The Institute of Research and Islamic Studies, 1987.

Katona, George. *Psychological Economics*. New York: Elsevier Scientific Publishing, 1976.

Keynes, John Maynard. *General Theory of Employment, Interest, and Money*. New York: Harcourt, Brace & World Inc., 1964.

Khalifa, Rashad, (translator). *Quran*. Tuczon, Arizona: Islamic Productions, 1989.

Klein, Lawrence R. *The Keynesian Revolution*. New York: The Macmillan Company, 1949.

Kregel, J.A. *Rate of Profit, Distribution and Growth: Two Views*. Chicago: Aldine Atherton Inc., 1971.

Kuhn, W.E. *The Evolution of Economic Thought, (2nd edition)*. Cincinnati, Ohio: South-Western Publishing. 1970.

Kung, Hans. *Infallible? An Inquiry*. Garden City, New York: Doubleday and Company Inc., 1971.

Lachmann, L.M. *Macro-economic Thinking and the Market Economy*. London: The Institute of Economic Affairs, 1973.

Laidler, David. E.W. *Essays on Money and Infl ation*. Chicago: University of Chicago Press, 1975.

Langholm, Odd. *The Aristotelian Analysis of Usury*. Bergen, Norway: Universitetsforlaget AS, 1984.

Le Goff, Jacques and Patricia Ranum (translator). *Your Money or Your Life: Economy and Religion in the Middle Ages*. New York: Zone Books, 1988.

Leffingwell, Georgia Williams. *Social and Private Life at Rome in the Time of Plautus and Terence*. New York: AMS Press, 1968.

Lekachman, Robert. *A History of Economic Ideas*. New York: McGraw-Hill Book Company, 1959.

Leontyev, L. *A Short Course of Political Economy*. Moscow: Progress Publishers, 1968.

Lindhal, Erik. *Studies in the Theory of Money and Capital*. New York: Farrar & Rinehart, 1939.

Lindsay, Robert. *The Economics of Interest Rate Ceilings*. New York: New York University, Institute of Finance, 1970.

Lockwood, William W. *The Economic Development of Japan*. Princeton, New Jersey: Princeton University Press, 1968.

Lutz, Friedrich A. *The Theory of Interest*. Dordrecht-Holland: D. Reidel Publishing Company, 1968.

Maccoby, Hyam. *Early Rabbinic Writings*. Cambridge: Cambridge University Press, 1988.

MacEoin, Denis and Ahmed Al-Shahi, (editors). *Islam in the Modern World*. New York: Saint Martin's Press, 1983.

Mandel, Ernest. *Marxist Economic Theory, (2 volumes)*. New York: Monthly Economic Review Press, 1968.

Marshall, Alfred. *Principles of Economics, (8th edition)*. Philadelphia: Porcupine Press, 1982.

Marshall, Howard D. *The Great Economists, A History of Economic Thought*. New York: Pitman Publishing Corporation, 1967.

Martines, Lauro. *Power and Imagination: City-States in Renaissance Italy*. New York: Alfred A. Knopf, 1979.

Marx, Karl. *Capital (3 volumes)*. New York: Vintage Books, Random House, 1981.

Marx, Karl and G.A. Bonner and Emile Burns, (translators). *Theories of Surplus Value: Selections*. New York: International Publishers, 1952.

McCall, Andrew. *The Medieval Underworld*. New York: Barnes and Noble Books, 1993.

McClory, Robert. *Faithful Dissenters*. Maryknoll, New York, 2001.

Mill, John Stuart. *Principles of Political Economy, (2 volumes)*. New York: The Colonial Press, 1900.

Meek, Ronald L. *Precursors of Adam Smith*. London: Dent, 1973.

Minkin, Jacob S. *The World of Moses Maimonides*. New York: Thomas Yoseloff, 1957.

Mins, L.E. (editor). *Engel's on Marx's "Capital."* Moscow: Cooperative Publishing Society of Foreign Workers in the U.S.S.R., 1936.

Mises, Ludwig von and H.E. Batson (translator). *The Theory of Money and Credit*. New Haven: Yale University Press, 1953.

Moore, George Foot. *Judaism 2 vols*. Cambridge: Harvard University Press, 1927.

Moss, Laurence S. *The Economics of Ludwig von Mises: Toward A Critical Reappraisal*. Kansas City: Sheed and Ward, Inc., 1976.

Muhammad and Zafrulla Khan (translator). *The Quran*. New York: Olive Branch Press, 1991.

Muhammad and Rashad Khalifa (translator). *The Quran*. Tuczon, Arizona: Islamic Productions, 1989.

Muller, Jerry Z. *Capitalism and the Jews*. Princeton, New Jersey: Princeton University Press 2010.

Mundell, Robert A. *Monetary Theory*. Pacific Palisades, California: Goodyear Publishing Company, 1971.

Murphy, Brian. *A History of the British Economy, 1086-1970*. London: Longman Group, 1973.

Nelson, Benjamin N. *The Idea of Usury*. Princeton: Princeton University Press, 1949.

Newman, Philip C, Arthur D. Gayer, and Milton H. Spencer, (editors). *Source Readings in Economic Thought*. New York: W.W. Norton & Company, 1954.

Nissim Da Pisa, Yechiel and G.S. Rosenthal (translator). *Banking and Finance among the Jews in Renaissance Italy*. New York: Bloch Publishing Company, 1962.

Noonan, John T. *The Scholastic Analysis of Usury*. Cambridge, Massachusetts: Harvard University Press, 1957.

Noonan, John T, Jr. *A Church That Can and Cannot Change*. Notre Dame, Indiana: University of Notre Dame Press, 2005.

O'Connell, Marvin R. *The Counter Reformation 1559-1610*. New York: Harper & Row, 1974.

Oser, Jacob. *The Evolution of Economic Thought (2nd edition)*. New York: Harcourt, Brace and World, Incorporated, 1970.

Patinkin, Don. *Money, Interest, And Prices. (2nd edition)*. New York: Harper & Row, 1965.

Patinkin, Don. *Studies in Monetary Economics*. New York: Harper & Row, 1972.

Pemberton, Prentiss L., and Daniel Rush Finn. *Toward A Christian Economic Ethic*. Minneapolis: Winston Press, 1985.

Perry, Arthur Latham. *Principles of Political Economy*. New York: Charles Scribner's Sons, 1891.

Pickthall, Marmaduke. *The Meaning of the Glorious Koran. (first published 1930)*. New York: Dorset Press (reprint).

Pirenne, Henri and I.E. Clegg (translator). *Economic and Social History of Medieval Europe*. New York: Harcourt Brace and World Inc., 1937; A Harvest Book.

Plato and B. Jowett (translator). *Five Great Dialogues*. Roslyn, New York: Classics Club, 1942.

Postan, M.M. *The Medieval Economy and Society*. Middlesex, England: Penguin Books Ltd., 1975.

Pounds, N.J.G. *An Economic History of Medieval Europe*. New York: Longman, 1974.

Rima, Ingrid H. *Readings in the History of Economic Theory*. New York: Holt, Rinehart and Winston, Inc., 1970.

Ricardo, David. *The Principles of Political Economy and Taxation*. New York: Dutton, (reprint) 1978.

Rist, Charles and Jane Degras (translator). *History of Monetary and Credit Theory*. New York: Macmillan, 1940.

Ritter, Lawrence S. and William L. Silber. *Principles of Money, Banking, and Financial Markets*. New York: Basic Books Publishers, 1974.

Robinson, Joan. *An Essay on Marxian Economics. (2nd edition)*. London: Macmillan Saint Martin's Press, 1966.

Robinson, Joan. *Economic Philosophy*. Middlesex, England, Penguin Books, 1966.

Robinson, Joan and John Eatwell. *An Introduction to Modern Economics.* London: McGraw Hill.

Rockwell, Llewellyn H. Jr. (editor). *The Gold Standard, Perspectives in the Austrian School.* Auburn, Alabama: Auburn University, 1992.

Rodinson, Maxime. *Islam and Capitalism.* New York: Pantheon Books, 1973.

Roeder, Ralph. The Man of the Renaissance. New York: Time Incorporated, 1966.

Roll, Eric. *A History of Economic Thought, (3rd edition).* Englewood Cliffs, New Jersey: Prentice Hall, 1956.

Rotwein, Eugene, (editor). *David Hume Writings on Economics.* Freeport, New York: Books For Libraries Press, 1955.

Salvatore, Dominick. *Microeconomics, Theory and Applications.* New York: Macmillan Publishing Company, 1986.

Saleh, Nabil A. *Unlawful Gain and Legitimate Profit in Islamic Law*: Riba, Gharar, and Islamic Banking. Cambridge: Cambridge University Press, 1986.

Samuelson, Paul A. *Economics, 3rd edition.* New York: McGraw-Hill Book Company, 1955.

Samuelson, Paul A. and William D. Nordhaus. *Economics, (18th edition).* New York: McGraw-Hill Irwin, 2005.

Say, Jean-Baptiste. *A Treatise on Political Economy.* New York: Augustus M. Kelley, 1971.

Schuettinger, Robert L. and Eamonn F. Butler. *Forty Centuries of Wage and Price Controls.* Washington D.C.: The Heritage Foundation, 1979.

Schumpeter, Joseph A. *History of Economic Analysis.* New York: Oxford University Press, 1954.

Seligman, Ben B. *Main Currents in Modern Economics, (3 volumes).* Chicago: Quadrangle Books, 1971.

Shackle, G.L.S. *The Years of High Theory.* London: Cambridge University Press, 1973.

Shapiro, James. *Shakespeare and the Jews.* New York: Columbia University Press, 1996.

Smith, Adam. *An Inquiry into the Nature and Causes of the Wealth of Nations.* Chicago: Encyclopedia Britannica, Inc., 1952.

Soule, George. *Ideas of the Great Economists.* New York: Viking Press, 1952.

Spiegel, Henry William, (editor). *The Development of Economic Thought.* New York: John Wiley & Sons, 1952.

Sweezy, Paul M. *The Theory of Capitalist Development*. New York: Modern Reader Paperbacks, 1968.

Synan, Edward A. *The Popes and the Jews in the Middle Ages*. New York: The Macmillan Company, 1965.

Takisawa, Matsuyo. *The Penetration of Money Economy in Japan*. New York: AMS Press, 1968.

Tamari, Meir. *With All Your Possessions: Jewish Ethics and Economic Life*. New York: The Free Press, 1987.

Tanakh, *The Holy Scriptures*. New York: Jewish Publication Society.

Taussig, F.W. *Principles of Economics, (3rd edition, 2 volumes)*. New York: The Macmillan Company, 1929.

Tawney, R.H. *Religion and the Rise of Capitalism*. New York: Harcourt, Brace and Company, Inc., 1926; Mentor Books, 1947.

Taylor, Overton H. *A History of Economic Thought*. New York: McGraw-Hill Book Company, 1960.

Trainer, Richard D.C. *The Arithmetic of Interest Rates*. New York: Federal Reserve Bank of New York, 1981.

Twersky, Isadore. *A Maimonides Reader*. New York: Behrman House Inc., 1972.

Van Horne, James C. *Function and Analysis of Capital Market Rates*. Englewood Cliffs, New Jersey: Prentice Hall Incorporated, 1970.

Various. *Catechism of the Council of Trent for Parish Priests*. New York: Joseph F. Wagner, Inc., 1952.

Various. *Economic Organization and Policies In The Middle Ages. Volume III: The Cambridge Economic History of Europe*. Cambridge: University Press, 1963.

Various. *Encyclopaedia Judaica*. New York: The Macmillan Company, 1971.

Various. *Medieval Callings*. Le Goff, Jacques, (editor) and Lydia G. Cochrane (translator). Chicago: University of Chicago Press, 1996.

Various. *Surveys of Economic Theory: Money, Interest, and Welfare*. New York: Macmillan, 1966.

Various. *The Talmud, The Steinsaltz Edition, Vol. IV, Part IV*. Jerusalem: Israel Institute for Talmudic Publications, 1991.

Various and Ben Zion Bokser (translator). *The Talmud, Selected Writings*. New York: The Paulist Press, 1989.

Vaughn, Karen Iversen. *John Locke, Economist and Social Scientist*. Chicago: University of Chicago Press, 1980.

Viner, Jacob. *The Long View and the Short*. Glencoe, Illinois: The Free Press, 1958.

Wagschal, Saul. *A Torah Guide to the Businessman*. New York: Feldheim, 1990.

Weber, Max and Talcott Parsons (translator). *The Protestant Ethic and the Spirit of Capitalism*. New York: Charles Scribner's Sons, 1958.

Wicksell, Knut and R.F. Kahn (translator). *Interest and Prices*. London: MacMillan and Co., Ltd., 1936.

Wilson, Thomas. *A Discourse Upon Usury: With a Historical Introduction by R. H. Tawney*. New York: Augustus M. Kelley, 1963.

Yang, Lien-sheng. *Money and Credit in China*. Cambridge, Massachusetts: Harvard University Press, 1952.

Periodicals

Anonymous. "Did Usury Ceilings Hold Down Auto Sales?" *FRB Chicago Economic Perspectives* 8/5 (September/October 1984): 24-30.

Chiu, Shirley. "Islamic Finance in the United States: A Small but Growing Industry." *Chicago Fed Letter, Federal Reserve Bank of Chicago* (May 2005), Number 214.

Collard, David. "Leon Walras and the Cambridge Caricature." *The Economic Journal* (June 1973): 465-476.

Cox, Stella, Karsten Junius, and Marc Piazolo. "Islamic Banking—A Promising Market for Conventional Banks." *Trends, Dresdner Bank* (April 1996).

Dewey, Donald. "The Geometry of Capital and Interest." *The American Economic Review*, Volume LIII, Number 1 (March 1963): 134-139.

Estrella, Arturo and Mary R. Trubin. "The Yield Curve as a Leading Indicator: Some Practical Issues." *Current Issues in Economics and Finance, Federal Reserve Bank of New York*, July/August 2006, Volume 12, Number 5: 1-7.

Fama, Eugene F. "Short-Term Interest Rates as Predictors of Inflation." *The American Economic Review*, Volume 65, Number 3 (June 1975): 269-282.

Fleming, Michael J. and Kenneth D. Garbade. "Repurchase Agreements with Negative Interest Rates." *Current Issues in Economics and Finance, Federal Reserve Bank of New York*, April 2004, Volume 10, Number 5: 1-7.

Friedman, Milton. "John Maynard Keynes." *Economic Quarterly, Federal Reserve Bank of Richmond* Volume 83, Number 2 (Spring 1997): 1-23.

Groenewegen, P.D. "A Re-Interpretation of Turgot's Theory of Capital and Interest." *The Economic Journal* 322 (June 1971): 327-40.

Hicks, John R. "Capital Controversies: Ancient and Modern." *American Economic Review* 64 (May 1974): 308-10.

Hollander, Samuel. "The Economics of David Ricardo: A Response to Professor O'Brien." *Oxford Economic Papers*, Volume 34, Number 1 (March 1982): 224-252.

Hollander, Samuel. "The Post-Ricardian Dissension: A Case Study in Economics and Ideology." *Oxford Economic Papers*, Volume 32, Number 3 (November 1980): 370-410.

Humphrey, Thomas M. "The Early History of the Real/Nominal Interest Rate Relationship." *Economic Review Federal Reserve Bank of Richmond* 669/3(May/June 1983): 2-10.

Humphrey, Thomas M. "Mercantilists and Classicals: Insights from Doctrinal History." *Economic Quarterly Federal Reserve Bank of Richmond* 85/2 (Spring 1999): 55-82.

Humphrey, Thomas M. "Nonneutrality of Money in Classical Monetary Thought." *Economic Review, Federal Reserve Bank of Richmond* 77/2 (March/April 1991): 3-15.

Hyse, Richard. "Richard Cantillon, Financier to Amsterdam." *The Economic Journal* (December 1971): 812-826

Ireland, Peter N. "Long-Term Interest Rates and Inflation: A Fisherian Approach." *Economic Quarterly, Federal Reserve Bank of Richmond*, Volume 82/1 (Winter 1996): 21-35.

Jamison, Dean. "Time Preference and Utility: A Comment." *The Economic Journal* (March 1970): 179-181.

Kahn, Mohsin S. and Abbas Mirakhor. "The Framework and Practice of Islamic Banking." *Finance and Development*, (September 1986).

Karsten, Ingo. "Islam and Financial Intermediation." *IMF Staff Papers* (March 1982): 108-42.

Keeley, Michael C. and Michael M. Hutchison. "Money and the Fisher Effect." *FRBSF Economic Letter* (August 7, 1987): 1-3.

Kula, Erhun. "Derivation of Social Time Preference Rates for the United States and Canada." *Quarterly Journal of Economics* (November 1984): 873-882.

Naughton, Tony, and Bala Shanmugam. "Interest-Free Banking: A Case Study of Malaysia." *National Westminster Bank Quarterly Review* (February 1990): 16-32.

O'Brien, D.P. "Ricardian Economics and the Economics of David Ricardo." *Oxford Economic Papers*, Volume 33, Number 3 (November 1981): 352-385.

Patinkin, Don. "Frank Knight as Teacher." *The American Economic Review*, Volume 63, Number 5 (December 1973): 786-810.

Reilly, Devin and Pierre-Daniel G. Sarte. "Changes in Monetary Policy and the Variation in Interest Rate. Changes Across Credit Markets." *Economic Quarterly, Federal Reserve Bank of Richmond*, Volume 96, Number 2 (Second Quarter 2010): 201-229.

Russell, Steven. "Understanding the Term Structure of Interest Rates: The Expectations Theory." *Review, Federal Reserve Bank of Saint Louis* (July/ August 1992): 36-50.

Santoni, G.J. and Courtenay C. Stone. "Navigating Through the Interest Rate Morass: Some Basic Principles." *Review, Federal Reserve Bank of St. Louis*, Volume 63, Number 3 (March 1981): 11-18.

Smith, Pamela Ann. "Where Capitalism Is Shaped by Islam." *Global Finance* (October 1992): 70-72.

Swanson, Eric. "What We Do and Don't Know about the Term Premium." *FRBSF Economic Letter* (July 20, 2007), Number 2007-21: 1-3.

Taylor, Thomas W., and J. Wynne Evans. "Islamic Banking and the Prohibition of Usury in Western Economic Thought." *National Westminster Bank Quarterly Review* (November 1987): 15-27.

Vandenbrink, Donna C. "Usury Ceilings and DIDMCA." *FRB Chicago Economic Perspectives* 9/5 (September/October 1985): 25-30.

Williams, John C. "The Natural Rate of Interest." *FRBSF Economic Letter* (October 31, 2003), Number 2003-32: 1-3.

Wood, J.H. "Money and Output: Keynes and Friedman In Historical Perspective." *Business Review, Federal Reserve Bank of Philadelphia* (September 1972): 3-12.

Wu, Tao. "Estimating the 'Neutral' Real Interest Rate in Real Time." *FRBSF Economic Letter* (October 21, 2005), Number 2005-27: 1-3.

Ziauddin, Ahmad. "The Quranic Theory of Riba." *The Islamic Quarterly* (January-June 1978), Volume 22, Numbers 1-2: 3-14.

INDEX

242-43, 245; rental of, 30,
154-58, 160, 194, 219, 224,
228, 230, 246-47, 250; variable,
170, 172, 185; wages fund, 209,
222-23, 243, 249
Carey, Henry Charles, 217-19
Cauwes, Paul Louis 147-48
Cesar, William, 154
Clark, John Bates, 208, 219-21,
223, 232
Chaucer, Geoffrey, 26
Church doctrine, 44-46, 58-59;
canon law, 23-24, 36, 45,
59; conciliar regulations,
21-22, 24, 32, 43, 83; papal
pronouncements, 21, 23-25,
37, 43-45, 63, 73-74, 79, 82,
85, 88; patristic views, 21
Child, Josiah, 98-99
Code of Hammurabi, 17
Cossa, Luigi, 153
Courcelle-Seneuil, Jean, 147
Credit practices: Asia, 19-20, 46;
Europe, 18-19, 23-24, 30-33,
38-41, 43, 58; Middle East
17-19; Northern Italy, 41-43
Culpeper, Thomas, 98-99

Dante, Alighieri, 25-26
Dietzel, Karl, 160
Diet of Nuremberg, 94
Droz, Francois Xavier, 146
Douglas, William, 216, 221

Eck, Johann, 72
English rulers, 38-40, 78, 95

Exchange banking, 18, 70-72, 83,
85, 101-02; bills of exchange,
70-71, 84-85

Factors of production, 114, 123,
127-28, 145, 155-56, 183,
218-20, 229; land, 145, 218,
229; labor, 104, 107, 121,
125-28, 145, 155, 162, 221, 246
Fetter, Frank, 232-33
Fisher, Irving, 205, 217, 224-28, 263
Franklin, Benjamin, 216
French rulers, 40-41
Friedman, Milton, 233-34

Galiani, Ferdinando, 152-53, 188
Garnier, Germain, 146
Garnier, Josef, 147
George, Henry, 219
Gerardo of Siena, 62
Gerstner, Franz Joseph, 126
Giles of Lessine, 69
Grotius, Hugo, 95

Haas, Jacob de, 149, 194
Hayek, Friedrich von, 208-210
Henry of Eutin, 69
Henry of Hesse, 69
Hermann, F.B.W. von, 158-59,
160-61, 180
Hicks, John, 199
Hinduism, 19-20
Hostiensis, Enrico Bartolomei, 67,
71
House of Fugger, 43, 74
Hume, David, 107-10, 116, 119

ABOUT THE AUTHOR

Fernando S. David was the Regional (Asia-Pacific) Economist of Citibank from 1964 to 1990 and a Financial Markets consultant to Citibank from 1990 to 2005. He studied at Boston, Harvard, and Fordham Universities and holds MA, MS, MA, and PhD (cand) degrees. He taught Economics at Pace University in Pleasantville, New York. The author also has several essays and short stories published. He lives with his wife in Scarsdale, New York.